Working-Class Kids and Visionary Educators in a Multiracial High School

Working-Class Kids and Visionary Educators in a Multiracial High School

A Story of Belonging

Karen V. Hansen
with Nicholas Monroe

LEXINGTON BOOKS
Lanham • Boulder • New York • London

Lexington Books
Bloomsbury Publishing Inc, 1359 Broadway, New York, NY 10018, USA
Bloomsbury Publishing Plc, 50 Bedford Square, London, WC1B 3DP, UK
Bloomsbury Publishing Ireland, 29 Earlsfort Terrace, Dublin 2, D02 AY28, Ireland
www.bloomsbury.com

First published in the United States of America 2024
Paperback edition published 2025

Copyright © 2025 by Karen V. Hansen and Nicholas Monroe

All rights reserved. No part of this publication may be: i) reproduced or transmitted in any form, electronic or mechanical, including photocopying, recording or by means of any information storage or retrieval system without prior permission in writing from the publishers; or ii) used or reproduced in any way for the training, development or operation of artificial intelligence (AI) technologies, including generative AI technologies. The rights holders expressly reserve this publication from the text and data mining exception as per Article 4(3) of the Digital Single Market Directive (EU) 2019/790.

British Library Cataloguing in Publication Information available

Library of Congress Cataloging-in-Publication Data
Names: Hansen, Karen V., author. | Monroe, Nicholas, author.
Title: Working-class kids and visionary educators in a multiracial high school : a story of belonging / Karen V. Hansen with Nicholas Monroe.
Description: Lanham, Maryland : Lexington Books, 2024. | Includes bibliographical references and index. | Summary: "In 1970s California, when many school communities resisted progress, visionary teachers and dynamic students at Sunnyvale High School created a vibrant, multiracial school community where students took on meaningful leadership roles, found common ground, and blazed multiple paths to successful adulthood"– Provided by publisher.
Identifiers: LCCN 2024032092 (print) | LCCN 2024032093 (ebook) | ISBN 9781666959680 (cloth) | ISBN 9781350581845 (paperback) | ISBN 9781666959697 (epub)
Subjects: LCSH: Sunnyvale High School (Sunnyvale, Calif.)–History. | Sunnyvale High School (Sunnyvale, Calif.)–Alumni and alumnae. | Children with social disabilities–Education (Secondary)–California–Sunnyvale–History. | Minority children–Education (Secondary)–California–Sunnyvale–History. | Multiracial education–California–Sunnyvale–History. | Student participation in administration–California–Sunnyvale–History.
Classification: LCC LD7501.S945 H36 2024 (print) | LCC LD7501.S945 (ebook) | DDC 373.794/73–dc23/eng/20240808
LC record available at https://lccn.loc.gov/2024032092
LC ebook record available at https://lccn.loc.gov/2024032093

For product safety related questions contact productsafety@bloomsbury.com.

∞™ The paper used in this publication meets the minimum requirements of American National Standard for Information Sciences—Permanence of Paper for Printed Library Materials, ANSI/NISO Z39.48-1992.

For our teachers

Contents

List of Figures	ix
Preface	xi
Acknowledgments	xvii
Introduction	1
1 A Vale in the Sun	13
2 Spirit by Design	23
3 Athletics before Title IX	39
4 A Fighting School	55
5 Tensions of Connecting across Difference	67
6 Was It a "Race Riot"?	83
7 Transformative Changes	95
8 Informal Support Bolsters Resilience	115
9 Legacies and Lessons	133
Appendix: Sunnyvale High School Interview Subjects	145
Bibliography	151
Index	159
About the Authors	167

List of Figures

	Paul Sakamoto pen and ink drawing, 2013	xx
Figure 1.1	Map of Sunnyvale, California, 1956	16
Figure 1.2	Plan of Sunnyvale High School	18
Figure 2.1	Paul Sakamoto, Vice Principal, 1966	28
Figure 2.2	Pep rally, 1972	36
Figure 3.1	Carolyn Buszdieker, Teacher and Coach, with Swimmer, ca. 1972	46
Figure 3.2	Dianna Good Making the Shot, Girls' Basketball Game, 1974	50
Figure 5.1	Black Student Union, 1970	72
Figure 5.2	Chicano Student Union, 1971	75
Figure 7.1	Sunnyvale High School Marching Band, 1972	98
Figure 7.2	Ed Lizardo, Drum Major, 1972	100
Figure 7.3	Doug Walker, Teacher and Coach, 1972	105
Figure 7.4	Slave Sale. *Skywriter*, December 14, 1971	110
Figure 8.1	Cece Padgett (right) Talking with Cheryl Whincup and Two Other Girls, 1972	118
Figure 8.2	Van McClung, Bob Hagg, and Gary Robinson, 1973 and 1974	119
	Paul Sakamoto pen and ink drawing, 2013	144

Preface

The grass on the neglected football field was splotchy and brown when I visited just before the school was closed in 1981. Sunnyvale High was built for the baby boom. After that generation passed through, the district decided to shut it down. I walked onto the dusty track in front of the empty bleachers and heard a familiar voice. "Karen! Karen, is that you? Where have you been? I've been dreaming about you." I turned around, saw my old friend, and gulped back the tears. I had been dreaming about her, too, about all our friends, and about this place.

Sunnyvale High School (SHS) taught working-class kids for twenty-five years, from 1956 to 1981. Today it has no formal way of reaching out to those whose lives it touched. Yet connections endure; alumni and former educators gather annually to pay tribute to it, each other, and the school's ability to weave us together.

Why did this seemingly ordinary high school hold such extraordinary meaning for the students who had roamed its halls? It had shaped my thoughts, feelings, and sense of purpose in life for many years. How did Sunnyvale High nurture and encourage a diverse group of disadvantaged adolescents? How did it create a strong community and sense of solidarity among kids from so many different walks of life?

Attending the fortieth reunion for the class of 1972 (the graduating class before my own) helped me understand its power and begin answering those questions.

"SUNNYVALE SAVED MY LIFE"

On a warm evening in 2012, after dinner at the reunion, I sat down next to Doug Walker, a dynamic teacher whose class on US Black history challenged and broadened the views of the school's predominantly Anglo and Chicano students. People lined up to shake his hand. Although I didn't intend to eavesdrop, I heard more than one person say, their voices quivering, "Thank you Mr. Walker. You saved my life." Then their stories would unfold, and Walker would reflect with them. He reaffirmed what he had told them at the time: that they had it within them to persevere and make choices that would lead them out of their current crisis. So many kids had felt on the edge, for so many reasons.

Not everyone took Mr. Walker's class, nor did everyone need his particular counsel. Sunnyvale High provided a refuge for many students. Sometimes motivation came from a coach or a teacher advising an after-school activity. For others, it sprang from the vibrant art department or pioneering courses in electronics. Friends were most important to others, supporting them emotionally and making sure they did the right thing. These people and spaces joined students together in cooperative endeavors that made them feel less isolated, taught them to ask questions that put things in a broader context, and enabled them to develop self-discipline.

Adolescents found many different paths through those troubled years. One boy discovered that the marching band gave him a sense of pride and transformed his internal feelings of worthlessness. One girl immersed herself in extracurricular activities promoting school spirit. Her ordeals at home receded, and her peers made her feel seen and appreciated. Another boy took refuge in sports. The gym was open for extended informal practice, shooting baskets, dribbling past teammates, and the coach was around to offer guidance. He found solace and purpose in being part of a team that surmounted challenges on and off the court.

Educators at Sunnyvale High connected with students and tried not to let them fall by the wayside. One girl might not have completed high school if her counselor had not regularly chased her down, brought her back to campus, and reminded her of how much her parents counted on her earning a high school diploma. She took her counselor's insistent message to heart because of the relationship of trust he established with her. In an oral history interview with me, she confided that "he did more listening than talking."

Another girl jokingly told me, "cheerleading saved my life," but her humor hid a deeper truth. She had been "hanging around with the druggies." After a year and a half of smoking marijuana in the bathrooms and stealing alcohol from her parents, she had an epiphany: "I realized this really was not the path I wanted to go down." Her friend ended up addicted to heroin, but she ran track and, dressed in a cheerleading uniform, jumped, yelled, and supported the boys.

Struggling in his remedial math class, one football player felt tormented by his math teacher. She made him stay after school to do his homework, which he otherwise failed to turn in. At times, she even sent him to the principal's office with instructions not to let him leave until he finished. She could not have known he would later win a football scholarship to college and become a math major. But she did know that if he learned to stick with a problem until he worked it through, he would learn how to learn. He came to imagine himself having a future.

When one girl got pregnant at the end of her sophomore year, instead of sending her away and banning her from campus, as was the norm in 1970, her counselor worked with her and her parents to enable her to finish high school on time. He empathetically withheld judgment. "He just made me feel like, oh my God, you're not this horrible person." She got married and kept the baby. For two summers running, she took classes and graduated with her class in 1972.

REUNIONS

Inspired by my experience at the class of 1972 reunion, I planned an intimate dinner the night before my own fortieth reunion in 2013. Reunions are "autobiographical occasions" filled with reminiscences and new realizations.[1] I wanted to explore the questions I had been wondering about with former classmates whom I had known since junior high. I gathered a small group to reflect on the long-term impact SHS had on us and the lives of other students. Jane Manley and Gloria Collins had been my good friends. Beginning in seventh grade, Gloria and I discovered we both aspired to become the first woman president. She was a petite Italian, and I was a tall Scandinavian—like a "Great Dane" dog, she punned. We played sports and did theater together. Jane, a year ahead of us, became my best friend in high school. Gloria and Jane lived around the block from each other and were devoted book fans, like me. In homeroom with Gloria and me in junior high, Dennis Gobets was a science guy who spoke a language we did not understand. Later, I reconnected with Dennis when he contacted me about writing a biography of his mother. I was delighted to discover how deeply our current interests aligned. At Brandeis University, I taught a class on "Gender, Biography, and Society."

I had mistakenly assumed that all of the students in the advanced track with me were aching to go to college, although not everyone had done so because they were too poor or unfamiliar with the process. After high school, good students like Gloria and Jane lived at home, worked day jobs, attended De Anza College for two years, and then transferred elsewhere to complete their bachelor's degree. Given the cost of attending a four-year institution and SHS's lack of counseling about financial aid, this path made higher education accessible.

But, Dennis told me, a college degree was not necessary for a successful career. The city of Sunnyvale, a burgeoning center of the postwar defense industry and the recent electronics boom, was a hotbed of opportunity in the early 1970s. He explained that the science and math guys who went straight from high school into electronics firms that became the core of Silicon Valley did not "lose time" like he did by going to college. Still others found viable paths to stability or upward mobility through the military or jobs in the skilled trades. In the early 1970s, it was possible for high school graduates to become apprentice electricians or plumbers, or to find other decently paying skilled jobs with prospects for becoming their own boss.

The crowd that showed up at our class of 1973 reunion the next day did not reflect the working-class futures I had imagined. Perhaps because disaffected people tend to shun these events, the alumni who came seemed to be solidly middle class, if not affluent. One was a financial planner, another a public school administrator. Many long-term public sector employees had already retired, although we were only in our late fifties. One man, who came from a family of doctors in Mexico, worked in medical insurance. A star among us, who was voted "most likely to succeed," was an award-winning television news reporter.

Even more striking than the examples of people who did better than their parents and thrived against the odds was our racial and ethnic diversity. That gathering reflected the demographics of California's Bay Area. If the state had thoroughly integrated its schools, they would all have had a multiracial student body that looked like us. Sunnyvale High students came from a mixture of ethnic and cultural backgrounds and lived in predominantly working-class neighborhoods. Because the housing market was stratified by property values and the cost of rent, lower-income families, including whites as well as people of color, clustered on the north side of town, from which the school drew nearly all of its students.

As young people, we recognized that our school was stigmatized because we were poor and rowdy. The better-off, predominantly white residents of the rest of Sunnyvale expected us to fail, or at least slog along at the bottom. Our families had been struggling financially, many of our parents had little formal education, and many of us were migrants from other regions or immigrants from other countries.

I felt indignant about the public aspersions cast on Sunnyvale High. I was fiercely proud of the school when I was there, a sentiment that educators deliberately nurtured. As a student body, we were proud of our diversity, our school, and what we created there together. Our defiant solidarity overrode racial and ethnic differences, in spite of tensions and divisions of the 1960s and 1970s. How did that happen? And how did so many of us succeed in making a different future than we and our families had anticipated?

PROVOKING INSISTENT QUESTIONS ABOUT SOCIETY AND HISTORY

I was one of a handful of graduates in my class of over 500 to go straight to a four-year college. My older brother had helped me set my sights on college, which was unthinkable to our parents, who had left school after the eighth grade.

At the University of California, I was drawn to the questions posed by history and sociology. I found it exhilarating to learn, even when that meant recognizing the systematic cruelty and violence that mark many societies, past and present. Yet, compassion and community exist alongside destructiveness. I kept wondering: Why are my smart, funny, and talented friends working at Hewlett Packard or Libby's Cannery instead of taking classes with me? Where have all the people of color gone? Why is everyone so blonde and rich? These disparities disturbed me.

I continued to pursue questions of community in the context of economic inequality through graduate school and as a historical sociologist teaching in a university oriented toward the liberal arts. What forces create and reproduce inequalities of race, class, and gender despite significant changes in the population, economy, and culture over time? Why do so many families enforce rigid ideas about gender and sexuality that generate misery and conflict in intimate relationships? How do people break free from constraints that limit their potential and develop resilience in the face of myriad obstacles? How do we come together across our differences and try to change society?

SHS transformed the lives of many young people, including my own. Granted, no school is perfect: it was underfunded; some teachers had given up on students. Students were sorted into courses by their perceived academic potential, which too often reflected their race and their parents' education. Yet Sunnyvale High made many of us feel like we were engaged in a common struggle to make a worthwhile future. How did its teachers and students enable us to feel that we *belonged*?

Today, schools are struggling with dilemmas that resemble those we faced and tried to resolve fifty years ago. We were a working-class school with a multiracial student body. We shared common economic circumstances because housing in the city of Sunnyvale was segregated by class. Families with limited or irregular incomes but a variety of races, ethnicities, and immigration statuses could afford to live on the north side of town, but not elsewhere. On campus, there were physical altercations and racial-ethnic tensions, and some students had trouble crossing social boundaries, though many insisted they did not.

The educators and students at Sunnyvale High profoundly shaped not only my curiosity about history and the world but also the questions I still ask today as a sociologist.

SHS was a community with its own culture and often felt like a self-contained circle. At the same time, it was deeply connected to the world outside, through the values expressed by its educators and students. Teenagers observed the labor of their parents and sometimes toiled alongside them, picking cotton, vegetables, or grapes in the Central Valley or processing fruit in the local canneries. They listened intently to teachers whose own lives had been shaped by migrant farm labor, work in the oil fields of southern California, internment by the US government, and civil rights activism. Students demanded respect, conveyed appreciation, argued and disagreed with each other, and sometimes fought physically. They felt the power of friendship and collective identity.

NOTE

1. Vered Vinitzky-Seroussi, *After Pomp and Circumstance: High School Reunion as an Autobiographical Occasion* (Chicago: University of Chicago Press, 1998); Robert Zussman, "Narrative Freedom," in *Narrative Sociology*, eds. Leslie J. Irvine, Jennifer Pierce, and Robert Zussman (Nashville, TN: Vanderbilt University Press, 2019), 141–61.

Acknowledgments
Karen V. Hansen

It is impossible to say enough about the extraordinary generosity of the Sunnyvale High School community, teachers, and students alike. As a young person, I was the beneficiary of their kindness and belief in me. In doing this research over the last ten years, I have been reminded at every juncture of their genuine desire to help and their willingness to trust me. I am deeply grateful to everyone who formally shared their stories, as well as those who spoke informally about their adolescence. From the project's inception, some have voluntarily conducted background research, helped me recruit people to interview, and even scoured through microfilm. Suzi Brink Logan, Carolyn Buszdieker, Bob Douglas, Bob Hagg, David Hernandez, Sharon Prefontaine, Adrian Stanga, and Nicholas Townsend have earned my utmost gratitude.

Sadly, several key narrators died before the book went to press: Terry Dyckman, Al Furtado, Pat Furtado, Walter Hale, Paul Sakamoto, and Adrian Stanga. Their wisdom and insight benefited me and this project enormously. Four dear friends and relatives celebrated the project from the start but did not live to see it in print: Anita Ilta Garey, Eva Hansen, Susan Klaw, and Debra Osnowitz.

Friends and colleagues have generously read iterations of this manuscript in its entirety, sometimes more than once. I am grateful for their critical eye and the time taken away from their own work: Margaret L. Andersen, Joyce Antler, Maxine Baca Zinn, Andrew L. Bundy, Nora Bundy, Mignon Duffy, Robert Handa, Nazli Kibria, Marya Levenson, Margaret K. Nelson, and Grey Osterud. David Hernandez and Jane Manley were willing to talk endlessly about the issues and read selected chapters. The lifeblood of my scholarly life is my stalwart writing group: Mignon Duffy and Nazli Kibria have willingly read flabby outlines and sloppy sentences while holding me in a close circle to explore ideas. While not formally a member of the writing group, Grey

Osterud has been central to the shape of this project and narrative, which have been deeply influenced by her belief in the value of oral histories and her skill at shaping up a paragraph.

When this project began as a harebrained scheme to study a school that I had attended but had closed forty years before, two colleagues at Brandeis University, Marya Levenson and Anita Hill, acted as my advisory board. They read interview transcripts, advised, and encouraged me. In our annual retreats to discuss work and life, Arlie Hochschild keenly found the potential gems, often buried in muck, and helped me excavate and polish them.

I discussed the project at length over coffee and dinner with Penny Cherns, Ricardo Cordova, Peter Del Tredici, Benjy Hansen-Bundy, Evan Hansen-Bundy, Adam Hochschild, Susan Klaw, Kim Marshall, Rhoda Schneider, and Doug Walker. Annette Lareau always had suggestions of relevant books to read. When Paul Kennedy discovered an Archie comic of a Roman slave sale, he immediately brought it to my attention.

At Brandeis University, I have had the good fortune to work with remarkable research assistants over the years. Nick Monroe has become a colleague, friend, and now coauthor. PhD student Jenny LaFleur's passion for education spilled over into this research. Master's students Jennifer McWilliams and Semra Malik provided research assistance as well. My appreciation extends to curious, skilled undergraduates Lilah Kleban and Ruhi Roy, who searched for relevant literature and discussed their own experiences in high school. Funding for travel, transcription, and hiring these remarkable young people came from Brandeis University's Theodore and Jane Norman Awards for Faculty Scholarship, a Provost Research grant, and the Women's Studies Research Center Student-Scholar Partnership.

No historical project can be completed without the able assistance of archivists and librarians. I owe a debt of gratitude to Laura Hibbler, Brandeis reference librarian, always ready to search for obscure sources, and to Jeanine Stanek (1932–2017) and Sue-Ellen Johnson at the Sunnyvale Historical Society and Museum Association, who diligently gathered Sunnyvale's artifacts to help others learn and remember.

The visual dimensions of this book are enhanced by the extraordinary photo editor and visual storyteller, Sarah Putnam. She brought many yearbook photographs to life. Marilyn Mason generously granted permission to use the Paul Sakamoto pen and ink drawings. SHS alums helped me locate and scan yearbooks. Thanks to Suzi Brink Logan, Gloria Collins, Mary Collins, Dianna Good, and Jane Manley, and to all those who granted permission to use their images from fifty years ago.

None of this research or writing would have had meaning without the circle of love provided by my family—Andrew Bundy, Benjy Hansen-Bundy, and Evan Hansen-Bundy. I am forever grateful for their support, their willingness to disagree with my interpretations of evidence, and to cheer, cajole, and distract me when the world felt like a dark place. My not-so-nuclear family merrily supported my early morning writing, even when I had to miss walks to the beach or a lively round of mini-golf.

Nicholas Monroe:
The bond between student and teacher is sacred. My father, James Monroe, embodies what I believe a teacher can and should be. A coach for nearly forty years, my dad is also an uncompromisingly devoted high school teacher in Chicago. His philosophy is exemplified by his pride in working with students who are written off as "underperforming" or "low-potential." For my dad, supporting students whom everyone else overlooks is viscerally personal. It's a point of honor central to his calling as a teacher, and it's what I'm most proud of about my father.

To my mother, Norma Monroe: you are my hero and the person most responsible for the opportunities and education I've received. One of my earliest and most cherished memories is of you reading to me in bed. Today, reading to your grandchildren is a cathartic experience that allows me to relive those moments and keeps you alive in my heart. You sacrificed and endured so much to provide your children with the best possible education. I am eternally grateful for and in awe of you. I live my life to honor you and make you proud.

Teachers are also role models. Nothing in my life has been more important than being a role model to my brothers Peter, Michael, and, more recently, Geo. This still holds true, and as an adult, I now appreciate how much I learn from and look up to all of you. I'm proud and grateful to call you my brothers.

Oberlin College cultivated my ability to understand the world, empathize with its inhabitants, and think critically and creatively. My professors remain some of the people I most admire. Gina Perez, you were a mentor and made me feel safe during an especially difficult time in my life. Booker Peek, your classes brought my two loves—teaching and learning—together in incomparable ways. Your wisdom has shaped every aspect of how I see and understand the world.

To my best friend, wife, and coparent Rachel Benson Monroe: it's no coincidence that we met at Oberlin. I've done more learning—personally, professionally, and academically—alongside you than with anyone else. There is no greater privilege or honor than sharing my life with you.

To my children, Noah Benson Monroe and Maya Evangeline Monroe: Words are inadequate to capture my gratitude for getting to experience life with you. My greatest joys come from teaching you and helping you navigate the world. To my delight, you are also my greatest teachers, having shown me more about the world and myself than I ever could have imagined.

Paul Sakamoto pen and ink drawing, 2013. *Source*: Sakamoto Designs: Paul's Pen and Ink Drawings, by Paul Sakamoto and Marilyn Mason, San Jose: self-published, 2014, p.10.

Introduction

"We were all alike." That phrase echoed like a mantra throughout my interviews with former students and educators from Sunnyvale High School (SHS). They did not mean we were all the same, but rather that in the ways that mattered most, we had a lot in common. Students and their families shared a working-class status that grounded their collective identity. In turn, SHS educators nurtured a sense of solidarity and community across a multiracial student body. This sentiment gave students a feeling of belonging.

PROUDLY REPRESENTING SUNNYVALE HIGH SCHOOL

Sunnyvale High differed profoundly from all the other high schools in the Fremont Union High School District. This predominantly white, middle-class district had six schools. Outsiders cast Sunnyvale High as the poor step-sister: darker, less successful, bound for neither wealth nor glory. Alumni recall that competing athletes feared visiting the campus because of its reputation for intimidation, violence, and crime. Adults in other parts of the district regarded Sunnyvale High students with disdain. Later, a district administrator confirmed this in an exchange with an alum: "They thought they were 'babysitting us until we were arrested.'" This book shows, in painstaking detail, that not only were SHS's detractors wrong, but when others reminded students of their second-class status, they bound together more tightly, strengthening their sense of solidarity and community.

Ed Lizardo '73 embodied the school's collective identity. As the student body president, Ed attended a district council of all the presidents. He recalled entering the room for the first evening meeting when boys from other schools were already seated. Heads turned. A bespectacled boy set the tone: "*And you are?*" The others silently stared, the room electric with tension. "Who are you?" Pause. No one greeted him. Every boy was white, and Ed felt them marking his difference. "Here I am, this Filipino kid."

In that moment, all the toxicity targeting Sunnyvale High flooded him. He felt "unwanted, unwelcomed, unnecessary and irrelevant." The others' hostility "was in their eyes and in their faces and what they *didn't do*." Ed had no preconceived notions about how he would be received, but the message was clear: "They don't think I'm worthy of being in their presence. I'm *low*." He was thrown, as many people are when confronted with prejudice. "For a flash, I felt ashamed."

But then everything changed. "I remember thinking in my mind, *I am Sunnyvale High School.*" "I'm representing Sunnyvale," he resolved, and "I need to show them *who we are*." He took a deep breath, stepped forward, and introduced himself: "I'm Ed Lizardo from Sunnyvale." And he felt a surge of pride. Boys on one side of the room rose and shook his hand; then others followed their lead. Ed started to relax as they recognized his dignity. He felt vindicated because he had altered the other presidents' perceptions of him and the school.

Ed took the disrespect being leveled at him, based on the hierarchy of whiteness over brownness and middle-class cultural capital over working-class deficits, and turned it around. His composure was grounded in his camaraderie with SHS students. Sunnyvale High cultivated pride in an enveloping "we." His was not an assertion of individuality; it was an embrace of collectivity. The pride he summoned announced that he and SHS belonged.

How did Ed Lizardo come to embody the dignity of an embattled school? How did he come to feel unqualifiedly that his classmates stood behind him in that room?

AGAINST THE ODDS

The structure of schooling tends to perpetuate inequality rather than ameliorate it. Today many policymakers think that good high schools produce high test scores and college-bound students who are well-positioned to excel in a knowledge-based economy. These measurable outcomes are one way that school districts and nations assess their excellence and ability to compete against other districts and countries.

We know, however, that widespread inequities in the quality of schools result from the fact that in most states, schools are funded by local property taxes.[1] Many schools and districts have inadequate resources to improve, deepening the existing inequality.[2] Schools in wealthy communities can afford to offer lower student-teacher ratios, enriched curricula, more counseling, individual and team sports, and the arts and music.

Within the United States, a student's zip code is an accurate predictor of academic achievement and test scores. In poorer neighborhoods, scores on standardized tests are lower and dropout rates are higher. Differences in household incomes and housing values have a major impact on what a school can offer its students.[3] These disparities are rooted in economic, housing, zoning, and educational policies and practices whose effects compound over generations.

Across the country, segregation by race and ethnicity has a major impact on student achievement.[4] Although the Supreme Court declared "separate but equal" schools unconstitutional in 1954, integration has not been attained. Although federal policies and financial support generated significant progress toward integration in the 1960s and 1970s, schools in many districts and states are as racially segregated now as they were seventy years ago.[5] Separate and unequal schooling perpetuates socioeconomic disparities between racial groups.

Because schools have been designed for a white, middle-class student body, this orientation can be especially damaging to Black and Brown students' academic prospects.[6] Their distinct experiences are ignored or excluded. Kids from the lower end of the economic spectrum often experience school as a constraining, even oppressive, environment. With the current emphasis on standardized testing, schools tend to lump together those students labeled as low achievers. In effect, the practice of tracking students reinforces structural inequalities based on race, class, gender, and native language in a self-perpetuating cycle.[7]

Vigorous public debates have focused on how we can expand educational opportunity and create greater equity in our multiracial democracy. Why do schools in low-income communities regularly fail to meet high standards? Why do so many of their students languish, even though they have the potential to flourish?

Sunnyvale High had none of the advantages of predominantly white schools in affluent neighborhoods. It faced conditions that parents, educators, and the public today understand as causes of school failure, not success. Its students came from a low-income area; most of their parents held blue-collar jobs, and few had gone to college.[8] Students and their parents considered graduating high school a major accomplishment. Given the student body's remarkable ethnic, racial, and linguistic diversity, cultural differences were impossible to ignore. In 1970, SHS students' families spoke twenty-two languages other than English, including Spanish, Portuguese, Samoan, Tongan, Fijian, French, German, Dutch, Tagalog, Mandarin Chinese, Cantonese Chinese, and Russian.[9]

Turnover rates among students were very high because so many parents had seasonal jobs or were temporarily stationed at nearby military bases. Official statistics no longer exist, but Adrian Stanga reported on the high turnover for the 1963–1964 academic year from the documents he kept as principal. "We had a 30% migratory rate . . . In other words, if we started school with 2,000 students, 30% of that, 500 to 600 of those students were coming in or going out." He asked, "Can you imagine the difficulty of a teacher with [so many] kids coming and going [making] an end-of-the-year evaluation of their achievement?"

Observers might politely call schools like Sunnyvale High "unpromising," predicting low test scores, a high dropout rate, disaffected students, and frustrated teachers. Indeed, when the school was opened in 1956, Fremont Union School District officials expected that its students would be mediocre and troublesome. Disparaged by outsiders, SHS did not get much credit for what it did to defy their expectations of failure.

How did SHS succeed in reaching its students, who were predominantly from poor and working-class families, including many immigrant, Brown, and Black families? Why wasn't it filled with alienated and disengaged students and burned-out teachers?

A GOOD HIGH SCHOOL

The alumni and retired teachers I spoke with insisted that Sunnyvale High was a *good* school. It mitigated some of the most debilitating and demoralizing consequences of poverty and racism. Educators worked with students to interrupt the forces that might otherwise have sent its disadvantaged students into a downward spiral. Many students thrived. If, as John Dewey memorably suggested a century ago, the best way to prepare children for adulthood is to ensure they live rich and full lives *as children*, then the best way to prepare adolescents for the future is to enable them to lead rich and full lives in high school.

Sociologist Sara Lawrence Lightfoot recognizes that education is more complex than any set of objectively measurable outcomes can capture. Many education reformers share a "tendency to focus on what is wrong rather than search for what is right, to describe pathology rather than health."[10] Instead, she poses alternative measures of "good schools," including self-assessment: good schools are "described as good by faculty, students, parents, and communities."[11] That is certainly the message we hear from Sunnyvale High's alumni and retired faculty. A good high school accepts, engages, and inspires its students. It helps them envision possibilities for their lives that they might not otherwise have considered.

In a comprehensive study of high schools, Michael Rutter and his research team found that the *ethos* of a school captures these unmeasurable dimensions of schools' successes. They conclude that it is "valuable to think of schools in terms of their characteristics as social organisations" and focus on their social dynamics.[12] In keeping with the democratic approach of John Dewey, America's most influential progressive educator, they argue that schools should be understood "as a form of community life."[13]

Using Lightfoot's yardstick and with an eye to the school's ethos, we can see what Sunnyvale High did right. This scrappy, multiracial public school transformed the usual trajectory of working-class and nonwhite students. It embraced rather than alienated; it recognized multiple forms of excellence; it nurtured students' voices and viewpoints, rather than treating them as passive recipients of instruction; it asked teachers to exercise initiative and creativity, rather than confining them to narrow, predefined tasks.

Sunnyvale High School provided an environment for students to learn, grow, and thrive, not in spite of their backgrounds, but in recognition and affirmation of them. It supported and enabled its students to develop their talents and interests in academic and non-academic pursuits. The most transformative SHS principals intentionally fostered connections between teachers and students by hiring diverse, young faculty who could relate to students. They encouraged students to come to school every day and motivated them to try and learn. Teachers nurtured young people, not in soft, fuzzy ways but by engaging them as people, holding them accountable for their actions, stimulating their minds, respecting their burdens, and pushing them to be better—as students, athletes, and human beings.

Considering the racial tensions that accompanied desegregation across the United States in the 1970s, Sunnyvale High created a remarkably open and inclusive community. It had multiple ways for students to get involved and to belong. The Othering & Belonging Institute at the University of California, Berkeley offers a definition of belonging: "Having a meaningful voice and the opportunity to participate in the design of political, social, and cultural structures that shape one's life."[14] Adapting it to a high school context, this definition identifies engagement, voice, and participation as key elements in creating the conditions for belonging.

Sunnyvale High School was not perfect. That is not a reproach, but a recognition of reality. Schools that serve working-class youth do not have to do *everything* right to make profound contributions to the lives of their students and communities. The educators and alumni I interviewed felt free to criticize teachers and counselors who judged students by their class, skin color, gender, or family backgrounds and segregated classrooms by race and ethnicity. When the school attempted to change, its progress was uneven and contested. The younger cadre of teachers clashed with the old guard. When biases surfaced, tensions between teachers could burst into open conflict. But students had learned to expect more of their school than it could always provide, so they pushed it to offer what they felt they deserved.

Sunnyvale High did not provide a surefire path to upward mobility, although it did for some. In the 1960s and 1970s, the young people at Sunnyvale High had more educational and economic opportunities than their parents had enjoyed. But many, especially those with less-educated parents, from immigrant families and families of color, faced daunting barriers that took cooperative efforts to overcome.

The school did not narrowly orient the curriculum toward higher education. Teachers developed a robust program in the creative and performing arts as well as industrial arts, and offered one of the first electronics classes in what became the Silicon Valley. Through its vocational education options, the school dignified manual labor and prepared many students for jobs in the emergent tech sector. In 1970, when racial and ethnic differences frequently created conflict, SHS hired an African American teacher to develop and teach a course on US Black history. Very few colleges offered such a class; Sunnyvale High made it part of its elective curriculum.

At the same time, the school helped students to learn and teachers to do their jobs in an effective, satisfying way. SHS offered students an array of avenues for involvement. It had an expansive sports program—including a robust set of offerings for girls, even before the mandates and funding changes brought by Title IX. Boys and girls could develop their physical capacities, acquire lasting competencies, and discover the power of teamwork. SHS had a comprehensive approach to student leadership and school spirit, with dozens of team-building and decision-making roles for students. The school's band program was an arts education venture, a core generator of school spirit, and a nationally competitive performing group. The school provided students with multiple opportunities to bond, lead, and thrive. Equally important, these activities gave students critical outlets for their creativity. Educators' and students' efforts to cultivate school spirit, evidenced in students' enduring identity as "the Jets," gave dignity to a beleaguered place and instilled both individual and collective pride. Educators and students deflected the stigma placed on the school by attributing it to others' misunderstanding and prejudice.

DOCUMENTING THE PAST

What I discovered at those reunions made me more curious about the school. I had thought I knew Sunnyvale High, but it had 2,200 students, and I had seen it only from my corner of campus. The school's story was much larger than mine. As I learned, many of us shared a collective story about how our four years together shaped us.

Exploring these questions prompted me to draw on my professional skills. I contacted alumni, teachers, administrators, and some parents to interview them about their experiences at SHS. I met some, like former principals Adrian Stanga and Paul Sakamoto, for the first time. I gathered those I knew well in small groups to reflect on our experiences and their enduring influence. Then I reached out to alumni I knew less well, and they connected me to other members of the Chicano and Black student unions, the boys who took classes in computer programming, and the girls who got called out to fight. Aware that memories are often incomplete and some of the school's formative moments had occurred before we arrived, I looked for documentary evidence. When I scoured the yearbooks from 1956 to 1981, I made shocking discoveries that revealed how unconscious white students were of the racism that pervaded the dominant culture.

How did Sunnyvale High sow the seeds of success in spite of the challenges we all faced? In part, we were growing up at a fortunate moment. Outstanding educators and excellent schools need adequate time and support. We benefited from living in California after it passed the Master Plan for Higher Education in 1960.[15] The state made a commitment to cultivating talent wherever it existed and created educational pathways for all kids, regardless of their skin color or parents' resources. And the job opportunities in the Bay Area offered paths to upward mobility. Big historical changes are made by the cumulative movements of many different people, so I set out to understand how SHS students and teachers actively participated in that history.

Over the past decade, I have interviewed fifty-five people. Those who agreed to talk to me are a self-selected sample from the school's twenty-five-year history: those who kept in contact with friends and teachers or who came to reunions and felt an attachment to SHS. All had earned a high school diploma. The disaffected are not included among those I interviewed, even though everyone I spoke with had some criticisms. The picture they paint reveals conflict as well as camaraderie. The selective nature of this set of narrators emphasizes students' engagement with SHS. Their positive experiences keep bringing them back and lead them to insist that Sunnyvale High was a "good school." A good school need not prepare all its graduates to earn college and professional degrees. What matters most is nurturing youth's confidence in their capacity to learn and to find their own pathway to a life they find fulfilling.

When I approached people for an interview or had others do so, only a handful declined. They insisted they had little to contribute or their memories had faded. Others had experiences they did not want to reveal. One was willing to speak with me in person but refused to be recorded. As teenagers, we had not always acted as our best selves. Some prefer not to expose their family's secrets. And not everyone enjoys being interviewed, no matter how compelling their stories.

I interviewed forty-one students; fifteen teachers or administrators, four of whom were also SHS alums; and three parents and community members. Approximately half were male and half female. (For details, see the appendix.)

Students had graduated as early as 1962 and as late as 1976. When we spoke together, narrators ranged in age from their mid-fifties to early nineties. The student interviewees represent a general cross-section of those who attended SHS; 52 percent are white, 20 percent Asian American/Pacific Islander, 17 percent Latina/o, 7 percent Black, and 2 percent "other." Five alumni had immigrated with their families from China, Mexico, Japan, Scotland, and Taiwan, while many others migrated to California from other parts of the United States. Many had at least one immigrant parent. My mother, from western Canada, held a green card as a resident alien until the day she died. Others' parents came from Germany, Greece, Ireland, Italy, Mexico, Norway, and Portugal. Some students had mixed ancestry. Not all students did well academically, but some did. Many dabbled in classes at De Anza College during and after high school or completed some college. Two-thirds of the alumni I interviewed completed a college or advanced degree, certainly a higher proportion than for the school as a whole. Most worked in industry, particularly food processing or electronics; some joined the military or went to business school.

The educators—almost one-fourth of the interview subjects—were teachers, staff, counselors, and principals, and some held several of those positions. Some began teaching in the 1950s soon after Sunnyvale High was founded; others joined the faculty at the end of the 1960s when school systems were expanding to accommodate the baby boom. Some kept teaching at SHS until 1981 when it was closed; others left to become principals, counselors, and superintendents in other schools and districts. Many got master's degrees in education or counseling; three earned PhDs or EdDs. Several educators later served on regional and statewide oversight bodies and were elected to office in professional organizations.

Interviews were as short as an hour or as long as three or four. I interviewed some individuals multiple times over several years. All of the recorded oral histories and transcripts will be deposited in the California History Center at De Anza College in Cupertino, an archive that documents the region's largely neglected working-class history.

At Brandeis University, I worked with Nicholas Monroe, a former middle-school reading and social studies teacher from Chicago. His PhD dissertation about first-generation college students assesses the skills and social capital they brought with them that helped them succeed. A first-generation college student himself, he watched his father return to school in his fifties to become a teacher. Deeply appreciative of what his interview subjects contributed to his project, Nick understood the value of what the SHS alumni said. As he read through the Sunnyvale High student newspaper, *The Skywriter*, he marveled at its high-quality reporting. He observed that it must have had an outstanding faculty advisor; Sara Accornero was indeed that. Nick was equally impressed by the innovative approaches adopted by teachers and students so many years ago, when similar reforms are now considered cutting-edge. Our conversations over several years convinced me he would be an insightful collaborator in writing this book. Nick brings the perspective of a younger educator committed to reform and who recognizes how audacious some of the educational experiments at Sunnyvale High were.

As a society that aspires to advance equal opportunity, to develop talent wherever it exists, and to promote upward mobility, the United States has ample reason to care about effective schools.

Sunnyvale High School created community and nourished camaraderie across differences, yielding what Heather McGhee calls a "solidarity dividend."[16] McGhee finds that when people with differing racial and ethnic backgrounds bond around common class interests and actions, they can accomplish a great deal for themselves and others. SHS alums say, *"we all got along."* At reunions, they observe the diversity in the room. Rather than either ignoring or fighting over their differences, they discuss them. Research on educational bias shows that "intergroup contact produced by more racially integrated environments in which children learn and live has been demonstrated to reduce intergroup prejudice."[17]

Creating this dynamic learning environment was an extraordinary opportunity for the educators who worked at SHS. Many just starting their careers gravitated to Sunnyvale High and its mission. From their involvement in the civil rights movements of the 1960s, they viewed teaching as a powerful way to make the world more just. In retrospect, many retired teachers, principals, and counselors claimed that the best job they ever had was at Sunnyvale High. They celebrated their colleagues and the school environment. They recalled how strongly they supported each other and their shared educational projects. They bounced ideas off of each other, designed new curricula, team-taught courses, and collectively sought new ways to engage the students. Innovative administrators let them experiment and make mistakes, and still backed them up.

This book explores the difference that dynamic educators made in the lives of students at Sunnyvale High. Some teachers were deeply committed to mentoring individuals. Others were skilled at facilitating intergroup communication, mediating conflicts that turned on race and ethnicity. The educators who were most effective in this multicultural, predominantly working-class milieu came from backgrounds that did not endow them with privilege. Some had attended Sunnyvale High and became the first generation in their families to go to college. For them, school had been a pathway to a better life, and they returned to SHS to provide the same opportunity for others. Indeed, they were convincing examples of what was possible, and they helped students develop confidence in themselves and encouraged them to explore the world beyond their parents' horizons. They created a sense of community and possibility among working-class adolescents.

We invite you to explore what lessons can be learned from a close look at a school whose innovative educators engaged students and gave them a place to belong, and we ask you to consider how schools can do this today.

NOTES

1. Richard Rothstein, *Color of Law: A Forgotten History of How Our Government Segregated America* (New York: W.W. Norton, 2018).

2. Greg J. Duncan, and Richard J. Murnane, eds., *Whither Opportunity? Rising Inequality, Schools, and Children's Life Chances* (New York: Russell Sage Foundation, 2011); Robert D. Putnam, *Our Kids: The American Dream in Crisis* (New York: Simon & Schuster, 2015).

3. See the Opportunity Atlas, 2018, https://www.opportunityatlas.org/ (Interactive Map, Charts, and Graphics with Data on Opportunities in the United States); Jo Blanden, Matthias Doepke, and Jan Stuhler, *Educational Inequality*, Working Paper 29979 (Cambridge, MA: National Bureau of Economic Research, April 2022).

4. Recognizing that language is constantly changing and that meanings are political, I begin with Maxine Baca Zinn's powerful explanation of the relationship between race and ethnicity:

> The term racial-ethnic refers to groups labeled as races in the context of certain historical, social, and material conditions. Blacks, Latinos, and Asian Americans are racial groups that are formed, defined, and given meaning by a variety of social forces in the wider society, most notably distinctive forms of labor exploitation. Each group is also bound together by ethnicity, that is, common ancestry and emergent cultural characteristics that are often used for coping with racial oppression. The concept racial-ethnic underscores the social construction of race and ethnicity for people of color in the United States.

Maxine Baca Zinn, "Family, Feminism, and Race in America," in *Families in the U.S.: Kinship and Domestic Politics*, eds. Karen V. Hansen and Anita I. Garey (Philadelphia, PA: Temple University Press, 1998), 39. With this historical backdrop, I recognize that there is no consensus within any racial-ethnic group about the best term to use to describe their identity. I use what I understand to be the most widely accepted terms and those that are most appropriate to the historical moment the book is describing. I use "Black" and "African American," as well as Latina/o and Chicana/o, interchangeably.

5. Gary Orfield, Jongyeon Ee, Erica Frankenberg, and Genevieve Siegel-Hawley, *Brown at 62: School Segregation by Race, Poverty, and State* (Los Angeles: Civil Rights Project/Proyecto Derechos Civiles, UCLA, 2016); Amy Stuart Wells, Jennifer Jellison Holme, Anita Tijerina Revilla, and Awo Korantemaa Atanda, *Both Sides Now: The Story of School Desegregation's Graduates* (Berkeley: University of California Press, 2009). See also Betty Cox, "De Facto Segregation," in *Encyclopedia of Educational Reform and Dissent*, eds. Thomas C. Hunt, James C. Carper II, Thomas J. Lasley, and C. Daniel Raisch (Thousand Oaks, CA: Sage, 2010), 260–61.

6. William F. Reese, *The Origins of the American High School* (New Haven, CT: Yale University Press, 1995); Theodore R. Sizer, *Horace's Compromise: The Dilemma of the American High School* (New York: Houghton Mifflin, 2004). Ethnographer Ann Arnett Ferguson explains that the asymmetries between the dominant middle-class white norms of a school and the communication styles of its working-class Black students create an environment in which teachers perceive students as having a "bad attitude." This in turn can reinforce some teachers' belief that many of their students don't have the cultural resources to be successful students. Ann Arnett Ferguson, *Bad Boys: Public Schools in the Making of Black Masculinity*, 2nd ed. (Ann Arbor: University of Michigan Press, 2020), 61–62. See also Prudence L. Carter, *Keepin' It Real: School Success Beyond Black and White* (New York: Oxford University Press, 2005).

7. Jeannie Oakes, *Keeping Track: How Schools Structure Inequality*, 2nd ed. (New Haven, CT: Yale University Press, 2005).

8. Nicholas Townsend, *The Package Deal: Marriage, Work and Fatherhood in Men's Lives* (Philadelphia, PA: Temple University Press, 2002). These neighborhoods also had an abundance of single-parent households. Judith Stacey, "Sexism by a Subtler Name? Postindustrial Conditions and Postfeminist Consciousness in Silicon Valley," *Socialist Review* 96 (1987): 7–28.

9. Jim Miller interview, August 25, 2014.

10. Sara Lawrence Lightfoot, *The Good High School: Portraits of Character and Culture* (New York: Basic Books, 1983), 10.

11. Lightfoot, *The Good High School*, 23. A host of excellent ethnographic and longitudinal studies of high schools points to similar recommendations: Gerald Grant, *The World We Created at Hamilton High*, rev. ed. (Cambridge, MA: Harvard University Press, 1990); Michael Medved and David Wallechinsky, *What Really Happened to the Class of '65?* (New York: Ballantine, 1981); Sherry B. Ortner, *New Jersey Dreaming: Capital, Culture, and the Class of '58* (Durham, NC: Duke University Press, 2003); C. J. Pascoe, *Nice Is Not Enough: Inequality and the Limits of Kindness at American High* (Berkeley: University of California Press, 2023).

12. Michael Rutter, Barbara Maughan, Peter Mortimer, Janet Ousten, with Alan Smith, *Fifteen Thousand Hours: Secondary Schools and Their Effects on Children* (Cambridge, MA: Harvard University Press, 1979), 182–84.

13. John Dewey, "Looking Back: My Pedagogic Creed," *Language Arts* 59 (1982): 541.

14. Othering & Belonging Institute, University of California, Berkeley, https://belonging.berkeley.edu/our-story, accessed January 13, 2024.

15. Clark Kerr, *The Uses of the University*, 5th ed. (Cambridge, MA: Harvard University Press, 1963).

16. Heather McGhee, *The Sum of Us: What Racism Costs Everyone and How We Can Prosper Together* (New York: One World, 2021).

17. Erica Licht, and Khalil Gibran Muhammad, "A Call for Anti-Bias Education," *Learning for Justice* 5 (Fall 2023): 31. See also Cherry M. Banks, *Improving Multicultural Education: Lessons from the Intergroup Education Movement* (New York: Teachers College Press, 2005); Patricia Gurin, Biren (Ratnesh) A. Nagda, and Ximena Zúñiga, eds., *Dialogue across Difference: Practice, Theory, and Research on Intergroup Dialogue* (New York: Russell Sage Foundation, 2013).

Chapter 1

A Vale in the Sun

The stories recounted in this book unfolded during the late 1960s and early 1970s in a place of sunshine and strife: Sunnyvale, California.

Sunnyvale sits at the northern end of the Santa Clara Valley, the homeland of the Ohlone people. Two hundred years ago, vast grasslands dotted with oaks covered the valley and the foothills, stretching up to the coniferous forests of the Santa Cruz Mountains. The region enjoys soft breezes off San Francisco Bay but does not get enveloped by the fog that shrouds the northern part of the peninsula. As Native people knew and settler colonists learned, the gentle climate and rich soil yielded an abundance.

Ohlone people harvested acorns from the carefully tended oak trees and ground them into flour, which was the mainstay of their diet. For thousands of years, they "practiced land management by using fire to keep brush from taking over meadowlands, and this provided grazing habitat for game and fostered certain grass and flower types for the dietary chain."[1] They also traversed the mountains to fish on the coast as far south as Point Sur.

Conflict and conquest, not peaceful coexistence, marked the valley after the arrival of Europeans in the eighteenth century. Spanish missionaries intent on Christianizing Native people enslaved them to perform all the labor on the ranchos. The decimation of the Indigenous residents resulted not only from Natives' lack of exposure and immunity to Europeans' endemic diseases but also from their forced labor and concentration around missions.[2]

The United States declared its sovereignty over the territory of California at the beginning of the Mexican-American War of 1846–1848. Its audacious claim took on greater meaning with the influx of white settlers from the east. The discovery of gold in the Sierra foothills in 1849 drew tens of thousands of gold seekers to California's mountains and seaports, as well as its fertile valleys. This invasion intensified the contest over land. Aiming to "eliminate the Natives," who belonged to approximately sixty distinct linguistic groups, white men hunted down and slaughtered the surviving bands of Indigenous people throughout California.[3]

At the same time, railroad companies recruited Chinese men to dig tunnels, build bridges, and lay track for the transcontinental railroad.[4] The United States intended the laborers' stay to be temporary, and Congressional legislation prevented them from bringing spouses to join them. With the passage of the federal Chinese Exclusion Act of 1882, after the completion of the railroad network, no more Chinese were allowed to immigrate. In 1913, the state legislature passed the California Alien Land Law, which prohibited Asian immigrants—Chinese, Japanese, Korean, and Filipino—from owning or leasing agricultural land.[5]

Farmers first planted wheat in the Santa Clara Valley, then discovered that orchards of apricots, cherries, and prunes were more profitable. In the 1890s, immigrants from Portugal, Lebanon, and Italy became small landholders and experts in growing fruit trees. The soil in Sunnyvale and Mountain View was especially good for cherries.[6]

Food processing companies started canning and drying fruit near the orchards and next to railroads that shipped their products to vast markets. Some manufacturers, such as Hendy Iron Works, also set up shop. Town boosters recruited businesses by touting the abundance of labor and took advantage of the 1906 earthquake that devastated San Francisco by attracting even more families seeking work and housing.[7]

In 1901, local residents and real estate developers chose the name Sunnyvale for the town, which was incorporated in 1912. That name conjured a California dream that concealed the violent past and the racial hierarchies that helped the town to prosper. "Sunny" fits the weather, while "vale" is ambiguous. It describes an extensive tract of flat land bounded by hills, but also means "the scene of life,"[8] as it was for the throngs of people who came to make Sunnyvale home.

California produced the vast majority of fruits and vegetables sold in the United States. The industry was concentrated in Santa Clara Valley, which "produced 90% of California's total fruit and vegetable output" in 1930.[9] That year, thirty-eight canneries operated in the valley.[10] Sunnyvale's four canneries—Schuckls, Libby's, California Canners, and Del Monte—were its major employers. They recruited seasonal workers, predominantly women, who sorted and packed fruit and tended huge, boiling hot vats that filled whole neighborhoods with a sickeningly sweet smell. The supply, wages, and conditions of labor were always an issue in the boom-and-bust economy, driven by war and depression: "1934 marked the peak year for Sunnyvale's canning industry."[11] For employers, recruiting enough temporary workers to meet seasonal demand was continually a challenge. For workers, conditions in the packing sheds and processing plants where they toiled "long hours for low pay" were "hazardous" and "unsanitary."[12] When the Great Depression galvanized widespread efforts to organize industrial unions, cannery workers staged their first strike in 1931 and by the end of the 1930s had formed the United Cannery and Agricultural and Packing and Allied Workers of America.[13]

In 1930, Sunnyvale became home to Moffett Naval Air Station and an array of defense-related industries.[14] During and after World War II, the cherry and apricot orchards were gradually displaced by factories, offices, and housing for their employees. Hendy Iron Works and the National Aeronautics and Space Administration (NASA) coexisted with Libby's and California Canners, which operated until the 1970s. After the war, federal efforts to sustain US military supremacy, combined with pork barrel politics, funneled massive government funding into California's defense industries. Sunnyvale and the entire Bay Area benefited enormously from the arms race with the Soviet Union. (See figure 1.1.)

Houses thrown up on the cheap for workers proliferated and were made affordable for white veterans by their modest prices, the GI Bill, and FHA loans. Federal housing support and loans went almost exclusively to whites, not other racial groups.[15] Between outright discrimination and real estate agents ushering African Americans to East Palo Alto and white families toward Mountain View and Sunnyvale, few Black families owned homes in the affordable subdivisions—Lakewood and Fairwood—north of the Bayshore Freeway.[16]

The combination of the baby boom and rapid in-migration of workers meant the city grew quickly, continuing to build over more of that prime cherry-growing soil. To accommodate the flood of children entering the school system amid an influx of new workers and the postwar baby boom, Sunnyvale needed a second high school.

FOUNDING A NEW SCHOOL

Until 1956, Fremont High School, built in 1925, was the city's only high school. The Fremont Union High School District decided to build a new school on the north side of town to serve the burgeoning housing developments where blue-collar Anglo, Mexican American, and Asian American families were concentrated. Although deeds did not restrict the sale of houses to nonwhites, the price of housing determined where people could afford to live. Zoning laws in Sunnyvale reserved a majority of land for single-family homes, and only a few neighborhoods in the northern part of the city allowed higher-density housing. In effect, the combination of zoning, discriminatory realty practices, and prices segregated neighborhoods by class and color. One

16 *Chapter 1*

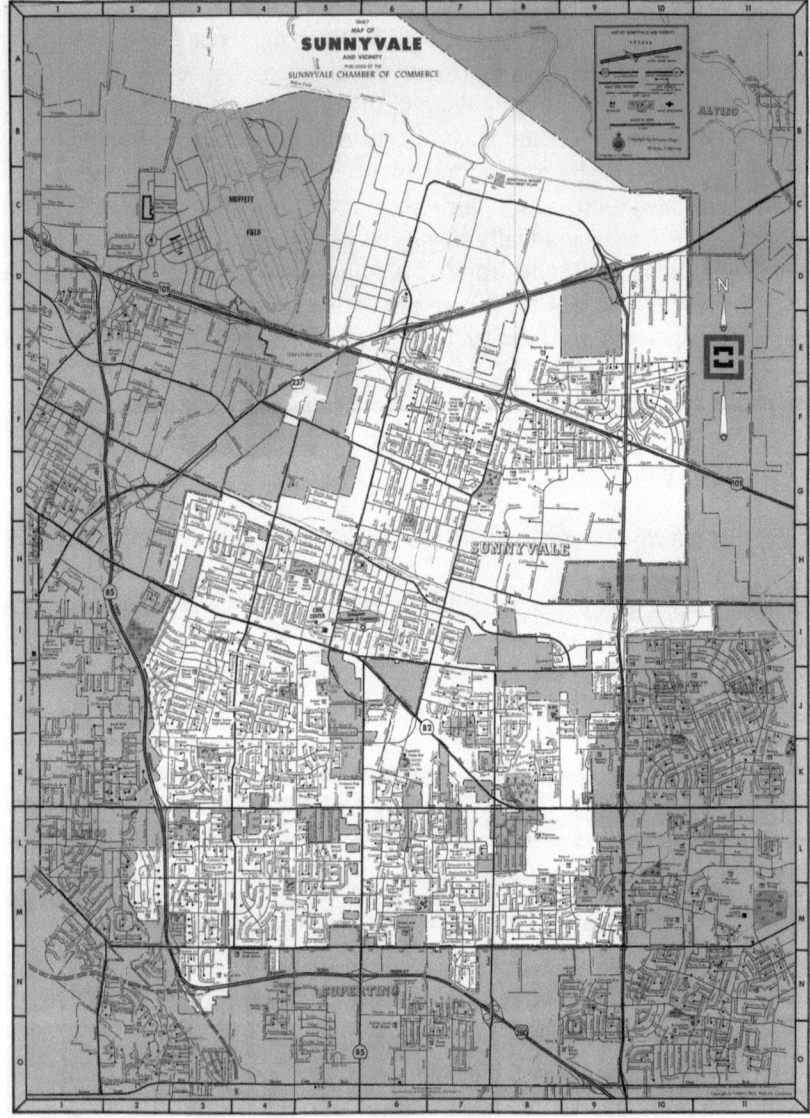

Figure 1.1 Map of Sunnyvale, California, 1956. *Source*: Sunnyvale Chamber of Commerce. Courtesy of Sunnyvale Historical Society and Museum Association.

student told me how his Mexican parents were swindled when they tried to purchase a house in Lakewood. The father paid a down payment, and the family moved in. The seller reneged on the contract and said the family had to rent the house from him. They lived there for twenty-two years, by which time they would have owned the house free and clear.

The city's financially stratified housing patterns concentrated nonwhite families spatially, and their children attended elementary school in their working-class neighborhoods. As a recent report from the Opportunity Institute at the University of California, Berkeley, *Unjust Legacy*, explains, "These policies and practices have directly contributed to the segregation of schools by both race and income since district boundaries and school zones closely mirror neighborhood patterns."[17] Those in Sunnyvale High's catchment area generated its racial mix. In effect, SHS was integrated because of the neighborhoods it served, not due to a court mandate.

Santa Clara County, which included the cities of San Jose and Santa Clara as well as Sunnyvale, was majority white in 1960. Over the next two decades, Sunnyvale's population more than doubled, from 52,898 to 106,618, and became more racially and ethnically diverse. The State of California counted "Spanish origin" persons separately (11.6 percent in 1980), but the federal census did not distinguish them from "Anglos," as non-Hispanic whites were locally called, until 1980.[18] First- and second-generation Mexicans formed the largest minority group. African American migrants from the South and a wide range of immigrants from Asia and the Pacific Islands made the population even more diverse. By 1972, in California as a whole, 30 percent of public school students were from racial and ethnic minorities, and that proportion was growing.[19]

Sunnyvale High School opened its doors in 1956, and its first class graduated in 1958. From its inception, SHS was under-resourced in comparison to Fremont High, which Paul Sakamoto described as the "mother school." Sakamoto, a Japanese American, had done his student teaching at Fremont and was hired to teach science at SHS in 1958. He remarked on "the constant comparison to Fremont. . . . We felt that we had a reputation to uphold there, to accomplish in the new school. . . . A pioneering spirit ran through the school and the faculty." From the beginning, he said, "the interaction between students and faculty was very close, and we all felt the same spirit."

The school's functional architecture communicated its intent to create future workers rather than aspiring scholars. (See figure 1.2.) Students criticized the buildings for looking like a factory. After the school closed in 1981, it became a Westinghouse factory.[20] Yet its one-story buildings, clustered on thirty-three acres and connected by open walkways, represented modern design. At its center, a rectangular rally court created a large public gathering space, with shade trees in planter boxes on one side, parallel to the cafeteria. The trees were encircled by elevated benches, ideal for groups of students to huddle and talk. A circular lawn commanded one end of the paved quadrant. Dubbed the "senior lawn," it was the exclusive territory of seniors, who threatened to dump trespassing underclassmen upside down in a garbage can.

An imposing gym bounded one end of the rally court, gateway to the locker rooms and swimming pools, complete with high diving boards. Behind the

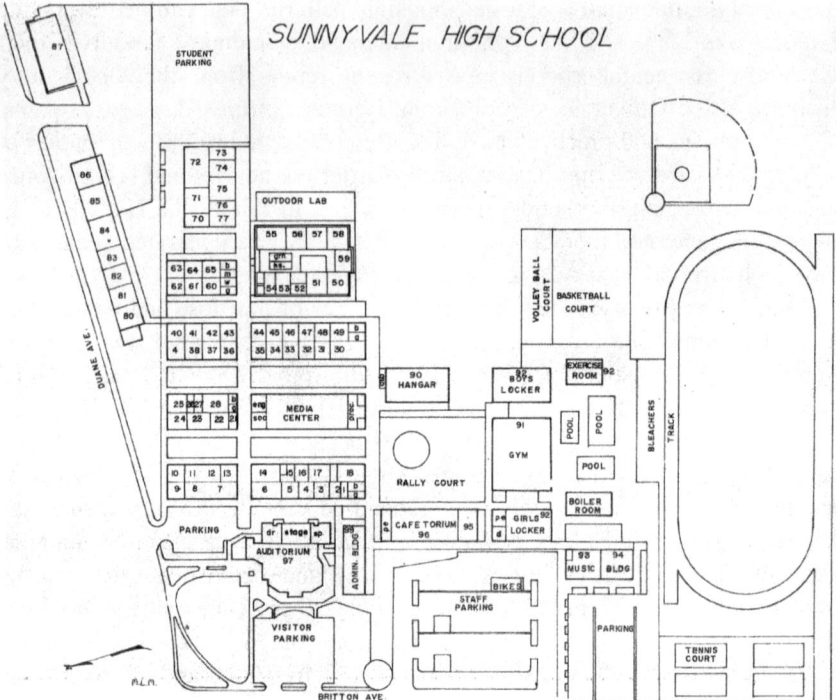

Figure 1.2 Plan of Sunnyvale High School. *Source*: Courtesy of Sunnyvale Historical Society and Museum Association.

gym was a track circling a football field with bleachers on the gym side. The student center, called the Hangar in keeping with the school's aerospace theme, was on the opposite side of the rally court from the cafeteria. Rows of lockers lined the open walkways that led to classrooms.

The location of classrooms was organized by subject matter. The art department and auto shop claimed cavernous buildings a long walk from the rally court, which gave these students a distinct sense of identity. Science classrooms with labs clustered in one wing and home economics with modular kitchens in another. The college-bound kids were a less visible minority, as college preparatory classes were interspersed with others in subjects like math and language arts.

ON THE WRONG SIDE OF THE TRACKS

Sunnyvale High School was built on the north side of town to serve the children of workers in the orchards and canneries, factories, defense plants, the military, and the service sector. It was the working-class school with a sizable minority population in a white middle-class district. Less was expected of the students at Sunnyvale High academically and athletically than their white middle-class rivals at Fremont High. It offered no advanced placement courses; math whizzes were sent to De Anza College in nearby Cupertino.[21]

The school was situated across the railroad tracks that traversed the peninsula north-south, parallel to and less than a mile away from El Camino Real, the historic roadway through the valley. These corridors separated middle-income homes from higher-density apartments and modestly priced houses of poor and working-class families. The boundaries that determined which school students would attend shifted back and forth depending on areas of population growth. Some years, in the neighborhood between El Camino and the railroad tracks, children in one household would go to Fremont, and several years later the boundary would be redrawn and younger children from the same home would attend Sunnyvale.

El Camino acted as a dividing line, especially for Mexican American youth. Growing up on the north side, David Hernandez '73 felt he could not cross El Camino because kids would call him derogatory names and shout epithets at him; people would stare at him; police would harass him. The road acted as a social boundary that dictated how young people moved through public spaces.

The Fremont Union High School District included five other high schools—Fremont, Monta Vista, Homestead, Lynbrook, and Cupertino. From the perspective of Suzi Brink '72, the other schools were "where the rich kids went." Stretch Lakely '73 remembered going to other schools for athletic events. "You just look in the parking lot. We look at all the cars. It's like, yeah, they got money." With its high proportion of students from struggling households, SHS qualified as a high-poverty school for purposes of federal assistance.

Because of the poverty, racial and ethnic diversity, and working-class background of most students, SHS had the reputation as a tough school. While at Fremont High for one experimental week, Black student Max Epps '73 heard students call SHS "the quote unquote ghetto school, lots of problems there."

The head of girls' PE, Carolyn Buszdieker, commented that this distinction affected athletic competitions: "You would be amazed at the number of kids" from other schools who "were afraid to come by the campus because of all of the things they had heard about how terrifying that [it] was to be there." That aversion was expressed even on neutral territory, like a football game at another school. JoAnn Vargas '73 danced with the Sabrettes, the SHS drill team. It was customary for girls in all the spirit squads to cross the field and greet each other at halftime of each game. JoAnn recalled when the opposing school's squads refused to come over. "We were told they were afraid of us, because we have razor blades in our hair."

Buszdieker described an incident that marked the psychological boundary signified by El Camino. As coach of the badminton team, she and the players waited for the arrival of the Homestead High School team. "They were late." When they finally arrived at Sunnyvale, the Homestead coach said, "We got held up at the border." She knew the other coach was alluding to the international border that kept Mexican families out of the United States. Buzz laughed as she told the story because it was so outrageously insulting. Her retort conveyed the antipathy that she, the other SHS coaches, and students felt toward this prejudicial attitude. "Well," I said, "I'm sorry they let you through then."

The economic and racial-ethnic segregation in the district went hand-in-hand with markers of second-class status. The SHS football field did not have lights for night games, so students trudged over to the rival's home field on Fridays. SHS did not even have its own buses. Sunnyvale teams were transported to events in what Carolyn Buszdieker described as "yellow, long, many-seated vehicles with the black racing stripes saying *Fremont High School*."

SHS students understood and resented their inferior reputation. Sharon Faeta '70 described Fremont as "the whiter school." Gloria Collins '73 referred to Fremont as the "arch enemy, in football and everything else." She, along with many others, perceived Fremont High as having "higher academic standards." She lived in the neighborhood between El Camino and the railroad tracks, where the school boundary lines shifted.

In that in-between neighborhood, full of homeowners, parents held decently paid jobs in the semiconductor, defense, and technology industries. Some had college degrees. One girl's father was a scientist at Ames National Laboratories. Yolanda Garcia's father worked at Westinghouse as a calibration technician for small instruments and appliances. Max Epps's dad was a military scientist whose work at Moffett Field was top secret; his mother was a registered nurse. Jane Manley's newly divorced mother worked as a secretary before she studied for a master's degree in social work. Cathy Coombs's father was a NASA scientist.

Many Sunnyvale parents hoped their children would earn a high school diploma, which they had been prevented from doing because of poverty or discrimination. In their eyes, graduating from high school was a real achievement. Other parents, usually those who were middle class and had some higher education, expected their children to go to college.

From the beginning, Sunnyvale High was an integrated school with an abundance of migrant and immigrant families. The district, mandated by the state of California and its courts to maintain "racial balance," used SHS demographics to signal its integrated profile. In the late 1970s, the influx of refugees from Vietnam and other war-torn countries in Southeast Asia brought even more linguistic diversity to the community.

Because the city of Sunnyvale had few African American families in the 1960s, SHS had virtually no Black students at first. That shifted gradually, although not dramatically. By 1970, about 2 percent of its students were Black. Several large families stood out as school leaders and athletes. Jackie Gooch '74, whose seven siblings also graduated from Sunnyvale High, reflected: "I always considered it to be a melting pot, because I looked at it as, we had Samoans; we had the Mexican Americans; we had our white population; you had the Black population, you had Hawaiians; you had Filipinos." Mexican American Dan Serna '71 described SHS as "a definite melting pot." His friend and fellow Chicano Student Union member Pete Araujo '71 noted that SHS distinguished itself from other schools by having "a mixture of many races. . . . We took in people from the north, from the south, from the east and the west. And they all came to Sunnyvale" and "all mixed in one pot." JoAnn Vargas '73, who was Puerto Rican, treasured the diversity at Sunnyvale High: "You can make friends with all ethnic backgrounds," something denied her in predominantly white schools she had previously attended.

Despite its dismal reputation among outsiders and the district's low expectations of its students, students and teachers defended their school and embraced a spirit of camaraderie.

NOTES

1. City of Sunnyvale, *Historical Context Statement* (Sunnyvale: City of Sunnyvale, 1988), 1–2. See also Mary Jo Ignoffo, *Sunnyvale: From the City of Destiny to the Heart of Silicon Valley* (Cupertino: California History Center & Foundation, 1994).
2. Elias Castillo, *A Cross of Thorns: The Enslavement of California's Indians by the Spanish Missions* (Fresno, CA: Craven Street Books, 2017); Brendon Lindsay, *Murder State: California's Native American Genocide, 1846–1873* (Lincoln: University of Nebraska Press, 2012).
3. Benjamin Madley, *An American Genocide* (New Haven, CT: Yale University Press, 2016); Patrick Wolfe, "Settler Colonialism and the Elimination of the Native," *Journal of Genocide Research* 8 (December 2006): 387–409.
4. Richard White, *Railroaded: The Transcontinentals and the Making of Modern America* (New York: W.W. Norton, 2012).
5. Erika Lee, *At America's Gates: Chinese Immigration during the Exclusion Era, 1882–1924* (Chapel Hill: University of North Carolina Press, 2003).
6. In a 2014 interview with me, Charles Olson reflected on his family's ties to the land. His Swedish father and Lebanese mother started a successful orchard and fruit stand. He explained that cherry trees "don't like clay or heavy soil. They like gravelly soil with loam because they don't like to get their feet wet." Compared to other parts

of the Santa Clara Valley, soil conditions were perfect. See the book written by his daughter, Yvonne Jacobson, *Passing Farms, Enduring Values: California's Santa Clara County* (Cupertino: California History Center Foundation, 2001).

7. Ignoffo, *Sunnyvale*, chapter 2.

8. *Oxford English Dictionary, Compact Ed.* (New York: Oxford University Press, 1987), 3584.

9. Ignoffo, *Sunnyvale*, 37.

10. Glenna Matthews, *Silicon Valley, Women, and the California Dream: Gender, Class, and Opportunity in the Twentieth Century* (Stanford, CA: Stanford University Press, 2003), 36.

11. City of Sunnyvale, *Historical Context Statement*, 6.

12. Vicki L. Ruiz, *Cannery Women, Cannery Lives: Mexican Women, Unionization, and the California Food Processing Industry, 1930–1950* (Albuquerque: University of New Mexico Press, 1987), 21.

13. Matthews, *Silicon Valley, Women, and the California Dream*; Ruiz, *Cannery Women, Cannery Lives*; Patricia Zavella, *Women's Work and Chicano Families: Cannery Workers of the Santa Clara Valley* (Ithaca, NY: Cornell University Press, 1987).

14. City of Sunnyvale, *Historical Context Statement*, 5. The base changed names and federal jurisdictions several times, and is now called Moffett Field.

15. Ira Katznelson, *When Affirmative Action Was White: An Untold History of Racial Inequality in Twentieth-Century America* (New York: W.W. Norton, 2005).

16. George Galster, "Racial Discrimination in Housing Markets during the 1980s: A Review of the Audit Evidence," *Journal of Planning Education and Research* 9 (1990): 165–75; Eli Moore, Nicole Montojo, and Nicole Mauri, *Roots, Race, & Place: A History of Racially Exclusionary Housing in the San Francisco Bay Area* (Berkeley: Haas Institute for a Fair and Inclusive Society, University of California, Berkeley, 2019).

17. Carrie Hahnel, Arun Ramanathan, Jacopo Bassetto, and Andrea Cerrato, *Unjust Legacy: How Proposition 13 Has Contributed to Intergenerational, Economic, and Racial Inequities in Schools and Communities* (Berkeley, CA: Opportunity Institute, June, 2022), 11.

18. Bay Area Census. http://www.bayareacensus.ca.gov/cities/Sunnyvale50.htm.

19. State Board of Education, "Racial and Ethnic Distribution of Pupils in California Public Schools, Fall 1971. A Report to the State Board of Education," 1972. https://eric.ed.gov/?id=ED070789.

20. A decade later, SHS's former campus housed a private Christian school.

21. Jack Schneider, "Privilege, Equity, and the Advanced Placement Program: Tug of War," *Journal of Curriculum Studies* 41 (2009): 813–31.

Chapter 2

Spirit by Design

Reflecting on the community that made up SHS, Robert Handa '73 posed a central question this book explores:

> When you look through a lot of the people who went to Sunnyvale High . . . there's a lot of successful people. They may be a blue-collar success. Some of them took it and translated it into white-collar success. But the point is . . . these people did not grow up with a lot of advantages.

So, Handa wondered: "What was it about that system that enabled them not to succeed, but to have the aspiration and the confidence to *try* to succeed, and then succeed?" Given its racially diverse students, working-class parents with little formal education and limited or no English, and high rate of turnover, how did SHS engage and motivate students?

FROM A PRISON TO A PLACE WHERE EVERYONE BELONGED

Founded only ten years after the end of World War II, SHS was first led by Marty Mathiesen, a military veteran and PE teacher. As the founding principal, he chose the school's mascot, the Jets, and the associated themes and colors, Columbia blue and white. Borrowing from the Air Force and connecting it symbolically to the nearby military base where many parents worked, Sunnyvale High's fight song began: "Off we go, onto the field of battle." The year after students came to the new campus, the Jets picked up cultural cachet from Stephen Sondheim and Leonard Bernstein's musical, "West Side Story." This modern adaptation of "Romeo and Juliet" opened on Broadway in New York City in 1957, featuring warring gangs—the Sharks versus the Jets. The visceral rivalry reflected an epic animus that tragically divided lovers and families. Being Jets connected Sunnyvale High to history and contemporary culture, while Shakespeare reminded everyone of the potential danger of vindictive conflicts.

Mathiesen believed in strict discipline. Head of Boys' PE Doug Boyd recalled, "He had a saying: 'Be fair, be firm, and be consistent.'" In practice, Mathiesen took a punitive approach to rule violations. As teacher Paul Sakamoto put it,

> He ran the school with an iron fist. I never forget the time that . . . I was at the main office and a woman came in to complain to him about Sunnyvale High School. She said, "My son tells me that you run the school like a prison." And Mathiesen responded, "That's because he's a prisoner."

Mathiesen's approach did not work. The district office noticed that an unusually large number of boys were getting expelled, particularly those who were Latino. Parents complained, prompting the district to investigate. Eventually, the district called on Adrian Stanga, then a business teacher at Fremont High, to investigate the situation with Latino boys. With his consent, administrators transferred him to SHS as vice principal and dean of boys.

Stanga's philosophy and approach to students contrasted sharply with Mathiesen's. Stanga believed in establishing personal connections with the students he disciplined. "As a dean, I never suspended a boy without being able to shake his hand 'cause he knew he got a fair deal. He knew he was wrong." Stanga sincerely respected his students and set high expectations for their behavior. By establishing individual relationships with students, he conveyed that he cared about them.

Two years later, in 1959, Adrian Stanga replaced Mathiesen as principal. Envisioning how to improve students' experiences at school, he realized he could tap into feelings of camaraderie stemming from Sunnyvale High's status as the city's "second-class school." Stanga knew what it meant to be the underdog. He grew up in a downwardly mobile white Louisiana family. He explained how his experience shaped his philosophy:

> My . . . grandfather was a wealthy man, owned much land in Southeast Louisiana. Not so when I was born. My father died in 1926, Christmas Eve, I was 4 years old. Mother died in 1938. I was 15, right at the peak of the Depression. The whole town had 400 people. Three miles away were 3,000 people. There was that dividing line. We thought they thought they were superior to us. At least *I* thought they thought they were superior. And so there was a white caste system in the South. . . . We fell down maybe [to] the lower middle or upper

lower class. . . . Simply put, I felt an empathy with those kids of Sunnyvale High School. I felt I knew what they were going through.

Relationship building was core to Stanga's approach to education. As Eric Paulson '62 said, he "tried to build relationships with all the kids, so each kid felt a part of the school." Stanga "made an effort to know us. He was always out on campus. He was always talking to kids. He was part of our lives. It was not like, 'Well, here comes the principal, we stay away from him.' . . . He was very, very positive." Carol Blasquez '62, who later married Eric Paulson, agreed: "He made us feel like whatever we were doing was important."

JET PRIDE

Under Stanga's leadership, working-class stigma morphed into school pride. He opened multiple doors for students to get involved at school and feel like they belonged. Stanga explained, "It was my philosophy to build a self-image and to say that we're as good as they are." Stanga understood that, even before academic achievement, it was important to address students' self-image and feelings of worth, to show them they mattered. He aimed to create an ethos of "oneness." He believed that fostering a connection to the school helped students develop pride, self-confidence, and motivation. They needed something to be proud of as well as something to define themselves against.

Fortunately, there was a ready-made common adversary on the more affluent side of the tracks. Fremont High's architecture conveyed its importance. Its football field had vast bleachers and lights so games could be held at night. It also had an outsized reputation.

The feeling of being disparaged had an impact on students' self-perception. Walter Hale, who taught math under Stanga and later became principal, explained: "Basically it was Sunnyvale against the rest of the district. We were tough, and we'd take them on, we didn't care where. And that attitude permeated the staff and brought us together." The sense of solidarity Stanga inspired came in part from being the underdog and resenting the indignities of an undeserved reputation. Suzi Brink '72 marveled at that bond:

> We had a unity. . . . We knew that we had to band together and be collectively better than *them*, better than what *they* thought of us. We bonded against the snobs who looked down on us, who had more advantages and more money, but less soul.

Malcolm High '67, a working-class Scottish immigrant, described how he felt crossing the border between high schools. When he dated a girl from

Fremont High he met in his church youth group, people there conveyed their dismay:

> I could name one hundred people that I'd met through my girlfriend who went to Fremont that wouldn't live in the house I lived in. They would think 'something really bad happened to us, and now we have to live there.' . . . Their homes seemed like they were three times the size of the homes on our side of the tracks in Sunnyvale.

He felt the profound class differences, and his girlfriend's parents treated him accordingly. They seemed to like him, but he always felt that they believed she "could do better."

Many high schools like Fremont, with majority white, middle-class student bodies, emphasized academic achievement above all else. That was not Sunnyvale's approach. While academics were important, success in the classroom was not the *only* way to achieve at SHS. The school invested in a broad curriculum that offered students many ways to discover their passions and talents, become involved, and succeed. For example, the music department provided a haven for those who wanted to learn to play instruments, sing, and perform, with a choir, an *a cappella* singing group, and many musical theater productions.

Representing a new school in the established Santa Clara Valley Athletic League, Sunnyvale High's sports teams often lost and, especially in the early days, anticipated defeat. School counselor Terry Dyckman observed that SHS students expected to lose in life as well as in athletic competitions. Adrian Stanga understood that losing lowered morale: "We had not won a football game in the first three graduating classes." Winning meant a lot to students. Even students who cared little for sports were proud of the effort their schoolmates put forth in competition. Jane Manley '72 took heart from Sunnyvale teams' fighting spirit. "We were scrappy and . . . I was proud of that."

RECRUITING TEACHERS WHO HAD RAPPORT WITH TEENAGERS

As principal, Adrian Stanga hired "a core of excellent teachers" who enjoyed working with teenagers and could connect with the blue-collar, racially integrated student body.

Stanga sought "people who understood the learning process, not only Track 3s but Track 1s." Using California's system of stratification, Stanga called Track 1 students "slow learners"; those in Track 3 were college bound. He wanted to build a school culture that incorporated *all* students. The principal could choose among the candidates the district office recommended for a teaching position. At that time, according to Paul Sakamoto, principals "had quite a bit of autonomy in running the school."

Teachers needed to have special skills in relating to adolescents. From SHS administrators' perspective, good teachers were "able to establish rapport with students, primarily. And we assumed that they knew their subjects since they were majoring in that subject. . . . We were more concerned about how well they communicated their subject matter to students." Sakamoto reflected:

> In Sunnyvale we did probably a better than average job of that, especially with teachers like Buzz [Carolyn Buszdieker], who had the ability to relate to kids in such a way that they didn't feel that it was like a prison.

Nearby San Jose State University became a logical source for new teachers. Its robust teacher training program placed student teachers in schools and collaboratively supported them. Its philosophy of experiential learning was innovative at that time. Those who earned teaching certificates at San Jose State were often the first in their families to attend college. In effect, they were good role models for Sunnyvale students. Later, the district also hired graduates from Stanford University's education program.

Carolyn Buszdieker was one of those San Jose State graduates who had done her student teaching at Fremont. She had known Adrian Stanga from the days when he was her high school typing teacher. She relayed a story they told about each other:

> He was just very charming and he walked around the typing room, and whenever he'd come by, he would put his hands on both sides of my desk and lean over and talk to me, face to face. And he did that with everybody. . . . So this one day he came up . . . and he leaned over and his tie went right in that [roller space]. It wasn't stuck. . . . I could flip it with my hand. And I reached up, looking at him, and out of the corner of my eye, I zipped the knob, pulling his head down.

In Adrian Stanga's version of this story, Carolyn then growled, "Give me an 'A'." She kept rolling his tie deeper into her typewriter, threatening him with every twirl. That story gets more dramatic with each retelling and the potential for strangulation more imminent, revealing their mutuality and playfulness.

Stanga hired Buszdieker, affectionately known as Buzz, to teach physical education at Sunnyvale High. She quickly became head of the department. Tall, comfortable in her body, and especially adept at cultivating social relationships, she had an easy laugh. Buzz's affability helped foster a culture where interpersonal bonds could form. She delighted in teasing students as lightheartedly as their loved ones and friends often do but was careful to never do so in a way that mocked or demeaned them.

It wasn't all fun and games. Buzz played a key leadership role across campus, setting a tone of respect while advocating for female athletes and girls in general. When she was hired in 1958, the Girls' Athletic Association (GAA) was treated as a club, not as organizing athletic competition. The 1959 yearbook devoted one-third of one page to the GAA and all of girls' sports, compared to the twenty-five pages covering boys' football, baseball, tennis, swimming, and everything else. Buzz set out to change that.

In 1966, after Stanga became a district administrator, Paul Sakamoto was promoted to principal. As dean of boys, head of the science department, and now principal, he embraced his predecessor's philosophy of bringing working-class students into a wide range of school activities and developing personal relationships with them. (see figure 2.1). As the eleventh child in a Japanese family who were sharecroppers on a farm they were forbidden to own, he knew poverty as well as vicious discrimination firsthand. Just eight years old when war broke out between the United States and Japan, Sakamoto and his family were evacuated to Rohwer concentration camp in Arkansas. Like all Japanese immigrants and their US–born children, his family fell

Figure 2.1 Paul Sakamoto, Vice Principal, 1966. *Source: Sabre,* 1966.

victim to President Roosevelt's heavy-handed Executive Order 9066 targeting Japanese and Japanese Americans. Forced to leave their homes and jobs, they had to work without pay while confined in remote locations. US citizenship offered no protection for native-born children like Paul. Although two-thirds of Japanese Americans incarcerated were US citizens, their civil and property rights were summarily disregarded.[1] Adding insult to injury for the Sakamoto family, three of Paul's older brothers served in the US military while his family was interned as "enemy aliens."

The emphasis on rapport with Sunnyvale kids favored teachers who were from working-class backgrounds themselves. Later in the 1960s, Sakamoto started hiring former SHS students who were first-generation college graduates. Remarkably, at least seven former students returned to work at Sunnyvale, including Eric Paulson, Sharon Prefontaine, Jim Miller, Joanne Shimoguchi, Steve McKeown, Rich Knapp, and John Figueroa. Jim Miller '64, who had been senior class president and captain of the tennis team, was the first Sunnyvale High student to graduate from Yale University. He returned to California and earned a master's degree in education from Stanford before teaching at SHS.

Miller pointed to a self-selection process that attracted him and other educators to SHS. The administration "thought it was important to be good mentors. . . . they really cared about making a difference." He reflected, "It was good to be young and enthusiastic. . . . Even in the math department, we tried to make things interesting." One of the shining stars of the class of 1964, Miller chose to return to Sunnyvale after finding his student teaching at Lynbrook High, a middle-class, racially homogenous school in the district, less exciting. According to Sakamoto, this dedication and set of values made "the faculty more committed than [at] most schools."

The changes Stanga and Sakamoto ushered in were not universally embraced by the faculty. Younger teachers faced opposition from some of the old guard who did not welcome innovation and lacked empathy for teenagers. Science teacher Bob Douglas recalled, "When I got to Sunnyvale, they had those senior teachers . . . who really controlled everything." Raised in Bakersfield, California, Bob, like his father, "worked in the oil fields to make money" while attending school. Unlike his father, he finished high school and then attended community college. In 1963, he transferred to San Jose State as a biology major, paying his way with the money he earned during the summer fighting "fires for the Forest Service."

When Douglas went to Napa for a one-year job as a science teacher, he was assigned students who had failed the course multiple times. He employed the compelling philosophy of his mentor at San Jose State who told him, "If you're gonna teach kids science, you have to have them *do science*. You don't lecture at 'em; you don't have 'em read it out of a book. You get 'em into a laboratory and you get their hands dirty." When he proposed taking his students on a field trip to the ocean for a marine biology unit, the school refused, believing the students too untrustworthy to let out of the building. So he created a science club, the students joined, and the administration relented. "Those kids lived 90 miles from the coast. They had never been to the beach, *ever*." Needless to say, they gained important insights from wading in tide pools and feeling the salty sea, and Bob Douglas demonstrated the power of experiential learning. "I brought that with me" to Sunnyvale High the following year, he concluded.

Loretta Gutierrez, also a product of San Jose State's dynamic teacher education program, remembers Sakamoto interviewing her for a job teaching English. When he found out she grew up as the youngest child in a large family of migrant farmworkers, she remembers him saying, "I was going to be *good* for their school because they didn't have very many Latino teachers. . . . He said, 'This is going to be great.'" Just twenty-three years old when she started teaching at SHS, Gutierrez faced bigoted teachers who dismissed her as a Mexican American woman. She and other young teachers supported each other to counter those senior faculty who resisted change and disparaged the students. Some "teachers . . . didn't give one iota about these kids, so we just had to keep our focus."

Bob Douglas elaborated: "Paul Sakamoto recruited a cadre of younger teachers that were second to none. I mean, they were incredible English teachers and physical education people and science people . . . very dynamic people." Douglas credited the school leadership, especially Sakamoto, for envisioning change and assembling an innovative team. In his view, Sakamoto, who later earned a PhD, "ended up being one of the strongest district superintendents in California before he retired."

According to Douglas, Sakamoto instituted key changes at Sunnyvale High. Above all, he put students first.

> He didn't always do things for the comfort of the faculty. He really looked at kids and looked at the kinds of experiences that kids needed to grow and become successful adults. And he tried to plug that into the curriculum.

Importantly, success was not narrowly defined. It included involvement in the community, citizenship, and doing meaningful work. In 1970, English teacher Peggy Hurt explained the approach to *The Skywriter*: "This foundation provides you with basic learning tools such as asking questions, listening to others' opinions, growing empathy with others and their views, and gaining awareness and confidence in yourself, your thoughts and your feelings."[2]

Sakamoto also made astute decisions in hiring his administrative team. His vice principal, Richard "Pete" Mesa, was the child of migrant farmworkers and played baseball in the Pacific Coast League before he became a science teacher and then dean of boys at SHS. Later, he became a superintendent in other districts and went on to become Chief Deputy Superintendent of Public Instruction for the State of California. Douglas called Mesa a "very, very talented guy." This leadership team had "a skill set and a commitment . . . that you rarely see." Counselor Terry Dyckman, who eventually went to work in private industry in the valley, shared that opinion. After working with technology firms' high-level executives, he described them as "some of the smartest people in the world and ostensibly great managers." In comparison, Sakamoto and Mesa "still stand out as probably the most inspirational and best leaders I've ever met."

Sakamoto explained their transformative approach. "At Sunnyvale we did more to reach the students. . . . We worked more diligently at including *all* students in programs, whether it be athletics, government, drama, speech, or homemaking." When Yolanda Garcia '72, who was Mexican American, transferred to Sunnyvale High from a Catholic girls' school her junior year, she found a welcoming environment. From school secretaries to teachers, "I felt supported. . . . Even in the beginning trying to find my classroom . . . I felt everybody was there to help the students, *all of them*." Including her.

CURRICULUM DESIGNED FOR EVERYONE

In a working-class and multiracial environment, Stanga realized that "something more should be done for those 'non-go-to-college students.'" Educating *all* students and the *whole* student was at the core of Adrian Stanga's philosophy, putting him on the cutting edge in the 1950s and 1960s. As he explained, "I hold that three domains—the cognitive, the affective, and the kinesthetic/psychomotor . . . should be educated."

Stanga promoted a broad curriculum with courses in art, choral and instrumental music, the industrial arts, home economics, and business in addition to math, science, history, languages (German, French, and Spanish), and English.[3] He saw work experience as foundational to vocational education. He linked students to jobs in the community, promoting on-the-job training and helping place students in local businesses. Classes involved hands-on activities. Malcolm High '67 relished his time in auto shop: "You're in there and you're smelling these solvents and oils and you're changing oil and learning about carburetors."

Tim Sanford '71 discovered theater at Sunnyvale High. The son of a third-grade teacher and a minister, he and his siblings worked summers picking beans in the fields of the Santa Clara Valley. After being artistic director of Playwrights Horizons theater in New York City for more than twenty years, he reflected on SHS's excellent music program, which allowed him to experiment and immerse himself in various genres. He recalled being part of a district-wide performance of Vivaldi's "Gloria." To outside observers' astonishment, it featured two outstanding vocalists from Sunnyvale: Peggy Gerboe had two solos and Kathy Nolan sang the duet. Sanford said, "We had a lot of really talented singers."

Other students found creative, hands-on experiences in SHS's vibrant art department. The art classrooms, located near the auto shop on the periphery of campus, were staffed by two full-time art teachers who each sponsored a student teacher. They taught pottery, drawing, and painting in a way that encouraged creativity and enabled students to discover and develop their talents. Paul Sakamoto commented that it "was unheard of" for a public school to devote so many resources to the arts, but "Ben Horachi and Herb Hart were great teachers." They inspired students and developed a loyal following: "Students would cut classes to go to their class." The art teachers often kept their classrooms open in the evening for students to work on their projects. Sakamoto observed:

> They were so casual about it that it caused some problems. . . . Some kid would say, "I need a piece of wiring." And Herb would look up and say, "Well, there's some wire up there. Why don't you cut that?" And that was the public address system.

When Stanga hired Sakamoto to teach math in the late 1950s, he was encouraged to be creative. "It was about the same time that the Russians sent Sputnik up." In 1957, the Soviet Union successfully launched the first satellite into earth's orbit. The United States was caught off guard and scrambled to catch up in the "space race." The federal government scoured the country for undeveloped talent and invested in science and math education. Sunnyvale benefited from those additional resources. Sakamoto said, "the students did well. The classes were small and the students were very bright."

After several years, Sakamoto discovered that the incoming class was especially talented. He appointed Bob Douglas to teach a summer biology class to help students accelerate and remain interested. Douglas said, "These kids' science skills were off the charts. I pushed them hard and presented them a week's worth of content every day. I pushed them and they always ran ahead of me." Douglas observed that the leadership team's innovations were research-based and data-driven:

> Those guys were well read and carefully studied what worked. They were intent on bringing those innovations into our academic and student services programs at Sunnyvale. They did that in science and mathematics, English and social studies, music and fine arts, student activities, and counseling and guidance.

Tracking students is widely criticized for creating and perpetuating inequality by separating students according to perceived abilities. Testing has often determined placement and thereby resulted in dividing young people by race and class.[4] In effect, tracking enriched and accelerated learning for some and led to underperformance and discouragement for others. Sunnyvale High recognized these dangers and employed heterogeneous grouping in some courses. As Sakamoto saw it:

> The benefit is that students learn from each other as well as from the teacher. In mixing students, they learn the culture of their fellow students; they get invited to homes of their classmates. And hopefully they learn a lot from just . . . sitting next to a student who is not like them.

Even as it saw the dangers and the potential to create inequality, Sunnyvale High sorted students. SHS had a special track for its small number of college-bound students.[5] Some were unaware of their separateness, but others noticed. Joe Leone '72, whose family was from Calabria, Italy, recalled: "We had a tiered system. . . . We had a set of Black students and a set of Chicano students that I never saw in classes," except for some Mexican and Mexican American students who were "intermixed." SHS offered no advanced placement courses, although it sent accelerated math students to take classes at the local community college.[6] One Mexican boy who did extremely well academically met with his counselor as a freshman. When the counselor found out that both of his parents worked at the cannery, he immediately enrolled the boy in auto shop and typing, rather than high-level math.

Some of the students who were sorted in to the lower tracks felt the distinction acutely. Walking into class his freshman year, Dan Serna '71 noticed immediately that all the faces in the room were Brown. Something was not right. "They put me in a class that you didn't have to do a damn thing. And it really upset me, man. . . . You're sitting in this class and you're going, 'What the hell's going on here?'" After his first year, Serna approached his counselor, Gerry Hanson, and told him, "I'm not gonna sit there for eight hours. . . . Put me in something. Either I make it or I break." That experience taught Serna a lesson: "I realized that a lot of things weren't as fair as they should be." When he spoke out, his counselor acted. Most students did not advocate so forcefully for themselves. Later, the Chicano Student Union (CSU) demanded that all students have equal access to a quality education regardless of their race or ethnicity.

The leadership team also paid close attention to students who were not performing well in key academic subjects. Bob Douglas reported that in the summer of 1968, Sakamoto and Mesa approached him and English teacher Tom O'Keefe about developing and team-teaching a new course that would cover the content of ninth-grade science and English. The students were all tenth graders who had failed science and English as freshmen. The course was scheduled as a two-hour block so it could take a practical approach. For example, the unit on nutrition and digestion was titled, "Where Does That Hamburger Go?" Douglas said:

> Students did a lot of hands-on science and literature and a ton of writing and speaking about science. It was an enormously successful attempt at motivating and rekindling interest in a group of kids who had given up and who had been labeled as low achievers by the system.

BELONGING BY PARTICIPATING

The ethos of the school encouraged connection and getting along. At its heart, that bond was built on SHS students' common class position. It was enhanced by opposition to other schools and a collective rejection of the stigma others placed on Sunnyvale High, its students, and, by implication, their families. As an example of that enduring ethos, the 1967 yearbook, the *Sabre*, was dedicated to the "Spirit of Sunnyvale High School." Its opening pages define that spirit as "enthusiastic loyalty" demonstrated by participation in student government, clubs, dances, rallies, and through victory and defeat in athletic competition.

Belonging was built on relationships between students. The shared economic circumstances of most families created a sense of equality for many. Black student Jackie Gooch '74 said, "Another thing I liked about Sunnyvale High School, . . . you might have had a few that had a little bit more, but most of us all came from the same side of the tracks." Robert Handa '73, whose Japanese American identity made him part of a visible minority, recalled: "There was no feeling like the whites are better off than us." Their collective underdog status bonded kids. "At Sunnyvale High, I don't think that people were really prejudiced, because who are you going to be prejudiced against? . . . We were all alike."

From Stanga's perspective, students had to feel like they belonged rather than being shunted aside as second-class citizens. The key, in Stanga's mind, was "to keep the kids interested and intermingling." Because everyone was required to attend school until they turned sixteen, the principal sought to engage them. "I'm adding activities and athletics . . . to give them a broader base, a foundation." Under his leadership, the school created a connective social tissue and offered many ways to get involved. "The nature of the activity brought people together."[7]

Stanga built a wide range of programs to engage students, not just sports teams but clubs, musical groups, theater, speech and debate, community service, and many groups to promote school spirit. That students got involved was more important than any specific activity. Eric Paulson '62 said that the principal "didn't care what it was, athletics, cheer, the band, choir, whatever. But you did *something*. And that connected you to the school. And if you're connected, you seemed to have better grades . . . you were more positive." Immigrant students like Malcolm High '67 treasured the opportunity "just to be a part of a group; you felt included."

Many clubs and activities were designed to induce students to identify with the school. From the beginning, girls served as cheerleaders and song leaders who supported boy athletes. They focused on football and basketball games. Letter girls stood at the back of the bleachers and spelled out J-E-T-S. The marching band was accompanied by flag twirlers and a dance and drill team, the Sabrettes, who performed in glittery short dresses and black net stockings in parades and at halftime.

Sharon Faeta '70 stepped onto campus in the fall of 1966 and immediately was captivated by the "goddesses" promoting school spirit. She was already performing with the Santa Clara Vanguard Drum and Bugle Corps, which marched in parades with flags, drums, and bugles and performed in competitions. Sharon felt drawn to the enthusiasm, the sense of purpose, the discipline and used her skills to stand up for her school. After shedding her shyness, she danced as part of an outstanding song girl squad her junior and senior years.

Of course, that rah-rah spirit did not appeal to all. But the vast school spirit apparatus offered expansive opportunities for involvement. The Pep Club was run by a student Commissioner of Pep and Rally, who belonged to the student government cabinet. She had an assistant commissioner and two commissioners for each class. There were varsity, junior varsity, and frosh cheerleading squads and dancing song girls. The school mascot—the Jetro, who dressed like a fighting pilot, with a one-piece uniform, a helmet, and boxing gloves—rotated by season. In addition to the marching band of sixty-plus, there was a pep band for basketball games.

The open call for tryouts did not reach everyone. Some found the effort to inculcate school spirit annoying and believed that it promoted hierarchy. When JoAnn Vargas '73 auditioned for Sabrettes and made the team, some Chicanas "gave me a static for it." She was surprised by their reaction because she was doing something she loved. But they called her a "rah-rah" and accused her of acting like "your shit don't stink." Somewhat offended, she confronted them and criticized their double standard: boys who got involved in school activities did not get the same kind of condemnation. "But being a female, it was like, 'Oh my God!'" She took pride in being one of the first Latinas to dance with the drill team and represent the school. Although urged by faculty and fellow Sabrettes to continue a second year and become a co-captain, she decided her need to work and help take care of her younger siblings overrode her delight in being part of the team.

The school scheduled all-school pep rallies during the school day. (See figure 2.2.) Every couple of weeks, the entire 2,000-plus student body, wearing white shirts, crammed into the gym bleachers to yell and scream and urge the team on. The substantial commitment of class time met some resistance. As Carolyn Buszdieker observed, "A lot of the teachers did not enjoy those pep rallies." The community outreach director, Vern Holte, quickly pointed out, "But the students did." Even skipping a class was not enough to mollify everyone. Jackie Gooch '74 resented the imposition; as she put it, "I didn't do cheerleaders very well." Girls' sports did not receive comparable support or enthusiasm. Indeed, they were almost invisible. (In other organizations, girls were often elected to leadership and constituted the bulk of many clubs' membership.) For many students, the pep rallies fostered a sense of "we" because virtually everyone participated. Sharon Faeta savored the collective experience: "I love that spirit, of your heart and your soul." To this day, she treasures her *Sabre* yearbook with SHS people and activities on display.

Adrian Stanga's vision of inclusiveness and involvement shaped the culture of the school long after he was promoted to the district administration in 1965. Paul Sakamoto picked up where Stanga left off, adapted this approach to the increasingly diverse student body, and deepened the possibilities for an

Figure 2.2   Pep Rally, 1972. *Source*: *Sabre*, 1972.

engaged education. Reflecting on her high school years, Cece Padgett '72 felt most proud of "being a part of a community and a class." Robert Handa '73 shared similar sentiments: "I remember thinking that I *belonged*."

NOTES

1. Erika Lee, *The Making of Asian America: A History* (New York: Simon & Schuster, 2015), 212.

2. *The Skywriter*, March 4, 1970.

3. Matthew B. Crawford, *Shop Class as Soulcraft: An Inquiry into the Value of Work* (New York: Penguin, 2009).

4. Jeannie Oakes, *Keeping Track: How Schools Structure Inequality*, 2nd ed. (New Haven, CT: Yale University Press, 2005).

5. Because the school records have been destroyed, these comments are based on teachers' and students' recollections. Students were often not aware of the system and whether had been placed in high or low tracks.

6. Schneider, "Privilege, Equity, and the Advanced Placement Program."

7. Contemporary research confirms the impact of extra-curricular activities. See Karlyn J. Gorski, "In School for After School: The Relationship between Extracurricular Participation and School Engagement," *Sociological Forum* 36 (March 2021): 248–70.

Chapter 3

Athletics before Title IX

Sports were at the center of SHS's extracurricular activities. As a magnet for restless teenagers and spectators eager to view competitive games, organized sports created an arena for belonging and interacting across racial and ethnic groups. An environment for students to make friends and learn to get along, athletics has been a bright spot in America's continuing struggle for school integration.[1] As in other schools across the country, sports at Sunnyvale High prompted students from different cultural, racial, and ethnic backgrounds to bond against a common adversary.

At the same time, the sports program was structured by gender inequities. Efforts to provide space and resources for girls' sports faced deep resistance. Schools underestimated the importance of athletics to young women. Sunnyvale High School denied girls' teams access to the gym and money for uniforms, and treated the women coaches like volunteers. Because sports help young people develop skills and self-confidence, this stark inequality had serious consequences.

THE BENEFITS OF PHYSICAL ACTIVITY

Sunnyvale High recognized the centrality of the mind-body connection to boys' development but disregarded its value for girls. Historically, masculinity has been deeply tied to athletic endeavors as well as to warfare.[2] Strong advocates within the school struggled to broaden opportunities for girls.

In the 1960s and 1970s, few parents attended their daughters' athletic events. Stretch Lakely '73 knew her mother could not watch her games because she had a full-time job. From Stretch's perspective, what mattered was that her mother did not object to her playing sports. Describing herself as "like the energizer bunny," Stretch played basketball, baseball, volleyball, and swam competitively. In contrast, two sisters being raised by their protective single father were not allowed to participate in after-school sports; he worried about hanky-panky involving boys watching their games and practices.

Boys' games were not universally supported either. Van McClung '73, whose father had played baseball in the Negro Leagues, was the exception. He taught Van to play ball and expected him to excel. In contrast, many immigrant and working-class parents did not value sports. Basketball coach Eric Paulson tried in vain to persuade the Mexican immigrant parents of three brothers to attend a varsity playoff game.

> Their parents *never* came to watch those boys play. So I called them and asked them to come. . . . Imagine having three boys on one team! Right? To see 'em play, right? They never did come. It wasn't part of their culture.

Paul Fong's parents, who were immigrants from China, donated flowers from their nursery for school floats, but they "never went to a game," even when Paul was quarterback on a winning football team. Dan Steward '73, whose father immigrated from Greece, said, "My dad let me do it, but he never went to a game."

Some working-class white parents needed their children's labor after school, which kept them from engaging in extracurricular activities. Mike Madden '72 played basketball and wanted to run track his senior year. But his father needed him to work in the family typewriter repair business. He insisted that Mike attend night school to finish his degree and forget about the foolishness of sports.[3]

Sports brought students and teacher-coaches into contact outside of the classroom. Being part of a team taught individuals how to coordinate strategy and work together.[4] For girls and boys alike, it taught skills, built physical strength, and developed leadership. For students used to losing, it offered a way to win.

Winning meant a lot to Sunnyvale High students, especially because it was unexpected. Alums and teachers alike remember the football team's first victory over rival Fremont High in 1964 as a "crowning moment." Jane Manley '72, who focused on academics, said: "We were considered the underdog," but when Sunnyvale put its talent on display, "I was proud of that." Malcolm High '67 recalled, "We liked to stand up for ourselves: 'Yeah, we are on the other side of the tracks! Deal with it!'" Dan Steward '73 said, "We tried harder because we weren't given things." He mused that growing up in a challenging environment created strong wills, which translated into exceeding others' expectations.

Sports provided students with opportunities for developing self-confidence. For Joanne Shimoguchi '64, sports were "the joy in my life." Mary Danziger '72, who competed in swimming, tennis, badminton, basketball, volleyball, and softball, had an aptitude for leadership and became an officer of the Girls' Athletic Association. She joined an innovative, year-long leadership class taught in the Girls' PE department. Stretch Lakely '73 remembers taking the class with Donna Chavez, who handpicked girls "she thought would be good teachers" and found avenues for them to cultivate their leadership skills.

Dan Steward remembers the bone-deep confidence he felt as a point guard on the basketball team. "I was always the leader. Right, everybody looked at me to guide them and lead them, and I was always the voice of the teams that I was on." He called plays, urged boys into position, motivated them. That sense of knowing what would work is something he has felt only episodically in his adult life. He uses it as a yardstick for how well he is doing: Is he in the right place, following the right path?

In athletics, girls used their bodies for power and self-expression. Through running, dancing, or playing volleyball, they could build strength and teamwork. PE classes inspired Jackie Gooch '74 to start a dance troupe. Teachers supported her by providing a space to rehearse, and she learned what it meant to perform at school and organize community events.

Playing sports instilled the values of sportsmanship and respect for others. Carolyn Buszdieker reflected: "I felt that the kids that we had at Sunnyvale were *always* the most respectful when they went to another school." She emphasized the importance of not swearing. "You'd hear these kids in the gym saying 'spaghetti' when they missed the bird or hit the shuttle out." They would be shocked when players on other teams did not uphold the same standards of sportsmanship. They would protest, "'Miss Buzz, did you hear how foul mouthed they are?' And I'd say, 'Yes, but we're not here to judge them, we're just here to beat them. And go home.'"

Many students benefited from the structure, discipline, and focus required to participate in organized sports.[5] Van McClung '73, who played football and ran track, said, "Having something to do, it kept me out of trouble." Paul Fong '71 acknowledged that because he was on the football team, he had to "go to class and all that, instead of hanging out." Gary Robinson '74 credited sports with getting him through school because he had to keep his grades up to be eligible to play and he enjoyed being on a team with friends. Pete Araujo '71, who ran cross country, track and field, played football, and wrestled, said athletics "kept me motivated."

For some, sports offered a place of solace. Kathi Romero '73 described sports as a "getaway" from the challenges of home. Similarly, Dan Steward '73 said:

> I could bury myself in sports and I was good at it and that made me feel good. . . . I just loved shooting and playing in the gym . . . that really probably more than anything helped me get through some of the tougher times, just having a place to go and shoot baskets. 'Cause I didn't want to go home, 'cause the home was not a good place to be.

Athletics spurred some boys to consider college. After Pete Araujo '71 won the Central Coast wrestling championship in his weight division, he was recruited for De Anza College's wrestling team, and after two successful seasons, he won a full wrestling scholarship to San Jose State, where he completed his bachelor's degree. "If you did not pass your classes in college, you're out. You can't be in sports. So that motivates you, too." Gary Robinson '74 loved playing football. When his departing Sunnyvale coach recruited him to move to southern California to play on the junior college team he was coaching, Gary felt pulled along. After two years there, he won a football scholarship to the University of Hawaii. Although he only stayed for a year, he later got his BA from San Jose State. Sports gave him a foothold in college and exposed him to a broader world.

In the 1960s and 1970s, colleges did not offer athletic scholarships to girls or recruit them for intercollegiate teams. Stretch Lakely '73 knew she wanted to play sports in college. Stanford University admitted her and offered her a tuition scholarship and financial aid, but it still cost more than she could afford. She chose to attend Chico State. At the beginning of fall term, she showed up for tryouts and made the team in basketball, swimming, and water polo. In her sophomore year, when the visiting female All American Red Heads basketball team saw her play, they recruited her to join them. At the time, most people did not think women could play competitive basketball, so the Red Heads and other barnstorming teams would play exhibition games against men's teams. They demonstrated their talents at hard-driving basketball, much in the spirit of the Harlem Globe Trotters, who would perform odds-defying feats on the court to entertain the crowd.

Excited at the prospect of being paid to play basketball, Stretch took a leave of absence from college to become one of a few hundred paid female professional players in the 1970s.[6] The grueling 200-plus game season demanded that they travel 40,000 miles around the country, often playing in a different town every night. After a year, Stretch returned home and enrolled at San Jose State, then became an athletic trainer and physical education teacher and coach. She was later inducted into the Basketball Hall of Fame with the Red Heads.

ARENA FOR INTEGRATING ACROSS DIFFERENCE

Sports were "the ultimate integrator and equalizer," as Terry Dyckman put it, because they brought students from different groups together to strive for a common goal.[7] At SHS, he said, "We had racially mixed teams. I never remember any incidents broken down around racial lines, Chicanos, Blacks, whatever." Athletics exposed students to others they might not otherwise have met. Carolyn Buszdieker said, "Doing an activity gives people a chance to get to know somebody in a different way." Students leaned on their bonds with teammates when racial tensions surfaced on campus.

Ed Lizardo '73 recalled:

> When I first started out for track . . . there's some whites, Blacks, Hispanics, a Filipino or two . . . Puerto Ricans. At that point there was no sense of racial prejudice or class. Benny Brown was Black but . . . he was a star of the track team and proved it later on when he left Sunnyvale High to become an Olympian. Everybody rooted for Benny. *Everybody.*

Van McClung '73 felt that "I kind of blended with the jocks" once he got to Sunnyvale High. Being one of the few Black students was challenging, and Van sometimes faced blatant racism. When he earned a place on the football team, he displaced a white boy who had held that position. The boy communicated clearly that he "didn't like Black folks." But "I really didn't let that bother me." When the tension culminated in an explosion, Van had to prove himself. "He was the only guy that I really fought at school. And I got along pretty much with everybody else." When he had conflicts with other white guys on his team, Van insisted, "we worked it out."

The team spirit of the football players buoyed him. Reflecting on his triumphs in high school, he highlighted two events. When the SHS football team beat Fremont in his senior year, "I was so happy to beat those guys, I didn't know what to do. Because they all talked crap." When he received the most valuable player award, he humbly praised his teammates. Van took the stage and said:

> We must have had a really, really good bunch of guys, because in order to win MVP as a running back, somebody's got the block for you. Somebody's got to make sure they take the guys out, so they don't tackle you.

He declared, "Hey, this is not just my trophy. This trophy belongs to all of us, because of the guys on the offensive line."

That spirit of generosity was also expressed at the wrestling awards later that year. Eddie Sanchez '73 was not the most valuable player. He was a slight, short Latino who hung around with jocks and played a supporting role as manager of the basketball team. He surprised everyone by going out for wrestling his senior year. The team had a robust mix of guys from many racial-ethnic groups. Over the course of the season, Eddie competed in twenty-two matches and lost every single one. But he did not quit; week after week, he showed up for practice and threw himself into the ring. Crowds gathered to cheer him on, celebrating his fighting spirit. At the awards banquet that season, coach Steve McKeown announced he had won the "most inspirational" award. As Eddie walked up to the stage, he received a standing ovation.

Coaches were key leaders in creating these multiracial environments. Doug Walker, who coached several sports, was acutely aware that he and James Omagbemi, a Nigerian who coached boys' track at SHS, were the only Black coaches in the entire district in 1972. The white coaches had to direct multiracial teams. Robert Handa '73 believed that merit counted.

> At Sunnyvale, certainly no coach could have survived and done well if they did not have that appreciation of cultural diversity. . . . Coaches are not going to say, "I want a white quarterback." . . . You might say that at another school, but you wouldn't have said that at Sunnyvale.

In 1971, when integration in high school and college sports was just beginning, a high school in Virginia reluctantly integrated its coaching staff and football team. The story was made into a Denzel Washington movie, "Remember the Titans." At Sunnyvale, Honda and Lizardo insisted, sports provided an ideal environment for overcoming prejudice.

After Sunnyvale High was closed in 1981 and Buszdieker started teaching and coaching at Fremont, former SHS students who were also transferred to Fremont confided in her: "'Miss Buzz, look at this,' and they'd pull up their shirt and, 'See this color? I'll never make that team.'" The kids felt they did not stand a chance because of the Fremont coaches' prejudiced attitudes.

Buzz recounted a story about the long-term impact of integration in the girls' sports league. In the late 1970s, as she walked across De Anza College campus to give a guest lecture, an unfamiliar white girl flagged her down. "Miss Buzz, Miss Buzz!" "I went over and she said . . . 'I know you don't know me, but I went to Lynbrook. When I came to De Anza, there were all these dark kids. . . . I was afraid. I was totally afraid to walk across campus by myself until I saw Rose Mendiola.'" Rose had played on the volleyball team at SHS and competed against Lynbrook High's team. Buzz asked her, "'Well, how are you doing now?' She replied, 'I found my niche and I'm fine. I can't thank you enough for the program you had there because I wouldn't have stayed at De Anza. I was that frightened.'"

What it took to change a white girl's fear of difference seems so simple, yet powerful. Sunnyvale High's integrated teams reflected its student body. The program that Buzz and other teacher-coaches built rippled outward. Playing against an integrated team in the district introduced a white girl to an athlete of color and helped her transform her fear of the unknown into a sense of safety and connection.

FIGHTING FOR GIRLS' SPORTS

Sunnyvale High's attempts to advance racial equity in and through athletics, however imperfect, were not matched by an institutional commitment to gender equity. If it was acknowledged at all, sex discrimination was seen as a problem only for female athletes, not viewed as a schoolwide issue with consequences for all. Before Title IX was passed by Congress in 1972, public schools were not required to provide equal educational facilities and programs for girls and boys.[8] At SHS, advocates for girls' sports accomplished a great deal, but prejudice, selfishness, and tradition stood in their way.[9]

On the national level, a few dazzlingly skillful women, like tennis sensation Billy Jean King, became professional athletes, and she and other women in tennis organized to demand fair wages as well as respect.[10] But women were prohibited from running in high-profile events like the Boston Marathon. Towns did not sponsor sports teams for girls, and they were not allowed to play Little League baseball with boys.

A study conducted by the National Federation of State High School Associations found that in 1970, only one in twenty-seven girls participated in high school sports, while their male peers were ten times as likely to do so. After Title IX was implemented, girls' participation soared. By 2018, 60 percent of all high school girls were involved, compared to 75 percent of boys.[11] As recent studies have shown, sports are physically, academically, and psychologically beneficial to girls.[12]

Head of Girls' PE at Sunnyvale High, Carolyn Buszdieker, who joined the faculty soon after it opened, had to counter a deeply embedded belief among coaches, teachers, and administrators: "They didn't think girls were capable." She was convinced that girls have the potential to develop athletic skills if given the opportunity and set out to prove that to everyone else. Buzz knew from her own experience what a difference having a wide range of choices

Figure 3.1 Carolyn Buszdieker, Teacher and Coach, with Swimmer, ca. 1972. *Source*: Scrapbook of the Girls' Athletic Association. Courtesy of Sunnyvale Historical Society and Museum Association.

could make. In her northern California high school in the early 1950s, with the advice and support of coaches, she tried everything. She loved tennis, basketball, and skiing, and she felt energized by competition.

At SHS, Buzz nurtured girls' confidence that they could learn. She told the story of one girl who walked into her badminton class with no apparent eye-hand coordination. "She couldn't drop the shuttle and hit it. Could *not*." From Buzz's point of view, her problem was that she had never held a racket and tried to hit a birdie or a ball. So, during class, Buzz had her take the birdie, stand in the corner five feet from the wall, and drop and hit it, over and over. It "usually fell to the floor"—until it did not. As the girl learned the skills badminton required, she came to love it and excelled. She joined the interscholastic team and rose to be the number one singles player in the league. Her success exemplified Buzz's philosophy at work. Recognizing the girl's determination to master a skill, she understood that all she needed was instruction and hour after hour of practice.

Few girls entered high school with any confidence in their athletic potential, while many boys arrived on campus with a sense of their physical capacity and expected to be respected for it. Paul Fong '71 boasted he had "physical prowess," which assured his acceptance among his peers. Girls were more often valued for their physical attractiveness but were also vulnerable to bullying from other girls and harassment from boys.

In the 1960s, the Fremont Union High School District treated girls' sports like a club, not an athletic league. They labeled girls' games "play days," the language parents now use when arranging activities for six-year-olds. Girls on teams did not wear uniforms but standard gym clothes. Girls who danced, twirled batons, or were cheerleaders at boys' games displayed their femininity in sparkling costumes but were often regarded as spectacles rather than skilled performers. Frustrated but committed, girls' coaches formed a district-wide Girls' Athletic Association to sponsor interscholastic games and tournaments. Coaches used their own cars to transport players and were not reimbursed for gas or their time. But they persisted.

Girls who loved sports supported their efforts. Stretch Lakely '73 had thought that her teams had no uniforms because the school could not afford them. But then she realized, "The guys had uniforms." She asked Buszdieker, "Why can't we just have their old uniforms?" Buzz responded that the boys' tank tops and shorts were "not very feminine." Exasperated, Stretch said, "I would just like to have something with a number on it." Was that too much to ask?

Before equity was an expectation, much less a right, girls noticed which teams wore spiffy uniforms and got leather basketballs and which did not. Gloria Collins '73 remembered, "We had to *beg* for stopwatches." She ruefully remarked that female athletes "were more disciplined" and "did better in sports." But "the guys had priority. They were the most important and the women came second or third." Stretch commented, "It was terrible . . . but we didn't know any different, because that's just how we were always treated." Dianna Good '76 agreed: "If there was any conflict, the guys always got priority." The disparity rankled: "It was the fairness thing. I thought, why don't we have people cheering for us? . . . That's just the way it was." There were no demonstrations or major student protests, but Dianna became a reporter for *The Skywriter* to cover girls' sports as well as boys'.

Before Title IX, gyms were considered exclusively male spaces. According to Joanne Shimoguchi, girls at SHS had to play volleyball and basketball "outside on the blacktop," with rubber balls, wooden backboards, and metal chain-link baskets. If it rained, coaches canceled the practice or game. Dianna Good, whose older sister played basketball in the girls' gym at Fremont, "wanted to be on the boys' team so I could play inside." Shimoguchi wryly observed that playing on the outdoor courts was evidence that girls were "certainly more hardy than the boys."

Behind the scenes, the battle over equipment involved subterfuge that verged on sabotage. The head of boys' PE would torment Marilyn Mason, the volleyball coach and PE teacher. She had a rolling bin of volleyballs to use for drills, but he would hide it, undermining her team's practices. Mason had to chase him down. When she finally found him, he'd say something like, "Oh, well, I put them in that other room."

In the late 1960s, one girl did not want her peers to know that she was in the Girls' Athletic Association. One of her teammates "would sneak me on the bus to the games." In retrospect, she felt sad about her shame and secrecy. "Nobody knew I was in GAA except the coaches and the other players." A decade later, Dianna Good felt differently: "I was known as one of the athletes in school, and there was a lot of pride around that, and it gave me a lot of confidence.... I was very focused on just doing the best I could.... And so you just play your heart out. You just give it your all."

With vision and fierce advocacy, Carolyn Buszdieker expanded athletic opportunities for girls in the region and gave them a new arena where they could excel and develop self-confidence. She raised girls' expectations of themselves and pressured the administration to support girls' athletics by funding coaches, equipment, space, and transportation. She understood how to act strategically. "I had to fight continually. I could stand there and scream and holler and it didn't do any good. I felt, you chose your battles.... To *demand* something just didn't work." She thought her eventual success came from being persistent. Administrators would ask themselves, "How can we keep Buszdieker's mouth shut?"

Throughout this adult conflict, girls watched the male coaches' denials and their female coaches' relentless pursuit of what they needed. Stretch Lakely recalled, "Ms. Buszdieker fought really hard to get us into the gym for basketball." Joanne Shimoguchi, an athlete whose own well-being depended on being physically active and excelling in competition, credited Buszdieker for creating space for girls' sports. Had it not been for Buzz's efforts, she said, "I don't know what I would have done." The students felt thwarted, but as Stretch put it, "You do what you do so you can play."

In 1964, SHS interscholastic teams had 448 boys, but girls' teams had only 60. The yearbook devoted four times as many pages to boys' teams as to girls' teams. In 1972, the boys still had 448 participants, but the girls had 217. Progress did not reach parity, but it represented improvement. When SHS closed in 1981, after the implementation of Title IX, the yearbook covered some teams that were coed, such cross country and badminton. It gave equal attention to volleyball and football. Boys continued to play a wider range of sports, such as wrestling and soccer.

Thanks to Carolyn Buszdieker's persistence and the contributions of her allies among the teachers and administrators, Sunnyvale developed a robust girls' athletic program. Beyond volleyball and softball, the Girls' PE department offered field hockey, swimming, badminton, gymnastics, modern dance, and tennis. "I thought we had a great athletic program," crowed Stretch Lakely. Buzz's conviction that girls were capable of athletic achievement was contagious. Through her example, humor, and perseverance, she opened doors.

THE IMPACT OF TITLE IX

Title IX was implemented very slowly after its passage in 1972.[13] The federal Department of Health, Education, and Welfare took two years to circulate its proposed guidelines; then each state had to draw up its own guidelines. Implementation in California took hold in the late 1970s. Historian Susan Ware observes, "Women athletic administrators, some of whom had been initially lukewarm about the law, began to sense its power when they saw how angry it made the men."[14] Even Buszdieker was shocked when she saw the rage male coaches expressed when they had to share resources and facilities they had guarded as their own.

Buszdieker recalled the Sunnyvale High meeting facilitated by Terry Dyckman to discuss how SHS was going to change its practices. "They never mentioned Title IX. It was just said, 'We're sharing the facilities.'" The boys' basketball coach started screaming:

> "I am not. I'm going to go right after school. I'm not going to stay and switch with her and have her go early one, two days a week and me go late." And he's just screaming, veins are sticking out on his neck. And Terry just very calmly said, "Yes, you will, Len. And will you sit down?"

Buzz felt a flood of relief when Dyckman said quietly, "That's how it's going to be." The coach's outrage tangled with his long-standing, congenial relationship with Buzz. He "walks over and kisses me on the cheek, and walks out." In his conflicted, self-interested way, he communicated his ambivalence. He was fond of Buzz, but he deeply resented the consequences of legal change and vented his feelings at her.

Although the legislation did not mandate gender parity in expenditures or numbers of athletes, it meant a major expansion in opportunities for women in sports. Buzz recalled an encounter with Doug Boyd, who had transferred to Fremont along with her after SHS closed, when he was angry about having to share resources the boys' teams had monopolized. He came over to her side of the shared office, put his hands on either side of her desk, and leaned forward. "I said, 'No, you can't do that anymore. And I'm going to report you if you do.' . . . He started screaming at me." One of the other teachers feared he was going to hit Buzz, he was that furious. Buzz reacted calmly: "I never thought he'd hit me. I really never had any fear at all." Minutes later, he backed off and acted as if nothing had happened. The rage he vented was against the new policy of equity, but Buzz was the face of the end of the privileges boys' teams and coaches had enjoyed.[15]

For the most part, girls did not play on teams with boys, but rather in separate divisions and competitions. But when they did try to integrate teams by gender, things did not go well. Stretch Lakely '73, eager to develop her skills and aware of the limitations of time and training for the girls' basketball team, approached Rich Knapp, coach of the boys' freshman team, to see if she could practice with them. She told him, "I need to get better, and I can't

Figure 3.2 Dianna Good Making the Shot, Girls' Basketball Game, 1974. *Source*: Courtesy of Dianna Good.

get better just playing, no offense, these girls." He agreed to incorporate her into their practices, "and then I got a taste of the gym."

The boys were less welcoming than their coach. "They thought it was just ridiculous." She assured them, "I want to get better, and that's why I'm here. I'm not here to school you." She was aware of being more skilled than some of them and, at 5 feet 10 inches, much taller than "these little freshmen puny guys that haven't even matured yet." Stretch found her ball-handling skills improved and she developed camaraderie with the coach, who invited her to play two-person volleyball with him in a teacher-student league. Later that year, her girls' basketball team won the league championship.

During Stretch's senior year, a short but equally talented frosh, Dianna Good, joined the boys' "C" team. (See figure 3.2.) According to her, "It didn't last because . . . the boys didn't really like me being there." The coach had tapped her to be one of the starting five. The boy she replaced, made to "sit on the bench," was especially distressed. Dianna loved playing basketball in the gym, but she understood the boys' resentment and felt guilty about taking someone's place. She decided to play only on the girls' team for the next four years.

It took well into the 1980s for Title IX to be fully implemented in California. Buszdieker did not wait; she moved the school toward equity in girls' athletics.

THE POWER OF COACHES' MENTORING

Sunnyvale High's remarkable physical education staff shared their life experiences with their students. Joanne Shimoguchi '64, who played multiple sports at San Jose State before she came back to teach and coach at SHS, had been in an internment camp with her Japanese American family during World War II. James Omagbemi, a track coach, had run in the Commonwealth Games as part of the Nigerian national team in the late 1950s. The water polo coach, Ed Szakacs, had been a young player in Hungary when the Soviet Union invaded in 1956. The Hungarian Olympic athletes managed to depart for the games in Melbourne, Australia, in the middle of that tense confrontation. The international conflict played out in the pool. Buszdieker remembers the aerial view of the "pristine-looking, magnificent swimming facility." During their semifinal water polo match, the pool "ran red with blood because the Hungarians beat up the Russians."

Those coaches played powerful roles in students' lives.[16] Jim Miller '64 said, "People in my class still talk about the fact that if some of the coaches weren't around, they wouldn't have graduated. . . . They became mentors for a lot of these kids." A decade later, Gary Robinson '74 described football and track coach Pete Tuana as a "father figure." Malcolm High '67 loved playing basketball for Tony Nunes. He became a "surrogate dad" when Malcolm's own father had to focus his energy on earning a living rather than watching his son's games. Kathi Romero '73 felt her coaches—Carolyn Buszdieker, Donna Chavez, and Joanne Shimoguchi—gave her an opportunity to thrive in a way her own family did not. Stretch Lakely '73 observed that the female coaches "were great people, and they were kind and smart, and they would just guide you in the right direction."

Some coaches helped students find jobs and introduced them to their families. Bob Hagg's wrestling coach, Herm Heller, "knew a little bit about what was going on at my home life. He actually gave me a job working at his Christmas tree lot." Carolyn Buszdieker and Marilyn Mason were aware that Mary Danziger '72, who had been selected as a foreign exchange student, had few resources and her mother had cancer. They invited Mary and her mother to Redding, where Buzz's mother owned a boutique, and outfitted her with the clothing she would need. Doug Walker brought home a student to meet his father, who had made a career in the Air Force by demonstrating his competence and persistence as "the first" Black officer on an assignment. This boy had his heart set on attending the Air Force Academy and received advice from the elder Walker about how he might achieve that.

JoAnn Vargas '73 "loved high school. I had a lot of good experiences there." Part of her satisfaction came from her PE teachers. JoAnn noted that they "encouraged me to do more," rather than looking down on her or others. They suggested she go out for different sports teams, lauded her dancing with the Sabrettes, and urged her to try out for song girl. JoAnn was an outstanding athlete, although because of her many family obligations she did not play interscholastically. Her senior year, she won the award for best athlete. JoAnn felt the PE teachers "had my back."

The girls' coaches modeled an excellent pedagogical approach, thought Gloria Collins '73, who sought to emulate them when she began teaching English at San Jose State. Swimmer Yolanda Garcia '72 found coach Marilyn Mason had a way of "pushing us to swim harder" by being encouraging rather than punishing. That inspired her to do better as an individual competitor as well as a teammate. Many considered Carolyn Buszdieker a great human being. Cece Padgett '72 felt she could confide anything to Buzz. Sharon Faeta '70, who taught dance for thirty years, described Buzz as "a natural leader."

Sharon Prefontaine '65 found a mentor in her dance instructor, Beverly Gaebel. Growing up with a father in the Navy and a mother who was not involved in her schoolwork or activities, she said she had basically "raised myself." Coach Gaebel took her students to professional dance performances in San Francisco and, she invested in Sharon's development and future. Gaebel had her choreograph a class and encouraged her to do the same for the school musicals. In addition to her supreme confidence in Sharon's creativity and abilities, Gaebel left her with another gift: "She gave me a necklace with the figurine of a ballerina with her skirt spread. Now, I never did ballet, but that was just a little tribute to my dancing."

In addition to their relationships with individuals, coaches went to extraordinary lengths to support their teams. In the late 1970s, when Joanne Shimoguchi's "C" volleyball team won a single game against Fremont after a long, discouraging season, she took them out to dinner to celebrate. Some had never before eaten in a restaurant. At that time, Vietnamese refugees were attending SHS and playing on the volleyball team. Shy about entering the unknown and worried about embarrassing themselves and Shimoguchi, they asked her to set up an etiquette session so they would know how to comport themselves. "So we actually practiced. . . . It was the first time some of them had had a steak in their life. They really appreciated that."

In the fall of 1973, Doug Walker's "C" basketball team won a league championship. As a reward, he took them to a Golden State Warriors basketball game at his personal expense. At the sports awards banquet, Walker insisted on sitting with his team, not on the platform for coaches.

These experiences at SHS demonstrate the critical support that organized sports offered students during their formative years. These stories signal the lasting impact of participation, the frustrations of gender inequality and the rewards of overcoming it, and the satisfaction students derived from their relationships with coaches and teammates.

NOTES

1. Janet Ward Schofield, *Review of Research on School Desegregation's Impact on Elementary and Secondary School Students* (Hartford: Connecticut State Department of Education, 1989); Robert E. Slavin, and Nancy A. Madden, "School Practices That Improve Race Relations," *American Education Research Journal* 16 (1979): 169–80.

2. Michael A. Messner, *Power at Play: Sports and the Problem of Masculinity* (Boston, MA: Beacon Press, 1992).

3. Annette Lareau, *Unequal Childhoods: Class, Race, and Family Life*, 2nd ed. (Berkeley: University of California Press, 2011).

4. Cheryl Cooky, and Michael A. Messner, eds., *No Slam Dunk: Gender, Sport and the Unevenness of Social Change* (New Brunswick, NJ: Rutgers University Press, 2018); Joan Steidinger, *Sisterhood in Sports: How Female Athletes Collaborate and Compete* (Lanham, MD: Rowman & Littlefield, 2014).

5. Jacquelynne Eccles, and Bonnie Barber, "Student Council, Volunteering, Basketball, or Marching Band," *Journal of Adolescent Research* 14 (1999): 10–43.

6. John A. Molina, *Barnstorming America: Stories from the Pioneers of Women's Basketball* (Sikeston, MO: Acclaim Press, 2016).

7. Martin Patchen, *Black-White Contact in Schools: Its Social and Academic Effects* (West Lafayette, IN: Purdue University Press, 1982).

8. Susan Ware, *Title IX: A Brief History with Documents* (Boston, MA: Bedford/St. Martin's, 2007), 7.

9. Ware points out that gender and racial equality in sports did not always go hand in hand. In expanding Olympic events, for example, "the very nature of the emerging sports might skew the racial proportion of female athletes to the disadvantage of women of color." Ware, *Title IX*, 17.

10. Susan Ware, *Game, Set, Match: Billie Jean King and the Revolution in Women's Sports* (Chapel Hill: University of North Carolina Press, 2011).

11. Nicole Zarrett, Philip Veliz, and Don Sabo, *Teen Sport in America: Why Participation Matters* (New York: Women's Sports Foundation, 2018).

12. Zarrett, Veliz, and Sabo, *Teen Sport*.

13. Ware, *Title IX*, 4.

14. Ware, *Title IX*, 13.

15. Ware, *Title IX*, 13.

16. Martin Camiré, Pierre Trudel, and Tanya Forneris, "Coaching and Transferring Life Skills: Philosophies and Strategies Used by Model High School Coaches," *The Sport Psychologist* 26 (2012): 243–60; Fanny Kuhlin, Natalie Barker-Ruchti, and Carly Stewart, "Long-term Impact of the Coach-Athlete Relationship on Development, Health, and Wellbeing: Stories from a Figure Skater," *Sports Coaching Review* (2019): 1–23; Christiane Trottier, and Sophie Robitaille, "Fostering Life Skills Development in High School and Community Sport: A Comparative Analysis of the Coach's Role," *The Sport Psychologist* 28 (2014): 10–21.

Chapter 4

A Fighting School

As a microcosm of American society, SHS experienced many of the controversies and conflicts that convulsed the country during the 1960s and 1970s. Its administrators, counselors, teachers, and students sought ways to facilitate mutual understanding within its diverse community, in contrast to the racial injustice and protests that were met with violence elsewhere. SHS drew on new models to promote inter-group communication, strove to balance class solidarity with racial and ethnic autonomy, and recognized that differences need not be accompanied by antagonism.

In 1968, widespread opposition to the Vietnam War mixed explosively with outrage about racial inequality. Major civil rights organizations disagreed about strategy and tactics. Debates about nonviolent civil disobedience, militant activism, coalitions with white allies, and racial-ethnic self-determination preoccupied activists and raised key questions for students.[1] Malcolm X, who symbolized Black pride and power, was assassinated in New York City in 1965. In April 1968, Martin Luther King Jr. was assassinated in Memphis. Two months later, Democratic presidential candidate Robert Kennedy, who supported racial justice, was assassinated in Los Angeles. In the wake of these shocking events, many Americans suffered a mix of rage and despair, raising questions about how to change a violent, unequal society.

Throughout the 1960s, SHS students were involved in ongoing conflicts on and off campus that sometimes led to fights. The student newspaper, *The Skywriter*, proclaimed "SHS Again Tries for Racial Harmony" in its November 1968 issue. "Racial harmony has long been a problem at Sunnyvale High but nothing concrete has ever been done to relieve the problem" except "when there was an outbreak of violence."[2]

Young people watched as the US government escalated an unjust war in Vietnam. SHS students worried about the draft for good reason. Like those in poor and working-class communities across the United States, many students were drafted as soon as they graduated from high school. One boy from the cross-country team got a high draft number, but his friends did not. None of them returned alive after being conscripted and sent to Vietnam.[3] At least one teacher, Jim Miller, left after being called up for military service. In 1971, he registered as a conscientious objector and did his alternative service with the Peace Corps in Latin America for three years.

PHYSICAL CONFRONTATION

The social dynamics of American high schools were remarkably durable over the twentieth century. Similar groups emerged everywhere: popular kids, jocks, cheerleaders, geeks, hoods, prom queens, and "average citizens."[4] These groups had their own versions at Sunnyvale High: stoners, nerds, the artsy crowd, football players, Black Power advocates, the debate team, drama groups, "*Viva La Raza*" Chicanos, spirit girls, and the band. As cheerleader Suzi Brink '72 observed, "Survival in high school was being associated with a group."

Sports teams provided a group identity for some students. On campus, team tryouts and competitions defined who belonged. Off campus, team members received respect. Dan Steward '73 recalled the way sports taught him to stick up for himself and behave in ways he could not at school. Washington Park, one of many nearby green spaces, had lights that illuminated basketball courts and tennis courts, so kids could play at night without supervision. Dan and many of his teammates would gather and play as often as they could.

> The way you stayed on the court is you had to win a game. If you lost, then you had to sit out. And so, we weren't going to lose. . . . There were a lot of fights and a lot of fisticuffs and a lot of threats. But I remember we never backed down.

Because there were no referees and no adults, players had to negotiate what counted as a transgression.

> There were many times where you had, "That's a foul." "No, that ain't a foul." "That's a foul." "That's not a foul." . . . You can't give in to 'em, cause you give in once, and you're over. And so, you had just to put your chest up, and if you had to put your fist up, you did it. Because you weren't going to back down, and so you had to learn to do that.

Like all high schools, SHS had fights on campus.[5] As Jets, students knew they were at the bottom of the heap in the district, but they still competed with each other for prestige. Who was on top? Who was the cutest? The fastest, athletically or sexually? Who was the toughest? The most popular? The smartest? Students made judgments freely and others reacted defensively, and sometimes aggressively.

Radically variable rates of adolescent development put spindly thirteen-year-olds on the same campus as hefty eighteen-year-olds. As a frosh, Ed Lizardo '73 described himself as "green" and "naïve." He said, "I felt really vulnerable, wow. I mean, little ol' me. I'm some little Filipino kid. So I just felt intimidated" by the tall and strong older boys on campus. Malcolm High '67 recalls his fear when he arrived on campus. "Quite honestly, I don't even know if I had hair under my armpits yet, and these guys looked like men, like they would have kids at home." The disparities in size and development shaped younger kids' experiences. Lizardo admitted, "I was terrified; I was *terrified*." But he managed the situation by not appearing scared and not backing down. "I never flinched," he insisted. He played sports, which helped develop alliances, and the following year he became drum major.

Students—mostly, but not exclusively, boys—established rank order through physical confrontation. A boy might get in a fight because he felt threatened, disrespected, or resented another boy talking to his girlfriend. Conflicts over girls sparked many fights. David Hernandez '73 recalled, "I fought everybody. It's just the way it was. We were really competitive guys." In that sense, SHS earned its reputation as a tough school.

Having a rough reputation helped some boys avoid fights altogether. Paul Fong '71, who had immigrated from China with his family when he was a toddler, grew strong by working in his family's nursery business. He made a name for himself even before he arrived at Sunnyvale High when he faced off with Latino student Charlie Trujillo. Walking to downtown Sunnyvale over the freeway overpass, he was confronted by Charlie, who demanded a quarter in order to pass. Paul replied, "I don't have a quarter." Charlie defiantly blocked his way. Paul picked him up, flung him aside, and kept walking. Later, they discovered they both lived in "little shacks" and became the best of friends. Paul did not need to fight in high school: "When new tough guys would come into Sunnyvale High School, they wanted to find out who the toughest guy was, and they would never get to me because Charlie would kick their ass." He described Charlie as a "good puncher." Paul repeatedly proved himself on the football field and commanded respect for his athletic skill. Nonetheless, he would still threaten to fight boys who crossed him. Later, when pushed to reflect on this pattern, Paul admitted, "I never touched anybody in high school." He didn't have to.

When JoAnn Vargas '73, a Puerto Rican girl who had begun picking in bean fields at the age of three, first arrived at SHS, she did not have high expectations. At Benner Junior High she had one favorite teacher, but two treated her with racist disregard and made no investment in her learning. She was quiet and raced home directly after school to take care of her younger brothers and sisters. Two older sisters attended SHS, but "I was still trying to get around my head so many different classes; and it's such a big school, and rushing, and the lockers, and all." Unexpectedly and for no apparent reason, during the first three weeks, she found herself challenged to fight by three different older Mexican girls known as *pachucas*. She was not a fighter, although her older sister Alva, who had dropped out of school, had earned that reputation. JoAnn described her surprise at their threats: "Wow, what did I do? I don't know who they are." She reasoned that they picked on her because she was quiet and "they always looked for the weakling." One of her best friends, "who didn't take anything," approached these girls and asked if they knew who Alva Vargas was. They did. She responded, "Well, that's her sister," and insisted, "You touch her, she's going to kick your ass." They backed off. JoAnn felt intimidated by the older girls who always traveled in groups. Fortunately, her friend's intervention and her sister's reputation "saved my skin"; they did not bother her after that.

In the district, Sunnyvale High students' behavior sometimes fed nasty stereotypes, even as they tried to counter them. Paul Fong became quarterback and captain of the football team his senior year, a leader among tough boys. One night during a game against Homestead High in 1970, Paul got incensed at the other team's trash talk about Sunnyvale and decided to teach them to show respect. After the game, he mobilized a bunch of his friends to return to Homestead, where an after-game dance was underway, and defend Sunnyvale's reputation. Paul recalled, "We were just trying to scare them." As they stood outside, the Homestead chaperones locked the gym doors to keep them out. A teacher came outside to defuse the situation, and Paul said accusingly, "You guys are a bunch of racists." After the fact, he insisted, "I was just representing the values of Sunnyvale High School." Standing up to the racist and classist taunts allowed him to hold his head high. He later fantasized about the possibility that Steve Jobs, who attended Homestead High in the class of 1973, was at that dance, cowering inside the gym before he went on to found Apple and conquer the world through technology. Perhaps a gang from Sunnyvale made him pause and consider the offensive behavior of his fellow students. It certainly did not make him or other Homestead kids think differently about Sunnyvale's roughneck means of settling disputes.

Counselor Terry Dyckman broke up fights on a weekly basis. He thought he was good at it, and students agreed. Like many of the staff drawn to SHS, he wanted to work in a multiracial environment with tough kids. Terry came from a white working-class family in rural northern California. Although neither of his parents finished high school, Terry's athletic prowess helped him secure a football scholarship to San Jose State. He discovered racial injustice as a teammate of Tommie Smith and Juan Carlos, the future Olympic athletes who raised their fists in a Black Power salute at the 1968 games in Mexico City. Terry met organizers from the United Farm Workers, who educated students about the working conditions in the fields and persuaded them to boycott grapes not picked by union labor. His college roommate later became a lawyer who successfully contested the torturous use of *el cortijo*, the short hoe, by field workers, in front of the US Supreme Court. Dyckman brought his nascent awareness of racial exploitation to his work at Sunnyvale, along with his aptitude for working with troubled kids.

Dyckman was regularly called to intervene in fights in Fair Oaks Park, which was adjacent to the school. "Sometimes the kids would tip us off." He described the scene, with "a heavy, heavy dose of Hispanic kids in it, but Anglos as well. Not so much with the African Americans." He would call the Sunnyvale police to back him up. But "they wouldn't go into the park without us." Dyckman knew all the students' names. "I said, 'John, come over here *now*.' [When] you can identify somebody by name, it's incredibly powerful. The police did not have that."

Although most girls abstained from violent conflict, they often used threats. Fights gained girls like Darci Daniels '72 reputation and status. Darci, who identified as Chicana, wore black clothes, strong black eyeliner, and hair ratted high, Chola style. Yolanda Garcia '72, a Mexican American who transferred to SHS her junior year, got called out by a jealous, white cheerleader. She found Yolanda's casual conversations with her popular African American boyfriend unacceptable. Yolanda remembered, "She threatened to hurt me. It all came through the grapevine 'cause she couldn't tell me to my face." The cheerleader targeted Yolanda with intimidating looks and let it be known that "she wanted to fight me on a certain day after school at a certain place." Yolanda was shocked. Yet, like many provocations, nothing came of them.

Some girls used intimidation as a survival tactic on campus. The head of Girls' PE, Carolyn Buszdieker, recalled a Samoan girl, Faaeegna, who had struggled to tamp down her anger. She had been suspended from her school in San Francisco and came to live with her aunt and uncle in Sunnyvale. One day after the varsity volleyball team lost its match, the coach, Marilyn Mason, came running to get Buzz. Faaeegna was angrily banging locker doors. When Buzz went to investigate, Faaeegna told her, "Miss Mason, she was so bad." Buzz demanded, "What did she do?" Faaeegna explained, "She wouldn't let me hit the girl." Buzz said, "What?!" Faaeegna explained, "Yes, that's what we did in San Francisco when, if we lost, we beat up the kid." Buzz insisted that Faaeegna refrain from fighting and be directly accountable to her. Faaeegna managed to stay on the volleyball team, made more friends in school, and was elected varsity cheerleader in her senior year. Her desire to fight and her impulse to express her frustration by banging lockers was channeled into more constructive outlets.

Once caught up in a fight, unlike boys, girls refused to stop. Terry Dyckman found it harder to break up fights between girls. "If they got into it, they really got into it. It wasn't for show." Dyckman recalled, "I've never been as scared as breaking up a girls' fight."[6] In contrast, Dyckman found it surprisingly easy to interrupt a fight between boys. Although boys mouthed off and needed to look tough, he could often pull a guy back from a tangle. Math teacher Jim Miller, who was young, short, and slight, explained that he learned how to break up a fight effectively by watching the female teachers. They would slowly approach a fight encircled by a crowd of onlookers. The cry of "teacher, teacher!" would invariably warn the two combatants, who would turn the heat down a notch. That prelude made it easier for the teacher to break it up.

GIRLS' BATHROOMS AS CONTESTED SPACES

Some girls came to school prepared to use intimidation and violence to control spaces on campus they believed belonged to them and their racial-ethnic social group.[7] They wore rings on every finger, ready to scratch, and girls like Darci strategically tucked pieces of razor blades in their hair so that if anybody grabbed it, they would be sorry.

Invariably crowded between classes, the girls' bathrooms at SHS were the most contested spaces on campus. As one of the few private places largely unsupervised by teachers, where girls could smoke, talk, and compete for dominance, the bathrooms were areas where some girls chose to hang out, and other girls worked hard to avoid.

One Asian girl, who ran track and excelled in speech and debate, prided herself on speaking her mind and freely disagreeing with people she thought were wrong. She was short and strong, but she avoided girls' bathrooms: "I didn't feel safe enough. . . . We just went to the bathroom in the gym because the teachers were there." Once, she recalled, "Things [were] said to me, and I thought, 'Well, I really needed to get out of here.'" She retorted with an invitation to take it outside. She thought, "If it was going to get violent, it will be in front of everybody." Fearful but determined to protect herself, she started taking martial arts classes with her friends. She did not fear boys on campus, only girls in the bathrooms.

When JoAnn Vargas got confronted in a bathroom, mentally she would calculate the distance from an office with adults where she might need to seek protection. She gauged how belligerently she could push back before being in danger. One girl taunted her by barking whenever JoAnn walked by. "I didn't think anything of it. Then it started again." When she entered the bathroom at a football game, she heard, "Woof, woof," and the message clicked.

"Oh, she's trying to say I'm a dog." The girls laughed. Fed up and angry, JoAnn snapped. She turned, cornered the girl, and began yelling, "Don't you ever bark at me again! I am not a dog." The girl "cried a little." Her friends threatened to intervene if JoAnn touched her. By now, JoAnn's friends had also entered the bathroom and made a reciprocal threat: "'You get her, we'll get you.'" JoAnn did not like to fight, did not want to fight, and admitted, "I can't do it—physically hit somebody." Nothing happened. But she, the quiet, unassuming girl, learned to stand up to those calling her out and got them to back down. The bold confrontation stopped the bullying, and afterwards the barking girl left her alone.

Even the fierce Darci Daniels had to gin up her courage to enter a bathroom. "When you're with your group, you're okay." But alone it was a different story. She recalled entering a bathroom on the outer reaches of campus where eight Black girls were hanging out.

> I had a beanie on because my hair frizzed. . . . One of them kept flicking my beanie. . . . I'm petrified, right? And I thought, I got to stand up to 'em because if I don't, they're going to hurt me.

Considering her options, she said, "Don't touch my *blanking* beanie again or I will . . . kick your *you-know-what*." Darci was afraid, but she insisted on respect. "You have to stand up."

Once she intervened when she witnessed girls picking on a shy red-headed girl in the bathroom. Darci challenged them, "Back off. Leave her alone." She conceded that those situations could have ended differently. "I always thought I was tougher than I was. . . . But I hated bullying. I *hated* it." At times, even teachers felt threatened. Despite being warned not to use the girls' bathrooms, Spanish teacher Loretta Gutierrez occasionally did so out of convenience. Once a Chicana student confronted her: "Hey, what are you doing in here?!" Looking back, she admitted, "I was afraid of the Mexican girls. This is a Mexican person [speaking]. . . . They had absolutely no respect for me."

At SHS, girls acted as gatekeepers of these contested spaces. The bathroom confrontations sometimes had racial overtones. Others arose when some girls invaded what others regarded as their territory. They effectively made outsiders feel uncomfortable and aware of their power.

FRIENDSHIP ACROSS BOUNDARIES

The physical and political confrontations at SHS could be seen as evidence that the school deserved its tough reputation. In truth, however, many students experienced it as a safe space. They weren't afraid of coming to school or encountering violence there. Nor did they cower in the halls. Some girls avoided the bathrooms, but unless they actively sought out combat, they rarely found it.

Friendships that crossed racial-ethnic boundaries coexisted with tension and conflict. Sunnyvale High was not a color-blind environment. Students recognized ethnic differences, openly discussing family heritage and individual identity. That established and affirmed differences, but did not always divide them. Instead, it became a normal part of how they navigated their interactions. They explored racial and ethnic differences in an effort to figure out what they meant. At the same time, they embraced friendship as foundational to their worlds.[8]

While groups coalesced around activities, many alumni characterized themselves as moving comfortably between friendship groups. Suzi Brink '72 said, "I was a floater. I had friends in all of the different groups, but I was never the core of any one group." Stretch Lakely '73 said:

> I wasn't just a dumb blonde athlete. . . . I had enough different groups of friends that I just felt like I could have gone anywhere. . . . I was doing stuff with the brainiacs, and then . . . I made stools for the song girls. . . . So I just was all over the place. I never ever . . . felt threatened, ever.

Jackie Gooch '74, who is African American, declared that most of her friends were Mexican American, and her best friend was white.
Many students forged friendships across difference. Van McClung, who is Black, recalled, "We mixed together very well. . . . Bob [Handa], he was Japanese. Bob [Hagg] was white, and Larry [McCracken] was white." Joe Leone, who is Italian with Calabrian roots and does not consider himself white, recounted a conversation he had with his Chinese next-door neighbor. "One day the gang showed up and it was Dale Matsumoto, Wesley Yamamoto, the Sakai Brothers. And I think Russell Kuna was there. And about three days later, Mr. Tang said to me, 'Don't you have any white friends?'"

Even with high turnover rates in the school, many kids had known each other in junior high and elementary school. Ed Lizardo '73, who is Filipino American, thought that friendship grew out of familiarity born of childhood activities and neighborhood connections: "I did not think in racial terms." But he also made new friends, including Max Epps, who is African American. Max began,

> This is a true story. . . . Ed actually asked me, "Do you want to be friends?" at our locker. [Laughter]. And I'll never forget it as long as I live. . . . And I said, "Sure." We were friends. He was the first person [I met] at Sunnyvale High School. And that was his opening line.

Ed told his own version of that story:

> Max has a face that I think anybody can befriend. . . . He's tall so I remember looking up at him, at his hair and that *kind* face. . . . I just remember giving him a smile and shaking his hand. I introduced myself to Max. . . . "I'm Ed, you want to be my friend?"

Perhaps that was an accident of personality, but it was also the culture of the school. Athletes and leaders had an open attitude toward kids from racial-ethnic groups other than their own. Ed's philosophy was unusual, but it shaped his leadership style as drum major and later as student body president. Differences and openness existed side by side.

Many became more than friends: they helped raise each other up. African American Jackie Gooch was inspired by her friends. They "helped me to grow. . . . I carry my friends with me." Bernie Moncallo '74, who is Puerto Rican, and John Norman '74, who has a Japanese mother and white father, became close friends with Gary Robinson, who is white. He confirmed, "These guys in a lot of ways raised me. . . . I was very lucky to have that type of peer group. And I think maybe it helped solidify really what's right and what's wrong." Their friendship proved a turning point in Gary's high school experience.

Darci Daniels, who presented as Chicana but actually had no Mexican heritage, went to live with the family of her best friend Kathi Romero, who was Mexican American. Darci's mother remarried and moved to Oregon, but Darci wanted to stay and finish her senior year at Sunnyvale High. In effect, Kathi, who was the eldest in her family, viewed Darci as her older sister. Darci claimed with pride, "Yeah, I took care of you." Kathi agreed, "She was my role model."

Deep ties between peers anchored these teenagers as they tried to manage their daily lives and make sense of their world.

SUCCESSFULLY CHALLENGING THE LAW

In the fall of 1969, one Sunnyvale student took the school's fighting spirit to a larger field of battle.

In the youth culture of the late 1960s and early 1970s, students defied authority, mocked rah-rah patriotism, and demanded freedom of speech. They exposed the hypocrisy of racial injustice in a country that proclaimed everyone is created equal. They opposed the escalation of the war in Southeast Asia. They expressed politics in part through their clothing, wearing US flag pants and fashioning tie-dyed tee-shirts that prominently featured a peace sign. To more conservative adults, young people's appearance undermined the social order, symbolizing anarchy, filth, and wanton sexuality.

In high schools, many administrators and some teachers used dress codes to hang onto a rigidly structured order. Some schools required strict, military-like comportment, especially in environments with lots of working-class kids and students of color. At Sunnyvale, the long-standing dress code mandated that girls wear dresses or skirts, which could not be too short, and boys had to dress neatly and keep their hair short. "They were trying so hard to keep us from being like the college kids," Jane Manley '72 reflected. Students understood the politics of clothing and saw where battle lines had been drawn between the administration's outdated, restrictive policies and students who sought freedom to wear what they pleased.

In October 1969, Sunnyvale senior Ramon Alarcón, who was Latino, was suspended because his hair hung below the top of his shirt collar. The *Palo Alto Times* reported that two years before, the Fremont Union High School District had declared "war against long hair."[9] At another school in the district, a boy had challenged the dress code in court. His legal suit failed, and the boy had to cut his hair or face expulsion.

At SHS, Ramon Alarcón contested that ruling. *The Skywriter* reported that he was "actively involved in the Youth Involvement Program of the city government and is the president of the Fremont Student Alliance, which consists of students from all over the district."[10] The Alliance met twice a week at Fair Oaks Park, adjacent to SHS, "with the purpose of protecting students' rights." When Alarcón was suspended, he sought the help of the Legal Aid Society and the American Civil Liberties Union; they took the case to federal court.

Alarcón's attorney argued that his suspension denied him his 14th Amendment rights to liberty, free expression, and privacy. In an affidavit, Alarcón stated, "I don't think my education should be conditioned on the way I choose to wear my hair." He pointed to gender inequity: girls "wear their hair longer than that prescribed for male students." The *Palo Alto Times* announced his initial victory: "Sunnyvale High School Senior Ramon Alarcón won his fight against the Establishment Monday. . . . Judge Robert Peckham in the US District Court in San Jose ordered the school district to reinstate Alarcón immediately."[11]

Ten days later, Alarcón and Sunnyvale High representatives appeared in court to make their arguments. The defense called Doug Boyd, boys' athletic director: "Although I feel it is an individual's basic right to choose how he or she wants to dress, if this choice endangers the well-being of the individual or others, it is therefore detrimental."[12] Boyd cited problems with sports like wrestling, personal hygiene, and swimming pool filters that got clogged with hair. The metal shop teacher warned that long hair was dangerous around power equipment.

Yet, Judge Peckham decided in favor of Ramon Alarcón. He ruled that long hair was not a health or safety problem, as the school claimed. Notably, the winning argument pivoted on boys' disadvantage compared to girls. They could wear their hair long, so why not boys? The issue of the double standard in clothing restrictions, which forbade girls to wear pants, was not explicitly part of the case. Nonetheless, the ruling had a major impact on girls as well as boys. Not only were boys allowed to wear their hair as they wished, but everyone gained the liberty to dress as they pleased. For the first time, girls had the freedom to choose: if they wanted to be warm on cold, windy days, or maintain their modesty by wearing pants, they could.

Students were thrilled. Sheree Furtado '72 exclaimed, "It changed *everything*." Jane Manley '72 expressed amazement that the dress code was not just modified: "The next year it was *gone*, totally gone." This triumph made Alarcón a hero on campus. He had led a principled fight against the school district and won. Students stood up straighter. Change was possible.

That contentious feistiness served the students at Sunnyvale High well. They stood up for themselves and each other when it mattered, insisting on their rights, dignity, and respect.

NOTES

1. Joshua Bloom and Waldo E. Martin Jr., *Black against Empire: The History and Politics of the Black Panther Party* (Berkeley: University of California Press, 2013); Barbara Epstein, *Political Protest and Cultural Revolution: Nonviolent Direct Action in the 1970s and 1980s* (Berkeley: University of California Press, 1993); Todd Gitlin, *The Sixties: Years of Hope, Days of Rage*, rev. ed. (New York: Bantam, 1993).

2. *The Skywriter*, November 1, 1968.

3. See list of dead from Sunnyvale: https://capitolmuseum.ca.gov/learn/about-the-capitol/capitol-park/vietnam-war-memorial/.

4. Sherry B. Ortner, "'Burned Like a Tattoo': High School Categories and 'American Culture,'" *Ethnography* 3 (2002): 122. See also Penelope Eckert, *Jocks and Burnouts: Social Categories and Identity in the High School* (New York: Teachers College Press, 1989); Amy C. Wilkins, *Wannabes, Goths, and Christians: The Boundaries of Sex, Style, and Status* (Chicago: University of Chicago Press, 2008).

5. Fights are ubiquitous at high schools. See Todd Michael Franke, Anh-Luu T. Huynh-Hohnbaum, and Yunah Chung, "Adolescent Violence: With Whom They Fight and Where," *Journal of Ethnic and Cultural Diversity in Social Work* 11 (2002): 133–58; Curtis Jackson-Jacobs, "Constructing Physical Fights: An Interactionist Analysis of Violence among Affluent, Suburban Youth," *Qualitative Sociology* 36 (2013): 23–52; Lisa Leitz, "Girl Fights: Exploring Females' Resistance to Educational Structures," *International Journal of Sociology and Social Policy* 23, no. 11 (2003): 15–46. The school environment in suburban Sunnyvale differed from the

inner-city school documented in Nikki Jones's study of a violence prevention program in Chicago: *Between Good and Ghetto: African American Girls and Inner-City Violence* (New Brunswick, NJ: Rutgers University Press, 2010).

6. Linda M. Waldron, "'Girls Are Worse': Drama Queens, Ghetto Girls, Tom Boys, and the Meaning of Girl Fights," *Youth & Society* 43 (2011): 1298–1334.

7. Julie Bettie, *Women without Class: Girls, Race, and Identity*, 2nd ed. (Berkeley: University of California Press, 2014).

8. Jasmin Sandelson, *My Girls: The Power of Friendship in a Poor Neighborhood* (Berkeley: University of California Press, 2023).

9. *Palo Alto Times*, November 10, 1969.

10. *The Skywriter*, November 14, 1969.

11. *Palo Alto Times*, November 11, 1969.

12. *Palo Alto Times*, November 11, 1969.

Chapter 5

Tensions of Connecting across Difference

By 1970, California had a long and contentious history of racial segregation in public schools. Some districts allowed children of Mexican descent to attend school with whites, but others sent them to separate schools along with Black children.

In 1931, a school board in San Diego County excluded all Mexican children from the school they had attended and insisted they go to an old building called "La Caballeriza," the barn. Parents organized a boycott and filed suit. *Roberto Alvarez v. Lemon Grove School District* was the first school desegregation decision in the history of the United States. In 1930, when the US Census set up a separate racial category for Mexican Americans, who had previously been classified as white, the League of United Latin American Citizens protested, and in 1940 they were again categorized as white. But some California school districts continued to segregate them.[1]

In a precursor to *Brown v. Board of Education* (1954), Mexican American parents successfully sued the Orange County school district (*Mendez v. Westminster School District*) in 1947, claiming that segregating schools based on students' national or ethnic heritage violated the 14th Amendment of the US Constitution. While the federal appeals court upheld racial segregation, it prohibited the segregation of children because of their "Mexican blood."[2] California's legislature responded by repealing state laws mandating segregation of Native American and Asian American students.

As California became more diverse, so did its schools. In 1963, a thirteen-year-old Black student named Jay Jackson was denied transfer to a white junior high school in Pasadena. Jackson and his parents sued the district, and *Jackson v. Pasadena City School District* eventually reached the California Supreme Court. The court ruled that the state was required to provide school facilities that avoided segregation and unreasonable racial imbalance and held local school boards responsible for alleviating segregation.[3]

In response to the new legal mandate and concerns about the treatment of teachers from minority backgrounds, the State Board of Education established a Bureau of Intergroup Relations in 1964. One of the bureau's main functions was to support educators in navigating this new, tricky, and potentially explosive terrain. Recognizing that racial divides were both structural and interpersonal, the bureau set guidelines for schools and trained teachers and administrators to facilitate interaction between racial and ethnic groups. It developed programming on how to prevent and defuse violent conflicts around race, and sponsored workshops for educators to learn about interracial understanding and bring practical tools for facilitating it back to their schools.

The new bureau drew on intergroup philosophy dating back to the 1920s.[4] At a time of heightened anti-immigrant and xenophobic attitudes, progressive educators had sought ways to mediate tensions between groups. Congress passed legislation in 1924 to dramatically limit immigration, while government-supported vigilante groups targeted Black veterans, African American communities, recent immigrants, and left-leaning publications and organizations.[5] In this context, the intergroup approach sought to create understanding between native-born whites and other racial-ethnic groups, avert violence, and encourage personal relationships between students from different backgrounds. A growing nationwide movement aimed to bridge racial divides by getting groups to realize their common humanity and cooperate "in the pursuit of shared goals."[6]

Several initiatives at SHS, led by Principal Paul Sakamoto, built on this intergroup philosophy. How did the school facilitate dialogue and understanding between different groups who had been fighting each other? What enabled peaceful engagement and even friendship across racial and ethnic lines?

PAVE: PSYCHOLOGY AND VOCATIONAL EDUCATION

Paul Sakamoto espoused intergroup policies and ideas as a path to "interracial harmony." He had personally endured virulent racism, not only in Rohwer concentration camp where he had been incarcerated during the 1940s but also upon his return to California where Japanese Americans faced acute discrimination.[7]

Sakamoto believed education was key to understanding across racial and ethnic divides. Building on the Sunnyvale High philosophy of engagement, he hired counselors like Terry Dyckman to assist with a new program. Dyckman described Sakamoto and Vice Principal Richard "Pete" Mesa as "the odd couple of education. Paul was a true intellectual." In contrast, "Pete was a street kid" who grew up in a family of migrant farmworkers. Together, they designed PAVE: Psychology and Vocational Education.

PAVE aimed to connect students with each other and with teachers, recognizing that those relationships could provide continuity throughout high school. PAVE classes sorted students alphabetically, which broke up cliques and randomized student groups. The PAVE curriculum reached beyond the confines of school to expose students to different experiences and various possible futures. It taught them tools for social and academic success.

Beginning with the class of 1974, freshman students were assigned to two counselors—one male, one female—who advised them until they graduated. In the classroom, they discussed study skills, group dynamics, discrimination, and communication. Bob Douglas, a young science teacher who became a counselor, described how PAVE worked:

> They got to know us as a teacher as well as being their counselor. . . . We built bonds and understandings of those kids and them of us, in ways that counselors in the old days could never do. And so it was very innovative.

As they matured from scared, uncertain ninth graders to seniors ready for college, a job, or the military, students developed trust in their counselors and considered their futures. Douglas detailed the range of activities:

> We had them take vocational interest questionnaires and screening instruments to determine their areas of strengths . . . and aptitudes. We brought in military personnel to administer the ASVAB (Armed Services Vocational Aptitude Battery) to explore how they might pursue vocational and civilian vocational training opportunities.

The counselors organized field trips to "the NASA research center at Moffett Field and to some of those emerging electronics/technology businesses like IBM and Hewlett-Packard." They brought in guest speakers to talk about their careers and their educational paths.

The program's longevity was key; it allowed students to establish foundational relationships with adults that supported them throughout the developmental and identity changes of adolescence. This trust, in turn, made it possible to discuss challenges and transformations that a single semester would not have allowed. PAVE became an anchor in the curriculum.

These principles and practices extended to other experiments on campus. Faculty collaboration, connective relationships with students, and multiple disciplinary paths to subject matter were the core of this approach. The speech and debate coach, Sharon Prefontaine, marveled at her ability to create the "Plus program" after only three years of teaching. Along with Mike

Mulvahill (social studies) and Dave McKean (art), they "combined social studies, English and math for entering freshmen." Prefontaine remarked that "life skills were still very much a part of education in 1970." The teaching team found "attendance improved, as you might expect. Kids showed up. Kids had a *person* right away."

The barriers to teacher-student contact were lowered. As Prefontaine put it, "You could be a human being. If a kid was crying, you could hug that kid. Without fear of accusation or court action. You could be human."

INTER-GROUP COUNCIL AND STUDENT UNIONS

In a similar vein, Sakamoto approached interracial coexistence as a long-term project: "It's something that you work at day and night for a long time. 'Cause you're dealing not only with school issues but general community needs as well." In 1968, Sakamoto founded an "Inter-Group Council" (IGC) on campus and experimented with ways to create interracial dialogue. *The Skywriter* announced IGC's mission: to create "a better relationship between racial groups at Sunnyvale High!" The IGC consisted of student representatives from the four main racial and ethnic groups on campus—"white, yellow, brown, and black," in the parlance of the day—and aimed to help students "get to know 'the other guy.' To work for true friendship." The group sought "to end ignorance" through engagement and communication.[8] Its members met regularly with Sakamoto, sometimes at his house, to talk and learn together. Symbolically and practically, the IGC represented the principal's approach to race relations. After only six months, IGC became *the* key organization addressing racial issues.

The national politics of race at that moment, in contrast, did not feature dialogue but demands for and resistance to change. In this climate, the fragile balance of recognizing political positions, learning histories, reconciling legitimate grievances, and mediating conflicts required determination and sustained leadership.

The Black Student Union

In the spring of 1969, Black students at SHS sought to establish a Black Student Union (BSU). They were a distinct minority; their small numbers prompted them to band together. Both De Anza College and San Jose State had established BSUs. The Black Panthers, headquartered just across San Francisco Bay in Oakland, had started organizing in high schools.

At SHS, a BSU could become a club, which meant seeking approval by the Associated Student Body (ASB) council. Being a club conferred legitimacy on a group and allocated resources. Those proposing a BSU attended a meeting in February 1969 to present their ideas. The ASB narrowly rejected the motion by a vote of eight to seven. Dennis Swanson, ASB's president, explained that the motion failed due to a "lack of understanding."[9]

One month later, a student leading the BSU campaign who became its first president, Willie Ratcliff, attended the ASB meeting. He aimed to clarify the proposal and persuade the council to reconsider. His answers to the questions posed at the meeting were reported in *The Skywriter*.

> Kathy Wisely (ASB secretary) asked: "What is the purpose of your organization?" Willie Ratcliff replied: "To help Whites understand Blacks a little better." Mike Katsarelis (senior class president) probed: "What is the difference between the Black Student Union and Inter-Group?" Willie Ratcliff responded: "Inter-Group is a discussion group, while the Black Student Union will have art and literature on Black History for students to read."[10]

The proponents insisted that BSU was open to white and Chicano students, not just Black students, which was a requirement for school funding. In this reconsideration, ASB approved the motion, and the BSU became an official club.[11] In keeping with the dominant ethos of that educational exchange, BSU representatives argued it would help white students learn about Black history and culture. Faculty advisors included James Jenkins, a new Black teacher who taught the innovative electronics class, and James Cruze, who was Native American and the Dean of Human Relations, a position intended to address racial issues.

Although the BSU was formally open to all, no white or Chicano students joined. They understood clearly that BSU was a space for Black students to get together. Learning about Black art, history, and literature did not gain much traction right away. Non-Black students recognized the value of autonomous organizations, but at the same time, they did not want to feel intimidated. Suzi Brink '72, who was white, recalled, "People used to say 'Don't let the BSU B.S. you.'" In other words, non-Black students should not let the club make unwarranted demands. She came from a family that was barely getting by—her mother was a typist and her stepfather unemployed—and thought that "prejudice comes in all shapes and forms" and does not just apply to race. She acknowledged BSU's usefulness, but also that felt many students shared a common condition—poverty—that shaped their lives in similar ways.

Terry Dyckman recalled the autumn day one of the BSU leaders, Don Kelley '70, electrified the campus by coming to school in clothing that announced his Black Power stance. Evoking the image of the Black Panther Party, he wore a black leather jacket, sunglasses, and a black beret tilted to one side. Dyckman interpreted his garb as a political statement that not only reflected a racial divide on campus, but created a new one. The 1970 yearbook, the *Sabre*, displayed group photos of BSU members in similar outfits. (See figure 5.1.) With boys standing behind them, the seated girls wore black leather jackets and big Afros. In the style of Angela Davis, a UCLA philosophy professor who belonged to the Communist Party, they made sure their dress expressed their politics. Some members are smiling, others proudly raising their fists in the defiant Black Power salute.

The BSU did not recruit all the Black students at Sunnyvale High. When Max Epps transferred to SHS in the fall of 1970, he attended a meeting "because I basically wanted to be around other Black people. I was new to the area and everything. And within five minutes, I realized I did not want to be in the Black Student Union." To Max, Black Power politics meant separation and division. It did not aim to negotiate ideas or discuss cultural differences. While it intended to inspire respect for Black people as citizens and human beings, Max believed that it emphasized confrontation rather than compromise. Max had lived in Washington, D.C. in April 1968, when rioting erupted after the assassination of Martin Luther King Jr. As fires ravaged a Black neighborhood, he witnessed acts of rage and destruction. "I did not want to go through this again." He asserted,

> I was *beyond* the Black Panther leadership part. Coming from a [military] service base where you don't get to pick and choose your friends because you're all kind of lumped together, I learned to assimilate and just make friends with a lot of different kinds of people.

Figure 5.1 Black Student Union, 1970. *Source*: *Sabre*, 1970.

Over the years, if annual yearbook photos are representative, the BSU ebbed and flowed. The last graduating class in 1981 had thirteen BSU members, slightly less than the fifteen it had in 1970.

The Chicano Student Union

Shortly after the ASB approved the BSU, Mexican American students formally proposed their own autonomous organization, which they had been planning for a while. Students with Mexican heritage constituted about one quarter of the SHS student body, so they had the potential for a sizable membership. In order to tap campus resources, they organized a club with an educational mission, and it was approved in March 1969.

The term "Chicano" was used by a political movement that emerged in the late 1960s. Activists in the United States reclaimed and redefined the term, which had a derogatory meaning in Mexico. They refashioned it to convey ethnic pride and reject the ideal of assimilation into white American society. Mario Garcia and Ellen McCracken explain, "To be a Chicano in the 1960s and 1970s was to be an activist in the Chicano Movement."[12] Turning to a long proud history, Chicanos claimed Aztlán as their homeland; the entire southwest region—now California, Arizona, New Mexico, Colorado—had belonged to Mexico before the 1846 Mexican-American War.[13] The far-reaching movement inspired poetry, theater, dance, and literature as well as political action like supporting the United Farm Workers unionization campaign. It insisted that Mexican American history and culture be included in school curricula from kindergarten through college. It called for a return to bilingual teaching and public services delivered in Spanish as well as English.

Members of the CSU at SHS engaged in serious debates about the meaning of Chicano. They aligned with activists throughout California, but they also worked to define it for themselves. JoAnn Vargas '73 was drawn to the cause "to help your fellow people." One perspective especially resonated with Pete Araujo '71: Chicano is "a state of mind. . . . It's how you felt about yourself." While this connected students to Mexican ancestry, it also embraced other Spanish-speaking peoples. Some students whose ancestors were from Puerto Rico, Guatemala, and other Central and South American countries joined the CSU. It gave them a place as well as a shared identity. JoAnn Vargas explained that she was ethnically Puerto Rican, but she was drawn to the term and the organization because "I like what we stood for." When she began picking beans with her family when she was only three years old, her mother dressed her in long-sleeved shirts so the plants would not scratch her as she worked her way down each row. When she started at Sunnyvale High, the organization and platform of the CSU spoke to her experience, so she joined.

Araujo described these debates as turning on a class divide among Latino students. Those whose families had been farmworkers rooted themselves in that agricultural history, which shaped their family's economic and social fortunes. Pete Araujo detailed his own background in California's Central Valley:

> Where I lived in Corcoran, I used to pick cotton for a living. My mother was picking cotton. All our relatives were all in cotton, out in cotton fields. . . . As we moved back to the Santa Clara Valley, then we started picking tomatoes. . . . I picked string beans. I picked pears. I mean, you name it, I picked it. . . . I went all the way to Idaho, picked potatoes when I was a kid.

The United Farm Workers grape boycott that began in 1965 was a rallying cry across the region and held special meaning for Araujo; he and his family had picked grapes in Delano, the heart of UFW organizing.

The students' agenda, connected to their agricultural and migrant heritage, was broad and powerful. In addition to educating others about Mexican history and Mexican American culture, it inspired youth to respect themselves, embrace their identity, and feel pride in their heritage. To Dan Serna '71, the CSU meant "I am exercising my rights. I'm exercising who I am, *what I am*."

Mexican and Mexican American students at SHS from middle-class families did not face the hardships and instability of migrant labor and were less likely to embrace Chicano identity. Yolanda Garcia '72, whose father was a calibration technician at Westinghouse and whose mother was a homemaker, explained: "I didn't wanna be labeled as the Chicana. I'm Mexican American first. . . . I was born here, my culture and my heritage is Mexican . . . which I'm very proud of. But I never, ever wanted to be labeled as a Chicana, because to me, they were very militant. They were aggressive. The girls scared me, frankly, with their makeup and hair and just the way they stood around." Among those who worked in the valley's canneries in unionized jobs that paid well above the minimum wage, many did not call themselves Chicano or Chicana either.

Several senior boys, including Jesse Guel, who had served on IGC, and Johnny Perez, led CSU organizing and outreach. They modeled a reasoned, strategic approach to solving problems. "They carried themselves with pride," Pete Araujo '71 recalled. "They were very calm, [when a] situation came up. They were just letting you know, 'Just wait. Wait. Don't just blow your head [and] start doing things.' So it made you disciplined." It also created solidarity. Araujo felt the difference in a world that disparaged and harassed Mexican American kids. "We figured that if we were together, it would be more difficult for someone from the outside to attack you, because now, if you attack one person, you're attacking the whole group." JoAnn Vargas '73 felt the strength that lies in numbers: "there's a lot of us. . . . We were a voice."

Figure 5.2   Chicano Student Union, 1971. *Source*: Sabre, 1971.

When David Hernandez '73 arrived at SHS as a freshman, he was eager to join the CSU. His older sister Vickie was treasurer, and David admired her friends; with their dignity and confidence, they could change things. He felt empowered by the CSU because it offered a positive image of people with Mexican heritage and connected students to a larger movement. The CSU anchored him, informed his worldview and political perspective, and made him proud.

Regardless of how long their families had lived in California, these students were not getting the education they were entitled to and deserved. One of the CSU's overarching goals was to obtain their rightful education and end the school's discriminatory practices, especially tracking and stereotyping that led to low expectations.

Many students aspired to become the first in their families to graduate high school. Their parents regarded this as a major accomplishment. Neither of Dan Serna's parents graduated from high school because "they were in the fields all the time." His father supported the family as a construction worker, and during the seasons when he was unemployed, his mother would cook tamales and have the children sell them in the neighborhood. Serna said, "We wanted education. We wanted to graduate from high school." CSU was demanding that the school live up to its legal mandate.

Students were particularly concerned about being tracked into classes on the basis of their skin color, heritage, and the language their parents spoke at home. Slotted into courses with teachers who set low expectations, they were deprived of opportunities to learn and become upwardly mobile. Educational success meant overcoming structural inequities and interpersonal prejudice at school. Despite employing many young, progressive teachers, SHS had an old guard of teachers and counselors who held stereotypical attitudes about Mexican Americans. Danny Serna '71 was advised to work at a gas station after he graduated. Pete Araujo '71 recalled one teacher who inappropriately assumed he was destined to perform only blue-collar jobs. As an audiovisual aide his senior year, he would deliver a projector to a classroom, show a film, and then return everything to the AV office. A teacher told him, "Oh, that's good that you try to understand the projector, and then after a while, you're gonna start understanding how to do the washing machines and refrigerators. So after you graduate, you can be an appliance repairman." Pete was stunned. "For that particular teacher, that's as far as I'm gonna get in life." In fact, not only was Pete the first in his family to graduate high school, but he became a championship wrestler, attended De Anza College for two years, then was awarded a full scholarship to San Jose State. After graduating, he became a firefighter.

The CSU broadened students' horizons, supported their academic aspirations, and encouraged them to envision a brighter future. As JoAnn Vargas put it, the message from their advisors and reinforced by members was, "There's more out there. You could do this; you could do that."

Mike Honda and Loretta Gutierrez became the CSU's advisors. Gutierrez, who began teaching at SHS in 1968 at the age of twenty-three, was the youngest daughter of migrant farmworkers. She had picked in the fields along with her older brothers and sisters. Always good at school, she earned a degree in English at San Jose State before coming to Sunnyvale to teach both Spanish and English. As a young, dynamic teacher, she understood the stakes of education and the power of what she called "the Brown movement."

Honda, who spent his early childhood interned in Camp Amache in Colorado with his Japanese American family, was fresh out of the Peace Corps in El Salvador. When he arrived to teach science, he volunteered to advise the CSU. Students were skeptical. As they milled about before a meeting, some boys made derogatory remarks about Japanese Americans in Spanish. Mike Honda, standing right beside them, responded in Spanish. Startled, they became extremely embarrassed, *vergüenza*, as Serna reported. They apologized profusely. Honda forgave them and demonstrated that he was an advocate for the students and knew how to mobilize resources on their behalf.

A while later, students discovered offensive fliers plastered on their lockers by students from nearby Peterson High School. The fliers made inflammatory comments, like "Chicanos eat shit," and "What's in their tacos?" Angry students began making plans to get revenge by going over to the school to "kick their asses." Mike Honda instructed them to chill and stay put. He immediately met with the principal at Peterson High. The new principal at SHS was "not very helpful," so he bypassed him. Along with Loretta Gutierrez, Honda took about fifteen students, including CSU leaders, to meet with the perpetrators' principal, who apologized on behalf of Peterson students. The SHS emissaries felt heard, respected, and satisfied. Having seen Mike Honda's effectiveness in action, Dan Serna '71 concluded, "He's a good man."

Honda became a leader among the faculty and connected with parents of color. Gutierrez observed that Honda could talk to *anybody* with persuasiveness and finesse. He used those skills after leaving SHS. In 1971, he won a seat on the San José Unified School Board and went on to serve in many elective offices, including the State Assembly for five years. In 2001, he was elected to represent the seventeenth Congressional District of California and served for sixteen years in the US Congress.

The BSU's and CSU's club status formalized the long-standing tensions between students and also prompted them to forge an alliance. They gained focus, considered the issues they faced, and set priorities. Both pursued learning and teaching opportunities. Black student Jackie Gooch '74 embraced their educational approach. She was involved in the BSU but also attended CSU meetings. She reasoned, "I am an all-round, openhearted person. 'Cause half my friends were Mexican American. So I would also go to this Chicano Student Union. . . . I was an equal opportunity girl."

For many CSU activists, its impact was long-lasting: educating students about their rights, giving voice to wrongs that had to be corrected, creating community, and demonstrating solidarity. Dan Serna '71 discovered the power of "demanding one's rights." At SHS, when he spoke up and insisted to his counselor that he be moved out of the low track, he was. As a teenager, Serna was brutally beaten and arrested without provocation by Sunnyvale police officers, suffering a concussion. After he got out of juvenile hall and recovered, he, Mike Honda, and other CSU members secured a meeting with the chief of police in Sunnyvale. Encouraged by his peers, he informed the chief about the unprovoked violence he endured and insisted that officers stop harassing and using excessive force with Chicanos in the community. Dan went on to work for the city of Palo Alto and became a shop steward for his local SEIU for thirty-seven years. Peter Araujo '71 celebrated the way CSU created a community that continues today. He learned that "we are a group and the more we stay together, the stronger we're gonna be."

JoAnn Vargas '73 translated that experience into a stronger, more forceful voice. Her combined experiences in high school, especially in the CSU, prompted her to rethink her parents' messages. They advised her "don't make waves" and "stay in the shadows." She began speaking out when she saw something she thought was wrong. She confronted girls who tried to put her down, and later spoke up about sexual harassment in her workplace. At SHS, she said, "I started getting a voice of my own."

By 1981, reflecting its diverse membership and the ongoing political debates about terminology, CSU had changed its name to Raza Latino but continued to pursue its mission. The club had a robust membership, with twenty-seven students in the photograph for the final SHS yearbook.

The Asian American Union

In 1970, there was no comparable club for Asian students, even though students with backgrounds in Asia and the Pacific Islands constituted over 6 percent of the student body. Together, there were three times as many Asian as Black students. Japanese American Robert Handa '73 reflected, "The Asians didn't really need to have a club and they didn't need to really be organized." He pointed to the impact of Bruce Lee, the Chinese martial arts sensation who became a cultural idol through his films. Kids of all races loved his toughness, his fearless warrior style, and his lack of compliance, whatever the situation. "At the time just having an Asian quarterback was almost enough." Chinese American Paul Fong was quarterback and captain of the SHS football team. Handa pointed to the symbolic power of Japanese Americans Mike Honda and Paul Sakamoto in positions of leadership and authority.

Consistent with a statewide ethos, students from Pacific Rim countries did not always see a reason to organize across national origins. This huge region had a recently been convulsed by international and civil wars.[14] Barely a generation after Japan's invasion of China and colonization of Korea, enduring tensions shaped the social dynamics among their descendants in the United States. In the wake of the Communist Revolution and the formation of the People's Republic of China, opposition groups sought refuge in California. Chinese and Japanese people shared a history of exclusion and discrimination, but that did not unite the older generations. Among the Japanese Americans who had recently been interned, a culture of silence prevailed.[15]

That changed in October 1970, when students, with the help of Mike Honda, founded the Asian American Union (AAU). *The Skywriter* reported:

> The club was started primarily to get together Asian-Americans which includes Chinese-Americans, Filipinos, Japanese-Americans, Guamanians, Koreans and Hawaiians to talk about their problems, heritages and cultures. Although the club is called Asian-American Union anyone is welcome to attend their meetings and participate in the activities.[16]

Like the BSU and CSU, funding was contingent on compliance with the ASB's principle of including all students. The SHS ethos of education prevailed. The AAU continued to grow over the 1970s until the school closed.

Born of a need for a collective identity in the context of racial conflict, a push for integration, and opposition to full inclusion, these unions were autonomous organizations that offered safe spaces for members of the SHS community. In some ways, they countered the IGC. In others, the unions complemented the IGC's ability to foster belonging in the school. The IGC set the tone and method of dialogue between groups on campus and accelerated the acceptance of the unions.

BROTHERHOOD WEEK, APRIL 1969

In April 1969, the IGC sponsored "Brotherhood Week." The women's liberation movement's critique of exclusionary masculine terminology had not yet reached Sunnyvale High. Despite vast numbers of girls leading organizations across campus, students who were concerned about social justice appeared less aware of sisterhood. Brotherhood Week celebrated the multicultural student body and gave each group an opportunity to teach others about its distinctive culture through speakers, entertainment, and food. IGC collaborated with the BSU and CSU to promote representation and dialogue across groups.

References to skin color did not offend students' sensibilities any more than "brotherhood" did. The week began with "White Day" and was followed by the other racial groups represented in the IGC. White Day featured a speaker from nearby Foothill College who emphasized the commonalities and cooperation between white people and people of color. Today, if a public school had the temerity to sponsor "White Day," it would signal white nationalism and advocacy of white supremacy and would be criticized as racist, anti-Black, and anti-immigrant. But in 1969, in the context of Brotherhood Week at SHS, White Day was part of a display of the rainbow that included all students and was not intended to separate racial groups or intimidate students of color.

The next day, "Yellow Day," featured *lumpia*, Filipino spring rolls, in the cafeteria, a display of Asian clothing, jewelry, and furniture in the Hangar, and a speaker on Asian history. Thursday was "Brown Day," honoring Mexican American culture, music, and food. The speaker, Mac Martinez from West Valley College, addressed how to combat prejudice. He argued: "1) Chicanos (and all people) should be accepted for 'what they are'; and 2) Chicanos should have self-pride and dignity."[17] On Friday, "Black Day" emphasized "Black is beautiful." Organized by BSU, activities included an exhibit of posters and clothing in the Hangar and a dance at noon. Chris Ross, the "minister of education" of the BSU at De Anza College, spoke.

Taking stock of the week's activities, *The Skywriter* reported, "The efforts put forth in this past week have provided hope" that race relations at SHS will improve.[18] Using that cautious but optimistic frame, *The Skywriter* editorial outlined two competing philosophies that existed side by side. The IGC espoused integration and multiracial understanding, while the BSU and CSU stood for autonomy and separate spaces, which implied confrontation. Could they coexist and complement each other rather than undermine each other?

The *Skywriter* editorialized:

> The formation of the Black Student Union and the Chicano Student Union has brought the student body to a moment of crisis. Although their purposes are

to increase harmony among the various groups on campus, they have become very controversial. The reason that the student body has a number of different feelings about these new clubs is this: a crisis is an opportunity to construct or destruct, to unite or separate. Some students feel that the student unions will only serve as cliques for different ethnic groups. That could do a lot of damage to intergroup relations. However, *The Skywriter* staff sincerely hopes that they will be uniting forces on campus. So far, they have shown that they really want to fulfill their goals.[19]

The editors concluded by saying they "will continue to support the student unions as long as they are the constructive organizations which they set out to be." Their position leaned toward intergroup politics, but campus relationships could go either way.

In retrospect, it is hard to tell whether Brotherhood Week had an impact, given the wide spectrum of opinion within as well as between racial-ethnic groups. It built on the intergroup philosophy and educational agenda. The next year, it morphed into a multitude of events with SHS-sponsored Black History Week and a Cinco de Mayo celebration.

Unfortunately for the school, Paul Sakamoto left SHS at the end of June 1969 to enter a PhD program in education set up by San Jose State, his alma mater, and Michigan State. His good fortune and ambition left Sunnyvale without leadership on race relations.

After the departure of this outstanding principal, Loretta Gutierrez saw tensions rising and worried that the situation would deteriorate. Even while Sakamoto was there, she had witnessed other teachers disparaging Chicano students and treating them unfairly. Counselors too readily tracked Chicanos into less academically advanced and vocational classes. Many parents were upset over the disrespect shown to their children. Gutierrez felt the resentment building and expected open conflict. "I knew it was going to happen sooner or later, because at the meetings that Mike [Honda] and I were having at night with the parents, their demands were justified."

NOTES

1. See Robert R. Alvarez Jr., "The Lemon Grove Incident," *Journal of San Diego History* 32 (1986). https://sandiegohistory.org/journal/1986/april/lemongrove/; Kristi Bowman, "A Different Shade of Brown," *Judicature* 88 (2004): 85–90; Reuben Donato, and Jarrod S. Hanson, "Legally White, Socially 'Mexican': The Politics of De Jure and De Facto School Segregation in the American Southwest," *Harvard Educational Review* 82 (2012): 202–25. For valuable classroom resources, see the Zinn Education Project, https://www.zinnedproject.org/; Vicki L. Ruiz, "South by

Southwest: Mexican Americans and Segregated Schooling, 1900–1950," *OAH Magazine of History* 15 (2001): 23–27.

2. *Brown v. Board of Education of Topeka*, 347 U.S. 483 (1954); *Mendez, et al., v. Westminster School District of Orange County, et al.*, 64 F.Supp. 544 (S.D. Cal. 1946), aff'd, 161 F.2d 774 (9th Cir. 1947).

3. *Jackson v. Pasadena City School District*, 59 Cal.2d 876 (1963).

4. Cherry A. McGee Banks, *Improving Multicultural Education: Lessons from the Intergroup Education Movement* (New York: Teachers College Press, 2005).

5. Adam Hochschild, *American Midnight: The Great War, a Violent Peace, and Democracy's Forgotten Crisis* (New York: Mariner, 2022); Erika Lee, *America for Americans: A History of Xenophobia in the United States* (New York: Basic Books, 2019).

6. Banks, *Improving Multicultural Education*. See also Martha Minow, Richard A. Shweder, and Hazel Rose Markus, eds., *Just Schools: Pursuing Equality in Societies of Difference* (New York: Russell Sage Foundation, 2008).

7. See Paul Sakamoto's oral history conducted by the Japanese American Museum of San Jose: https://www.jamsj.org/manabu/paul-sakamoto.

8. *Skywriter*, November 1, 1968.

9. *Skywriter*, February 28, 1969.

10. *Skywriter*, March 17, 1969.

11. *Skywriter*, March 17, 1969.

12. Mario T. García, and Ellen McCracken, eds., *Rewriting the Chicano Movement: New Histories of Mexican American Activism in the Civil Rights Era* (Tucson: University of Arizona Press, 2021), 4.

13. Cherríe Moraga, and Gloria Anzaldúa, eds., *This Bridge Called My Back: Writings by Radical Women of Color* (Watertown, MA: Persephone Press, 1981); Chon A. Noriega, Eric Avila, Karen Mary Davalos, Chela Sandoval, Rafael Pérez-Torres, and Charlene Villaseñor Black, eds., *The Chicano Studies Reader: An Anthology of Aztlán, 1970–2019*, 4th ed. (Los Angeles: UCLA Chicano Studies Research Center Press, 2020).

14. Yen Le Espiritu, *Asian American Panethnicity: Bridging Institutions and Identities* (Philadelphia, PA: Temple University Press, 1992).

15. Erika Lee, *The Making of Asian America: A History* (New York: Simon & Schuster, 2015).

16. *Skywriter*, October 23, 1970.

17. *Skywriter*, April 18, 1969.

18. *Skywriter*, April 18, 1969.

19. *Skywriter*, April 18, 1969.

Chapter 6

Was It a "Race Riot"?

The winter and spring of 1970 proved a turning point for SHS. In the wake of Principal Paul Sakamoto's departure and the arrival of his ill-prepared successor, several conflicts coalesced to create a moment of crisis. The dynamic faculty worked with administrators to move the school forward, accommodate legitimate student demands, and heal some of the ruptures.

From the start, Bob Bargman, who was hired to replace Sakamoto in the fall of 1969, was a bad fit for the multiracial, multiethnic, working-class school. Not only was he an inexperienced administrator, but he was unaccustomed to working with blue-collar families and Brown and Black students. A white man who had taught drama in a white, middle-class school, Bargman had little common ground with SHS students. As teacher Bob Douglas, who witnessed the principal's biases, frankly put it, he didn't know how to relate to "kids [who] were not college prep." Douglas speculated, "If he had really known my background, he'd probably [have] fired me, because he had no respect for human beings like me that were not of the middle class." Bargman refused to recognize the value of hiring teachers whose backgrounds were similar to the students'. Above all, he abandoned his predecessors' practice of building relationships with students to create community. By all accounts, he spent his days sequestered in his office, barking orders at the faculty, and making announcements over the public address system. Racial justice and dialogue across differences were not on Bargman's agenda, and the IGC was not convened after Sakamoto's departure.

Chapter 6

SMOG-FREE LOCOMOTION DAY

In February 1970, a new student organization invited everyone at Sunnyvale High to save the earth by participating in "Smog-Free Locomotion Day." It was scheduled for the end of Black History Week, when the BSU was sponsoring lectures, giving presentations, and selling soul food. Inspired by a dawning awareness that people must stop polluting the planet, the group worked with a science teacher, who served as faculty sponsor, and challenged students and teachers to get to campus without a motorized vehicle and join a festive parade. SHS students were exercising leadership in a nascent nationwide movement: two months later, activists organized the first Earth Day, which led to global activism and policy changes.

On that sunny Thursday morning, the plan was simple: circle around the neighborhood and return to the school before classes began. Five hundred students, fully a quarter of the student body, showed up riding bikes, gliding on skateboards or kick scooters, or on foot; one pulled a friend in a little red wagon. Several white boys carried a sedan chair on their shoulders with Johnny Gooch, the African American president of the junior class, sitting proudly atop. A sizable group from the marching band, including faculty director John Riggle and much of the drum line, brought up the rear.

This joyful parade returned to campus ten minutes after the bell rang for the first period. When the throngs began sauntering into the rally court, the principal reprimanded everyone for arriving late. Bargman ushered everyone into the cafeteria, threatening to issue unexcused tardy slips. Some students balked, irritated at the petty, unwarranted imposition of power. Don Kelley, a senior and an activist in the BSU, refused to go into the cafeteria, "claiming his teachers would let him have an 'excused' absence." Bargman reverted to his practice of making an announcement on the PA system. Athletic director Doug Boyd recalled his orders: "If you're not now in class, report to the cafeteria, and you'll be given detention for being tardy." Then, Boyd continued, "All hell broke loose." Students responded, "Up yours. We're not going back to class."

Don Kelley, a Black student who had not been part of the march, joined the growing number of students confronting Bargman. He accused the principal of being a puppet of the district administration.[1] Bargman promptly suspended him. Doug White, also African American, "grabbed a microphone in the school's closed-circuit television studio and urged students to 'come out and join the rally'; don't be a puppet!" Some students left their homerooms, milled about talking, and joined the chaotic resistance. The *Palo Alto Times* reported that 1,000 students—nearly half of the student body—refused to attend classes.[2]

In effect, the principal's actions that day turned a positive, hopeful event into a tense confrontation. By the end of the day, the principal had fatally undermined his authority and provoked a serious crisis.

THE FACE-OFF

In the crowded cafeteria, the smog-free parade participants converted their mass detention into a public forum for their complaints. At that juncture, a group of "radicals" who had been meeting earlier in the week—environmentalists and members of the BSU—"realized they had something in common." Together, students demanded ethnic studies and an open campus.[3]

For two hours, students voiced their many grievances, asking questions and demanding answers from administrators. The principal and vice principal were joined by the district superintendent, who made an emergency visit to SHS. Several male leaders articulated the students' perspective, notably Michael Ratcliff, chair of the BSU, and Ramon Alarcón, who had just overturned the restrictive dress code in court. Although girls held leadership positions in many campus organizations, not a single girl spoke during the confrontation with administrators.

Discussion centered on the issue of racism on campus and in the curriculum. Ratcliff read a list of demands: "1. Open campus; 2. Modular scheduling; 3. Better ethnic program; and 4. Better food in the cafeteria."[4] SHS students had been aware of protests at high schools up and down the state, whose leaders took a systemic perspective and made similar demands. By rejecting the stultifying structure of high school, they were searching for creative ways to facilitate engaged learning.

THE FIGHT

Meanwhile, in the rally court, simmering tensions between two senior boys—Chico Serna and Don Kelley—spiraled into a fight. Precisely how it was connected to the confrontation in the cafeteria is unclear; perhaps it was not. Students' recollections of the fight that day were more vivid than accounts of the conflict with the principal over reforming the school or the collective action to save the earth. Perhaps this brief confrontation unleashed another layer of fury framed by racial strife. Counselor Terry Dyckman observed: "Clearly there was tension on the campus. There was something brewing. I mean there always was. Maybe this was all on pre-boil and it just took something" like Smog-Free Locomotion Day to make it boil over.

In other settings, Chico Serna '72, an activist in the CSU, and Don Kelley '70, a leader in the BSU, were friends. Both were athletes, Chico a wrestler and Don a football player. The CSU and BSU at SHS were informed by, but not affiliated with, the Brown Berets and the Black Panthers, which had their own disagreements as well as distinct constituencies. Black and Chicano students, like the organizations they belonged to, could disagree about politics and strategy. Underlying their shared militancy, they competed for respect and resources.

Like many conflicts on campus, this fight between two friends seemed to erupt spontaneously. Paul Fong '71, who was on the edge of the fray, recalled: "It was just a really quick thing, but Chico grabbed Don and carried him through the glass of the Hangar," shattering the window. Robert Handa remembered the loud boom when Don's body hit the glass, immediately followed by the rain of shards hitting the pavement. A hush fell on the rally court as everyone tried to figure out what happened.

The commotion drew some students in and repelled others, filling the rally court with fear and excitement. The confrontation did not turn into a large-scale brawl, perhaps because Paul Fong and science teacher Mike Honda intervened to break it up. Fong later explained, "We were the middleman minorities. So we were used to breaking up fights." In the 1960s and 1970s, nonwhite people who were neither African American nor Latina/o were often marginalized both by the dominant, white middle-class culture and by the larger and more visible minority groups. Yet they sometimes served as mediators.[5] Here, the conflict between a Black and a Chicano student was interrupted by a Japanese American teacher and a Chinese immigrant student. As in much of California, the racial and ethnic landscape was too complex to accommodate a narrow Black-white binary.

The fight sparked other acts of defiance. Students milling around the rally court set garbage cans on fire. At one end of the rally court, a Black girl tried to join the ruckus. Barbara Brown ran into the girls' locker room. White teacher-coach Carolyn Buszdieker, who was in the PE office, jumped up. "I had heard there was noise outside but I hadn't bothered to go and look."

She demanded, "What are you doing?" Barbara replied, "I'm getting something out of my locker," then opened it and reached for some razor blades. Buzz said, "No, you're not." Barbara replied, "Yes, I am." Buszdieker described their next moves: "She got out of one door and I cut through the office and managed to get her." Buszdieker swung the chain-link gate to the rally court shut and then hollered to another teacher, "Call Mrs. Brown right now!" Buszdieker knew Barbara's family, so her immediate response was to reach out to her mother.

While Buzz kept her boxed in, two kids approached the gate from the rally court. One boy held a shingle hammer in his hand, which he began rhythmically slapping into his palm as he advanced. He demanded, "You let Barbara go." The other teacher opened the door to report on her call, saw the confrontation, screeched, and retreated. The boy braced to throw the hammer. Instead of protecting herself, Buszdieker burst through the gate and charged him. "He took off running." She stopped, returned to the girls' locker room, and "locked Barbara in our office till her mom could get there."

What were Buszdieker's options as a teacher in a dangerous situation? In 1970, California schools did not have security systems or police officers on campus; those measures came later, in response to fears of gun violence and actual shootings. Buszdieker could have backed off and let Barbara escape to join the fray in the rally court. Alternatively, she could have called the principal, which surely would have led to Barbara's suspension. Or she could have called the police.

Acting on the relationship ethos that characterized SHS, Buszdieker instead summoned Barbara's mother. Her astute assessment of the principal's ineffectiveness and her personal connection with the student's family shaped her reaction. Spontaneously, she intervened in a way that she believed was in the girl's best interests. Had she not done so, the commotion in the rally court would have had two more participants, one armed with a hammer and the other with razor blades. Mrs. Brown came to campus and took her daughter home. Buszdieker reflected afterward, "Her mom was so appreciative."

By the end of the day, some angry students sought ways to build on the confrontation's momentum to call for change. Having witnessed student protests in southern California high schools, they considered a boycott of classes. They knew that boycotts hit schools in their pocketbooks because the state funded schools based on attendance; fewer students in class meant less money for the school. They decided to call for a boycott and began taping up signs in the rally court. After school, one of the environmental activists convened a meeting and proposed forming a United Student Union. On short notice, about hundred students, most of them Anglo, showed up.

THE RASHOMON OF CONFLICT

In the years that followed, the group confrontation with the principal and the fight between an African American and a Chicano student became entangled in people's memories. Both overshadowed the environmental inspiration for the day. Media accounts reinforced the school's reputation as troubled and unruly. The question became not so much what had actually happened, but how, individually and collectively to interpret and respond to these tumultuous events.

Perspectives about what happened depended on people's positions and angle of vision. Today, some remember the conflict as a "race riot," a point of view hyped by TV news broadcasts and regional newspapers at the time. Others insist it was a political dispute. Still others argue that it was a typical high school fight between two boys, who were feeling belligerent that day but were otherwise friends.

Many teachers blamed Bargman for escalating the conflict. Eric Paulson, the boys' basketball coach, recalled, "The lack of leadership in administration . . . let that get to th[at] point." Teacher Loretta Gutierrez observed that the new principal had consistently rebuffed students' and parents' requests for more communication and had failed to consider their grievances about unequal treatment. He took a law-and-order approach to running the campus and was disconnected from students. Gutierrez emphasized, "The administration would *not* listen. They wouldn't listen. They kept saying no." The "Black Student Union and Chicano Student Union didn't feel that the school was doing much to help them. . . . There was still too much discrimination by teachers."

Bargman had abandoned interracial dialogue and the school's philosophy and practice of engagement. Crucially, he was unable to deal with working-class kids and students of color. Reflecting on the district's choice to place Bargman at SHS, a subsequent principal said he was a "nice guy," but the wrong person for the job. It was clear to the teachers that Bargman was in over his head. Counselor Terry Dyckman described him as "the most pathetically inept person I've ever seen in any role."

The Media Version

In the winter of 1970, mobilization against the US escalation of the war in Vietnam intertwined with racial tensions in contentious national politics. Teacher Mike Honda said, "At that time, racial confrontation was the thing." Young people's rage "was . . . all around you," as Jane Manley '72 put it. "It did seem militant, but . . . it seemed like it was possibly necessary." At that moment, the media readily framed a fight between high school boys—an ordinary occurrence all across the country—as a race riot between Black and Brown communities.

The front page of the *Sunnyvale Standard* linked the racial and environmental issues. Under the headline "Sunnyvale High Students Protest," the lead paragraph began, "About 200 Sunnyvale High School students cut classes this morning, protesting the possible suspension of a Black student and demanding changes in the school system."[6] The article continued, "The sometimes near-riot crowd formed today after Principal Robert Bargman told student Don Kelley that he was suspended." The rest of the story focused on the confrontation between Kelley and Bargman, the threat of suspension and its retraction, and Mr. Kelley's demand to know why his son was being disciplined.

Three photographs illustrated the story. The largest photo's caption read: "RIGHT ON! Protesting Sunnyvale High School students surrounding their principal, Robert Bargman, raised their clenched fists in the 'power to the people' symbol." The photo featured the principal facing a cluster of four Black students, all as tall or taller than him. Don Kelley stands to the left, pointing at Bargman. His father, Oliver Kelley, stands slightly outside the circle, wearing a suit and tie. The smallest photograph featured student Cathy Zukov in a vintage World War I gas mask, which she wore in the Smog-Free Locomotion Day parade. The environmental protest that kicked off the day was but a minor part of the story.

The SHS protest shared the front page of the *Sunnyvale Standard* with stories of unrest at San Jose State and the University of California at Santa Barbara. Together, they communicated the notion that out-of-control students were a menace to educational institutions. One headline declared, "Bomb Set Off at SJS," and the text detailed the damage to the old Journalism building.[7] On the back page of the front section, headlines announced: "Rampage Injures 16 Officers." A photo showed a crowd of 1,500 students facing off against 450 helmeted police in Goleta as the Bank of America and a laundromat burned to the ground. Adjacent, a smaller headline read, "Sunnyvale High Students Cut Classes in Protest." The juxtaposition of buildings being bombed and burnt down aroused fear that the high school protest could turn violent.

The following morning, the *San Jose Mercury News* proclaimed, "Anti-Pollution Parade Explodes into Sunnyvale Student Protest."[8] Its story focused on the demands for school reform and reported that Don Kelley's suspension was dropped after the principal met with his parents. The students' concern for the environment was buried by the issue of race as a group of Black students challenged a white principal.

Students were aghast at the newspapers' sensationalized distortion of their confrontation with authority. Bargman corralling parade participants into the cafeteria morphed into "students cutting classes." Ron DeMedeiros '72 remembered the papers "magnified how bad it got." Students were indignant at being unjustly misrepresented by outsiders. Gloria Collins '73 sarcastically asked, how do they define a riot? "Four people standing on the curb?"

The Politics Version

The issues that sparked conflict that day were fundamentally political—wanton neglect of the earth, the war raging in Vietnam, and the US history of racial injustice. All fueled demands for change. The *Palo Alto Times* reported, "Students contended the protests were not primarily along racial lines."[9] As math teacher Jim Miller put it, "I remember it as a fight, not as a riot. . . . There might be a racial component, but it wasn't *all* about race."

Paul Fong '71 attributed the fight to "a misunderstanding" that positioned Brown and Black students in opposition to each other. He saw national Black

Panther politics as "really divisive," so even though the Panthers and the Brown Berets shared an anti-establishment stance, the BSU and the CSU at SHS were on "two different wavelengths." David Hernandez '73, an active member of CSU, saw the conflict as based on a long-standing divergence in strategy and tactics between the two groups.

Tensions between Black and Brown students had escalated that year. A Puerto Rican girl who was active in the CSU, JoAnn Vargas '73, was shocked at the way Black pride ended up dividing students who were formerly friends. "All of a sudden, the color of your skin" turned you into "'enemies without cause.' That was new."

Of course, different racially inflected histories shaped the politics of patriotism. On another day, Mike Honda was summoned to intervene in a fight between Don Kelley and Charlie Trujillo. This conflict centered on the American flag, which "the Latinos were trying to protect." They were proud of their US citizenship and had relatives serving in Vietnam. But "the Blacks wanted to take it down. . . . They wanted to burn this thing" because it was a symbol of their oppression. As always, students gathered around. From the perimeter, another boy thought the conflict had nothing to do with race. Can politics with racialized actors ever *not* be about race?

Mike Honda counseled the students, "You both are fighting for the same thing." He convinced them to back off and talk before things escalated.

"It's the People" Version

Some insisted that the Serna-Kelley fight was between these two individuals, not about politics or race and ethnicity. According to one account, their falling out centered on Don's treatment of Chico's girlfriend. Many boys' fights were triggered by territoriality, competition for girls, and assertions of masculinity. Mike Honda acknowledged that the political moment framed how people interpreted quarrels. Later, after political tensions had abated, an argument between two boys might simply be called a personal disagreement.

Reflecting on what she heard from her older brothers at SHS before she arrived, African American student Jackie Gooch '74 said: "It sounded more like a brawl. Because they got over it quick. Does that make sense? And when I went there, that was not an issue at all." Black student Max Epps '73, who also enrolled at Sunnyvale High after these tumultuous events, recalled that students told him stories about that day as a way to explain the school's culture. Max had the impression that the conflict was particular to two people: "It started with a fight. . . . I don't think it was a racial issue." Japanese American Robert Handa '73 agreed with Max's perspective. It was "a conflict between *these guys*," a "*personality conflict*," rather than one racial group against another. Students knew each other across racial-ethnic boundaries because of their shared experience. Filipino American Ed Lizardo '73 observed that Don and Chico "knew each other" from elementary school. When conflicts arose, students had relationships to fall back on.

Fights continued to break out episodically, as they had before. Yet many students still found SHS a safe space, especially if they knew how to navigate it. Kathi Romero '73 said, "I don't remember wanting to stay home from school, or being afraid. 'Cause . . . I had friends in both groups." Students who had not been involved in the fray said it did not change how they felt about the school. Ron DeMedeiros '72 said, "I didn't feel like it was a safety issue." Jane Manley '72 said, "I never felt intimidated. I never felt afraid. I never felt threatened." Avoiding contested spaces and having friends across campus insured safety.

Some alums thought that the confrontation that day had precipitated a catharsis. Kathi Romero '73 reflected that it "has to happen; and then there's peace." Darci Daniels '72 recalled that afterward people knew the rules and treated each other with respect, but did not necessarily mix more. If they had trouble, they took it off campus.

Looking back, Carolyn Buszdieker remarked that one could easily have expected *more* conflict given the mix of students and the times. The real question was not, why did fights break out? But, *why weren't there more*?

CRISIS AS CATALYST FOR CHANGE

The next day, Friday, February 27, 1970, the principal went on campus TV and invited everyone to spend the first two periods discussing what had just happened, or "rapping," as the student paper put it. On the screen, visible to all, sweat ran down his face as he laid out an agenda.

Most significantly, Bargman announced a major concession to student demands: "Some ethnic studies will begin next year." This decision must have had district office approval. In 1970, only a handful of colleges offered ethnic studies. In the wake of a five-month student strike in 1968, San Francisco State was the first to establish a Department of Black Studies. At Sunnyvale High, a white faculty member, Len Hansen, had developed and taught a course in Black history, but no other ethnic studies classes were offered.

At the same moment, the call for a boycott of classes inspired some students to act. About forty students, mostly from the BSU and the CSU, marched around the open-air walkways during morning classes. First they went to the art studio, painted signs, and carried them past classrooms as they urged other students to join them. By noon, when few had done so, Chicano students decided to return to classes. The paper reported:

> One black girl told a knot of black, brown and white students, 'This isn't a matter of race. I don't care if you are pink or purple or white but you have to support me.' She referred to the fact that white students were not taking part in the class boycott. Then the girl said, 'You had better face it; most of the things you got are because of black students.' Several Mexican-American students walked off at that point.[10]

CSU members disagreed with BSU students about aims and tactics, and the boycott fizzled. But student demands for reform had already made a powerful impact.

Students demanded that the school hire more teachers who reflected the racial and ethnic diversity of the student body. Like their counterparts on college campuses, they denounced the biases and misrepresentations of minority groups in history textbooks and the absence of people of color and women from the curriculum. Students wanted to learn about people like themselves, substantive knowledge that spoke to larger truths.

Students and teachers used formal and informal channels to process the conflict's meaning and find ways to move forward. The district set up sensitivity training for teachers. Students talked in groups with counselors. Most importantly, they talked with each other about what happened and what it meant.

The ill-equipped principal fell apart. Dyckman reflected, "He had no clue what to do. He was hiding in his office." The counselor recognized that Bargman "was incapable of coping with the staff; the kids intimidated him." Bob Douglas recalled, "He would lock himself in his office and tell his secretary, 'I don't wanna see anybody.' . . . That, frankly, set a tone for the rest of that year."

The principal's personal crisis turned into an opportunity for teacher leadership.[11] Administrators, counselors, and teachers stepped up to run the school because they realized the principal no longer could. The counseling staff approached the vice principal, Ed Bangle, and the head of student activities, Bob Ferrera, and said that with the principal paranoid beyond functioning, the school was "on float, and we were all filling the cracks."

They organized a weekend gathering of ten to twelve people off campus to "figure out how to fix this." Bob Douglas reported:

> We spent an entire day talking about what was wrong with the high school. I mean, we took that school apart piece by piece and thought through it and problem solved it, and developed a strategy about what we were gonna do to keep the place running for the rest of the year.

The group asked the administrators among them to approach the district administration with their plan. They assured their superiors, "We can last till the end of the year, but . . . this place next year needs to look way different than it does now." As Douglas put it, they mobilized their skills and fervent commitment to "not let anything happen to our kids."

They recognized that healing divisions within the school community was vital. Math teacher Jim Miller observed, "Sunnyvale . . . handled some of that diversity much better than some of the other schools in the district. . . . It didn't hurt to have some very young, bright people and some very smart educators." They thought many of the students' demands were warranted. According to Bob Douglas, "Some of us in the faculty agreed with them, frankly."

Loretta Gutierrez and Mike Honda held evening meetings with parents to build bridges. Gutierrez recalls those conversations, which began with the teachers asking: "'What is it that we can do to help you? And to help the kids?' . . . We sat around and they talked a lot. . . . Good things came from that." Honda was buoyed by parents who were committed to helping change the situation: "Most of the parents were powerful, cooperative and effective. I think that's the reason that we were successful."

This group of administrators, counselors, and teachers ran the school and helped to calm tensions between students. They did not perceive the confrontation as a race riot. They believed that the clashes could be resolved, and they had the skills to facilitate reconciliation. Jim Miller said, "Sunnyvale, I think, in many ways was a transition school for the district. . . . Not in the way they expected, believe me." What did it do differently? "In many ways it treated people . . . like human beings."

While conflicts within and between student groups were inevitable, the consequences were less severe than in the decades that followed. Yet to come were the crack epidemic of the 1980s, the proliferation of guns, and the militarization of schools, which made disagreements more explosive and going to school more dangerous.

NOTES

1. *The Skywriter*, March 4, 1970.
2. *Palo Alto Times*, February 27, 1970.
3. *Skywriter*, March 4, 1970.
4. *Skywriter*, 4 March 1970
5. Edna Bonacich, "A Theory of Middleman Minorities," *American Sociological Review* 38 (1973): 583–94; David J. O'Brien, and Stephen S. Fugita, "Middleman Minority Concept: Its Explanatory Value in the Case of the Japanese in California Agriculture," *Pacific Sociological Review* 25 (1982): 185–204.

6. *Sunnyvale Standard*, February 26, 1970.
7. *Sunnyvale Standard*, February 26, 1970. This level of violence and destruction seems unimaginable now. But "in 1972, there were 1,962 actual and attempted bombings in the United States, with twenty-five people killed." Jeffrey Toobin, *American Heiress: The Wild Saga of the Kidnapping, Crimes and Trial of Patty Hearst* (New York: Doubleday, 2016), 12.
8. *San Jose Mercury News*, February 27, 1970.
9. *Palo Alto Times*, February 27, 1970.
10. *San Jose Mercury News*, February 27, 1970.
11. Marya R. Levenson, *Pathways to Teacher Leadership: Emerging Models, Changing Roles* (Cambridge, MA: Harvard Education Press, 2014).

Chapter 7

Transformative Changes

The confrontation on Smog-Free Locomotion Day catalyzed the district to address the problems at SHS. Students demanded block schedules, an open campus where they could freely come and go, and a more robust multicultural curriculum. The self-styled leadership team of faculty not only ran the school but supported changes and folded in creative ventures of their own. Some of these innovations already had advocates in the district office, including former principal Adrian Stanga. His support was crucial to SHS, which continued to be an outlier in the district. At the same time, federal programs and philanthropic investment brought additional funding and emboldened educators to experiment.

The district hired Walter Hale as SHS's new principal. Unlike his predecessor, Hale had taught at SHS when Adrian Stanga first established the school's relational and inclusive approach. In the early 1960s, he became dean of boys and then moved to Fremont High for several years. Aware of the turmoil, Hale saw his job as "pulling the school back together again."

BLOCK SCHEDULING, OPEN CAMPUS, AND A STUDY CENTER

Hale used the flexibility and autonomy often afforded to principals in the 1970s to build on the faculty's innovations and add some of his own. He supported PAVE's implementation, appreciating the importance of continuity in counselor-student relationships. In addition to securing a budget from the district for reforms, he assigned Gerry Hanson, formerly a counselor and now the Model Schools director and Title I coordinator, to write grants to raise money from the federal government and private philanthropic foundations.

Hale claimed that he removed thirteen ineffective teachers and replaced them with more competent, dynamic ones. Despite his philosophical objections to affirmative action, he recognized the value faculty of color brought to SHS's diverse campus. He insisted that he did not fall into "the trap" of thinking, "You got to be Black to teach Black kids. No, you had to be a good teacher. So I was after good teachers and trying to give them what they needed to do their job."

Like other California high schools, SHS opened its campus so students could easily go to and from work. Gone was the infantilizing requirement of a pass to walk through the halls or leave for lunch at nearby restaurants.

Under Hale's leadership, SHS adopted a new scheduling system that slotted classes into longer periods and rotated between days. Classes met for ninety minutes rather than forty, which facilitated subjects like PE, art, and music that needed more setup time. The new schedule helped faculty in lab classes, like science and home economics, and supported project-based learning. Most importantly, the structure encouraged innovative teaching. For example, math faculty used team teaching, bringing several classes together for a lecture in a large space followed by small group work to solve problems.

Hale envisioned transforming the library into a study center by restructuring the building and creating a space to hang out. The flexible space went hand-in-hand with block schedules and an open campus. The study center offered new resources, like musical recorders for students to borrow. He remembered administrators at other schools warning him, "Hale, you're nuts. They're going to steal. Those Sunnyvale kids are going to steal all those recorders." Hale insisted it would work and then felt vindicated. "We would let them sign out for them, take them home on the weekend, take them home at night, and bring them back. We never lost one."

COMMUNITY OUTREACH

Hale recognized the power of building bridges with parents and the community to strengthen the school. Before Hale started, science teacher Mike Honda had lobbied the school to hire community liaisons for the Black and Brown kids and their families. The district provided funding, and SHS hired an ombudsman, Ed Ochoa, for this role. According to Loretta Gutierrez, Ochoa's job was to:

> work with the kids, walk around during brunch and lunch and stick around after school. . . . That's what the parents demanded. To have someone the kids could go to if there was a problem before it festered and got out of hand.

Using resources secured from the Mott Foundation, Hale created the position of Community School Director to develop the school's connections and communication with parents, local residents, and area businesses. In 1971, he hired Vern Holte, a second-generation Norwegian raised on a North Dakota farm. Holte understood the community he tried to reach.

> North Sunnyvale was blue collar. A lot of really hard-working people. And I came from a land where we worked very hard. You grew up on a farm and everybody pulls together. And you don't make any excuses. . . . I never saw anybody in that community ever complaining about their job. I didn't. I don't ever remember students complaining about their parents.

He continued: "*My people* in North Sunnyvale . . . lived and played in the same community. Okay? I mean they didn't have a lot of money." Vern proudly declared, "The kids weren't spoiled." When I asked him about racial tensions, he said that except for isolated instances, "I never saw any really major, all-out racial tensions."

He began outreach with adult education, inviting Barbara Clark, a popular home economics teacher, to lead the first class. Then Holte asked one of the students, Pam Martin, the drum majorette who had twice won the state championship for baton twirling, to teach a class along with her mother. On the first day, sixty-five girls showed up. The evening education program was so successful that "we started putting classes on in mobile home park homes and over at the elementary schools." Moreover, he organized English as a Second Language courses for parents and sponsored guest speakers. He arranged for a manager from Bumbleberry Pie Restaurant to lead a session on baking and a local butcher to instruct folks on how to select meats.

Sunnyvale High was surrounded by factories as well as homes. Holte built reciprocal relationships: "I worked with industry and they donated materials for the shops. They loved that." He believed, "If there's a need, it was my responsibility to go out there and tap it and then see if I could come back and work it out with the faculty." Sharing the resources of its open campus, the school invited nearby workers to use the gym at noon. As community interest in health and fitness grew, jogging and exercise courses became popular.

Holte's myriad efforts to bring students, parents, area residents, and local businesses together were amazingly successful. He hosted activity nights where community members and students could play games and interact. He started a monthly newsletter, *The Jetstream*, to reach parents. At a "principal's coffee," parents could come to campus, meet Walt Hale, and observe classes. Holte advertised a new Career Center that facilitated work experience for students. One issue of *The Jetstream* closed with his heartfelt message: "I offer an invitation to you to share openly with us concerning how our community may be strengthened and a better place in which to celebrate life. Will you join us?"

THE SUNNYVALE HIGH SCHOOL MARCHING BAND

Like high schools that coalesce around a winning football team, Sunnyvale's stunning marching band was a keystone of its community-building efforts. The band director, John Riggle, met with Hale soon after he began in 1970 and told him, "I want to build the best marching band in the United States. Not California, the United States." He had started at SHS the year before, and the previous administration was preparing to fire him. Hale ignored their plans, understanding that Riggle was "a different guy, and music guys are different." Treating Riggle's ambitious goal as reachable, he asked, "What do you need, John? . . . I'll get it for you."

With new resources invested in the band, Riggle and the students delivered. (See figure 7.1.) He drilled the participants, establishing discipline and *esprit de corps*. Parents organized car washes and bake sales to buy new uniforms and send the band to competitions near and far. The band won the

Figure 7.1   Sunnyvale High School Marching Band, 1972. *Source: Sabre*, 1972.

Santa Clara Parade of Champions three years in a row. They competed in the prestigious invitation-only All-Western Band Review in Long Beach, California, and won their division. When they traveled to Hawaii for the annual Aloha Parade in 1972, they were judged the "best mainland band."

The band auditioned and was chosen for halftime performances at San Francisco 49ers football games; its live appearance on national television filled everyone with pride. It even got cast as the marching band in the movie *Harold and Maude* (1971), for which it was paid $200.

Riggle selected rising sophomore Ed Lizardo '73 to be the drum major. (See figure 7.2.) Lizardo recalled:

> The drum major has to be the other point of leadership. And you can't have a leader who's just an equal or goofball as the next guy who wants to be a clown. . . . You need someone who someone's going to respect and perhaps even look up to. I guess he saw that in me. And I was up for that.

Expressing students' sentiments, Max Epps '73 felt proud of SHS because of Lizardo's leadership: "I always loved watching him work because he was so perfect. His posture was extraordinary." He also celebrated the new addition to the marching band: Pam Martin, a statewide champion baton twirler.

Riggle was an outsized figure for Ed and the rest of the marching band. He taught:

> *life lessons* about interacting and as a group, learning that you're a group, a family unit, and learning that you can have a common goal, and when you work together, you can achieve those goals. And when you do, you can enjoy the fruits of your labor.

Like other extracurricular activities established early in Sunnyvale High's history, the band provided a way for students to work together across race-ethnicity and form friendships outside the classroom. The band was racially integrated. As Ed Lizardo put it, "In band, race was not an issue. It never came up. . . . It was our own blessing and we didn't even know it." Their shared goals and common interests were more important than their differences.

OUTWARD AND UPWARD: WILDERNESS LAB AND NEIGHBORHOOD YOUTH CORPS

In the 1960s and 1970s, community activists and government agencies across the United States created numerous programs to improve learning, mitigate the effects of poverty, and facilitate skills development to broaden the outlook for young people. These alternative, activity-based learning environments

Figure 7.2 Ed Lizardo, Drum Major, 1972. *Source*: *Sabre*, 1972.

had life-changing benefits. They sought innovative ways to keep kids in high school and get them to think about college. Educators implemented two such notable efforts at Sunnyvale High: Wilderness Lab and Neighborhood Youth Corps.

Science teacher and counselor Bob Douglas, an Eagle Scout, outdoorsman, and naturalist, was inspired to develop meaningful off-campus, outdoor learning experiences for students. His approach aligned with the principles of Outward Bound, a national program founded in 1962 that took young people into the wilderness, taught them skills, and gave them a chance to explore their personal potential. Already committed to experiential learning in Sunnyvale's work with troubled youth, Douglas recruited two educators to help design the three-week adventure. Counselor Terry Dyckman had considerable expertise in group dynamics, although he was unfamiliar with camping. French teacher Rita Barton was an avid rock climber and adventuresome outdoorswoman. The school's leadership team approved the pilot course for twenty-five students. One week involved physical training, safety instruction, and gear packing at the school. That was followed by a ten-day, 100-mile backpacking trip through the high Sierra Mountains. "As educators, we were dumbfounded at the growth we saw in these students." Afterwards, the team proposed an annual summer school course called the Wilderness Lab. The superintendent enthusiastically approved.

The faculty team had complementary strengths. Douglas taught "nature study, mountain geology, plant and animal identification, and ecology." Dyckman led campfire discussions about relationships, group dynamics, conflict resolution, and self-confidence. "Along the way, he became an accomplished rock climber and climbing instructor. Rita Barton focused on rock climbing, confronting and overcoming fear, and acted as a role model and counselor for young women on the trips." Seeing many Wilderness Lab students "demonstrating significant growth in self-esteem, self-confidence, science and psychology knowledge, and a deep appreciation for nature and wilderness, the school district offered it for multiple summers."

Two stories stand out for Douglas. The first centered on a petite girl who was:

> studious and a good science student, but was quite shy and fearful of trying new things. She challenged herself on the 100-mile backpacking and the rock climbing, neither of which she believed she could do. She overcame her fear and even excelled. As a result of her newfound confidence and experience with mountain geology, glaciers and rock climbing, she applied . . . for admission to a summer institute in Glacier Study at the University of Minnesota.

The last contact Douglas had with her, she was working on a master of science degree in glaciology at a research station in Antarctica.

The second story Douglas told involved a small, quiet boy.

> He was a below-average student, but he loved the outdoors and all things nature. He was a very serious self-taught naturalist. On the 100-mile trek, as they reached a very high-altitude meadow and lake surrounded by 10,000-foot peaks, he started telling the other kids what they were seeing and how it all worked. This guy, who has been invisible to all of them before, suddenly is the person who is the expert

and the go-to guy answering their questions about what they were observing. For him, the transformation was remarkable, it was like seeing a flower bloom. The experience for this student would never have occurred in a regular classroom setting. The self-esteem and self-confidence he gained came from the dynamic between him and his classmates where he assumed the role of expert and teacher.

This uniquely challenging experience "stimulated rapid personal growth." Douglas likened the development of these students to that "shown in nineteen- and twenty-year-olds as a result of military training or from living in a college dorm." The Wilderness Lab team felt buoyed by their teaching experience and vindicated that it proved to be a "great preparation for the next steps in life."

Sunnyvale High sponsored a federal program, the Neighborhood Youth Corps (NYC), designed and launched during President Lyndon Johnson's War on Poverty.[1] The program provided low-income students with summer employment in community service positions, providing them with job experience and study skills. Students were encouraged to contemplate college and taught them the nuts and bolts of applying and attending. At SHS, Sandy Matteucci '70 emphasized, students received *no* help with applying for college and financing their education, which was essential for working-class kids. Pete Araujo '71, who joined NYC, said, "It was a great program. It got us ready for college" and "helped a lot of people graduate" high school. "It helped me. I was the first in my family to graduate." As part of the program, he took courses at De Anza College. "After a while you start thinking, 'Well, they're not difficult. They're like 13th and 14th grade,'" which made college less intimidating.

In Nicholas Monroe's interviews with first-generation college graduates, one white man, ten years after graduating, said that Upward Bound, a program similar to NYC, had changed his life. "That program did more to prepare me for success in college than high school did." It "got me thinking that 'college is a realistic thing.'"[2]

The program's pay was an incentive to attend and freed students from the need to take other jobs. In the process, it exposed them to new opportunities that they might otherwise never have considered. It demystified college and the process of applying for and getting funding for postsecondary education. Since most parents had never attended college, this kind of cultural capital made a crucial difference.

MULTICULTURAL CURRICULUM

Student demands for ethnic studies echoed around the country's colleges and universities. Their forceful logic pointed to the lopsided portrait of American society featured in most history courses: a "victor's" story of conquest that ignored the multitudes of poor, working-class, white, Black, Asian, and Brown people whose labor had built the country. Students insisted that classes teach about those who suffered from injustice in a nation that promised freedom and equality. It owed its prosperity to the backbreaking labor of enslaved men, women, and children as well as the masses of free people who cultivated its food, built its skyscrapers, fought its wars, and bore its children. Those men and women of the past and present were rarely glimpsed in history classes that focused on presidents and battles and skipped over the experiences of Indigenous peoples, enslaved people of African descent, Mexicans whose land was occupied by the United States, Chinese laborers who dug railroad tunnels and the ditches that turned swamps into farmland, and Japanese Americans confined in internment camps.[3] English classes ignored great writers who were not white males. Students wanted a curriculum that embraced their full humanity and offered an honest accounting of the country's vast wrongs and major achievements.

The combination of structural changes, diversified activities outside the classroom, and a broader curriculum transformed the school. Outstanding teachers who could emotionally connect with the students as well as teach cutting-edge subject matter helped students aspire to a better future, together as well as individually. An open approach to teaching and learning was transformative. Speech and debate coach Sharon Prefontaine reflected that this was an "era of creative teaching. Probably some of the most creative teaching we'll ever see.... People were really allowed this sort of intellectual freedom and to engage kids. It was a wonderful time to learn." School leadership had enough confidence to let teachers experiment, even if sometimes they had to learn from their failures.

Mexican American Literature

One new course resulting from students' demand for ethnic studies was Mexican American Literature, designed and taught by Loretta Gutierrez. With waist-length dark brown hair and a husky voice, she cajoled students in Spanish after having taught in the English Department and with English language learners. Growing up as the youngest child of a large family of migrant farm workers, she had a profound sense of what it meant to work in the fields. Like many Sunnyvale students, as a child, she had trouble envisioning options for her future. She found inspiration in the Chicano movement that strove for Mexican American dignity and organized for fundamental change.

She brought passion to the classroom and to her role as advisor of the CSU. Gutierrez believed that students needed to learn about Mexican history and

Mexican American culture in her Spanish language classes. She was keenly aware of the long, proud past and how profoundly it shaped the present.

She recalled, "Mike [Honda] and I pushed for Chicano Studies, which I then took on." She laughed at her own audacity: "I knew nothing about Mexican American literature." But Honda encouraged her, and she set out to learn: "I had to go up to Berkeley and find material and get it all. But I *loved* it." Gutierrez credited Honda with helping her get the class approved by the district.

> He's very good with people so he was able to calm down the parents and everything because they wanted to get involved, take the principal out . . . and he'd say, 'just take one step at a time. We'll do this . . . and if that doesn't happen, then you can go ahead and do what you have to do.' But he kept everything under control.

Gutierrez first taught the course in the fall of 1971. Students learned about the 1848 Treaty of Guadalupe Hidalgo, which turned California into US territory with a stroke of the pen, and read pathbreaking new novels like *Bless Me, Ultima*, which illuminated the experiences of Mexican Americans, who were otherwise absent from the curriculum.[4] "Kids took it and they liked it. And they had a *voice* and that was very important." She reflected, "This was a time when . . . classes like that were barely being introduced into the colleges, let alone at the high school level."

US Black History

As an African American educator, Doug Walker deliberated about accepting the job at Sunnyvale High because it was predominantly Anglo and Chicano. (See figure 7.3.) He was surprised when he arrived for an interview with principal Bargman in the spring of 1970. "I said, 'How many Black kids do we have here?' 'Oh, I think we might have 50'—we *might*. Out of 2,400?!" Walker had watched the television news coverage of the protest in February and wondered what was happening on campus to make it erupt in that way. At the time, teaching at a junior high on the peninsula, he was recruited by Mary Lou Lyon, head of the history department at Homestead High, who asked whether he might be interested in teaching in the Fremont Union High School District. Intrigued, he applied for a job and was offered a position at either Homestead or Sunnyvale. He picked Sunnyvale High. "I felt I could make a difference. I didn't know how I was going to do it, but I felt that I could do something."

He recognized that "a lot of kids there just . . . hadn't been around too many Black people. Hey, I was there, and they found out a lot." Walker explained how he worked with students:

Figure 7.3 Doug Walker, Teacher and Coach, 1972. *Source: Sabre*, 1972.

There were no kids like Sunnyvale kids. . . . These kids were real people. . . . I could relate to them . . . because they were out there working themselves. . . . They may not have understood this person who was Black. . . . But they started to think about that.

Just twenty-five years old when he began at SHS, Walker not only instilled knowledge but also inspired students to think. A tall African American man with warm brown eyes, Doug Walker was born in Tuskegee, Alabama, the son of a school teacher and an Air Force officer. His stock in trade was provoking curiosity, posing critical questions, and inspiring mutual respect. Walker took an inclusive and positive approach: "We're going to get there because you're going to figure this out." He did not talk down to students but invited them to inquire. He was deeply committed to teaching students their own history and the history of other groups while creating an environment where they could ask sensitive questions.

As a Black man from the South, Doug Walker's personal history and desire to teach others about segregation's impact powerfully affected the learning process. Conjuring scenes from his own childhood, Walker described the ordinary act of going to the movie theater: "It had a partition down there. Black people went to the left, white people went to the right. We all bought tickets at the same" window and paid the same price.

Walker oriented his students to a particular kind of learning.

> One of the first things I would say to them is that "You're in here for an experience. You're in here to get to know other people. You're in here to get to know *me*. I'm no different than you. This guy's no different than you."

Walker laid a foundation.

> I always told everybody in class, I said, "I respect you; you respect me. It's a two-way street." I don't think I ever embarrassed anybody in class. I never attacked people in class. I never did that. Kids might say something, and I'd say, "Now, explain that. What was that all about?"

Walker built rapport by bringing people into the conversation and prompting students to take ownership of their learning. They tended to be cautious: "Well, I don't want to say the wrong thing." Walker would insist, "'Well, by saying nothing, you're saying the wrong thing. So I need for you to talk.' How do you resolve issues? You have a dialogue."

Understanding that growth inevitably generated a certain level of discomfort, Walker was unafraid to push his classes to consider questions they might otherwise have avoided. In his classroom in 1971, a familiar image of Jesus hung by the door. Sunnyvale High School was a public school, so the image was not meant to inspire devotion but rather to provoke a question. Walker asked, "Was Jesus white?" This imagined likeness of Jesus was popularly displayed in white churches and homes everywhere. Students knew who it was without a label. He had long, wavy, almost blonde hair, with a concerned expression, compassionate blue eyes, and pale skin. "How do we come to think that Jesus was white?" Walker asked. "Where was he born?" Bethlehem in Judea. The Middle East. "How did this image of Jesus get created? Who paints it? Who circulates it? Why do we accept it?"

Even with the best of intentions, leading students to question previously held assumptions requires sensitivity and care. Teachers must demonstrate well-developed emotional intelligence. To get students to ask and answer uncomfortable questions, Walker had to create a safe space in the classroom.

> *Whatever you can do* to influence somebody . . . in a positive way, to motivate them to take another step. . . . A lot of kids were afraid to venture out because they never saw anybody in their family venture out. So, this is safe in here.

Robert Handa '73 recalled: "That class helped shape a lot of the way people looked at things. . . . You're in a classroom environment where you can now ask this question that would seem totally out of left field in just about any other kind of classroom."

After establishing norms for discussion, Walker put history in a structural context. He believed that students had to learn what they did not already know about slavery, the compromises adopted at the US Constitutional Convention, the end of Reconstruction, and the imposition of Jim Crow. He helped students to see historical patterns and understand that economic and political processes did not unfold accidentally. Instead, he showed them how these patterns result from people's actions, the passage of laws, the profits that accrued to businesses, and the fact that certain groups held power and excluded others.

Walker's principal goal was for his students to gain analytic distance. "I want you to go through a thinking process as opposed to just let the emotions take over, 'cause when emotions get in the way, you can't make decisions. It's just that simple."

Sheree Furtado '72, who is white, talked about her relationship with Walker: "He and I got into this dispute. And he told me just point blank, 'cause I was stubborn, that 'Just because it isn't right for you, doesn't mean it's not right for somebody else.'" Sheree described herself as "stunned" by his answer. Walker's ability to get her to think beyond herself affected her approach to the world. Max Epps '73, who is Black, said Walker's class "was like an awakening for me. . . . He taught me . . . ways to learn, opportunities that could be created that I never thought about before."

Walker sought to root out misconceptions stemming from unexamined bias and lack of exposure to different worldviews. Black students would assert a pecking order.

> "Hey, we were here first," and this and that. "Yeah, you know what? You're all here, so don't worry about it. Let's learn about each other's history and then communicate and learn how to do that. You might not like somebody, but respect somebody. Okay? Get on down the road."

Most importantly, Walker could discuss racial issues without silencing or explaining away pain and conflict, and he could challenge misconceptions without putting students on the defensive.

> When I think people are just going too far with the racial thing, if it's wrong, I'm going to call it. If it's BS, I say, "Look, you got to look beyond that. . . . Take

the high road and understand what's going on, and have dialogue. Maybe you'll learn something about yourself, too."

That kind of honesty and directness would be interpreted differently coming from a white teacher. Walker knew that, and so did the students.

By his second semester, US Black History became the most popular course on campus. He taught five periods of the class instead of one. "I went from having 34 kids to 180, and I had to cut back because I didn't have anywhere for them to sit." As Walker and Gutierrez developed ethnic studies courses, they attracted increasing numbers of students. People who belonged to different racial and ethnic groups felt they shared a common struggle for social justice. These courses not only taught an invisible history, but also served as a forum to create mutual understanding.

THE SLAVE SALE

Despite its many far-sighted innovations, other aspects of the school's culture were so backward-looking that today they seem stuck in the distant past. For example, prevailing mid-century notions of gender and sexuality persisted throughout the school, so that people routinely failed to recognize or acknowledge the existence of diverse sexual orientations among students and faculty. Walker and Gutierrez crafted a new multicultural curriculum, but racial and ethnic tracking of students continued. While Buszdieker and others were actively challenging expectations for female athletes and supporting girls' leadership, conventional sex-role stereotypes remained evident in school culture.

One perplexing annual event deserves closer scrutiny and raises a set of provocative questions that are difficult to answer.

In late fall, Pep Club annually sponsored a dance called the Twirp Twirl. It was part of the SHS version of Sadie Hawkins Day, a popular American event that temporarily turned gender hierarchies upside-down. Inspired by Al Capp's comic strip "Li'l Abner," this day was marked by what cultural historians call symbolic inversion: girls take on the male role of initiating heterosexual romance. In the comic strip, Sadie Hawkins, the "homely" daughter of the mayor of an imaginary town in Appalachia, was empowered to chase the single men of her community; should she catch one, she could demand that he marry her. In the SHS version, girls asked boys to the dance, bought matching shirts that they and their partners wore, and paid for everything. No queens or princesses were crowned, only a cute boy voted "Mr. Irresistible." The topsy-turvy week upended other everyday practices. Students dressed in wacky, mismatched outfits and performed stereotypes of backwardness, mimicking the characters in the comic strip and in the popular television show, "The Beverly Hillbillies."

To raise money for the dance, Pep Club organized what was routinely called a slave sale. The day before the dance, a succession of girls was auctioned and sold to the highest bidder. Students gathered in the rally court at lunchtime and watched girls parade onto a large wooden stage that had been erected by school staff. Those who stood on this simulated auction block were generally cheerleaders, song girls, and members of the larger multiracial and multiethnic spirit organization—in other words, popular girls with large circles of friends. In agreeing to be auctioned off to the highest bidder, these girls were participating in a humorous fundraiser. The chief concern of girls being auctioned was whether boys would place a high enough bid in what amounted to a very public popularity contest. The boys sometimes bid as individuals, but more often they pooled their resources. They pulled coins and crumpled dollar bills out of their pockets and consolidated their funds to buy their schoolmate on the platform.

The sale was a gendered phenomenon: girls were for sale, and the buyers were exclusively boys. Boys were not sold in the auction during the early 1970s.

The slave sale had undeniable but contradictory racial undertones. The framing of the event as a reenactment of selling and buying human beings is unmistakable. But, in an important racial inversion, most, but not all, of the girls were white, and some were Latina and Asian. There is no available record of a Black girl being auctioned. Their male buyers were a mix of white, Black, Brown, and Asian.

Former students, looking back, explain that some of the fascination with the ritual had to do with the consequences of being sold: being subject to the whims of others. The girl had to do whatever the buyers asked of her. Common challenges involved chugging root beer, throwing pies in people's faces, and rolling a piece of chalk with one's nose while crawling on hands and knees along a campus walkway.

Significantly, while reflecting on this event fifty years later, every person who remembered participating in the slave sale reported that, at the time, they had found it inoffensive. One girl who was sold along with two other senior song girls in the fall of 1969, Sharon Faeta '70, who identified as white, recalled being purchased by a much younger African American boy.[5] "How ironic was this? Robert Brown . . . bought us." For the whole week, in keeping with the rules of the event, Sharon walked Robert to class and carried his books. "No complaining. And we got a good laugh out of it."

These events, which entangled racial and gender hierarchies—at times subverting them and at others reinforcing them—seem crude, shocking and objectionable today. How could SHS's progressive school leadership permit this to happen? Why did neither participants nor observers express *any* concern about the origins, symbolism, or implications of this annual event? Perhaps their matter-of-fact approach to this student fundraiser illuminates something not only about the 1970s but also about our current political moment.

It is difficult to evaluate the full spectrum of the slave sale's intent and impact, in part because the historical evidence is spotty. Precisely when SHS students began staging a slave sale fundraiser is uncertain. The earliest record is from 1969, and the last from 1978. The 1981 yearbook did not cover it, so perhaps it had ended before the school closed. The sparse and uneven documentation makes it difficult to assess its meanings in this particular space. How can we evaluate the full spectrum of the ritual's aims and consequences without more historical evidence?

Some context can be established. SHS students were imitating contemporary all-white college fraternities and sororities throughout California and across the country. These Greek societies commonly organized events with a nod to an imagined Greek or Roman history, including toga parties, rather than alluding to American slavery. As with Sadie Hawkins, the slave sale as a student fundraiser could be found in comic culture. One 1967 Archie comic book featured a high school–based Roman version: Betty is up for auction, and Veronica jealously outbids Archie for Betty, in an effort to interrupt any romantic connection between them.

In the student paper, no article did more than announce the Twirp Twirl dance until a single photograph appeared in December 1971. (See figure 7.4.)

Figure 7.4 Slave Sale. *Skywriter*, December 14, 1971. *Source*: Courtesy of Sunnyvale Historical Society and Museum Association.

The Skywriter printed this striking image without an accompanying story. With a female auctioneer at the microphone, two girls in pigtails stand in the middle of the stage, and a boy in a varsity letter jacket stands nearby. Two Black students walk in front of the platform. While the photo raises a bristling array of racial and gender questions, its caption is fraught with sexist and racist tropes: "Two pretty slaves show their teeth as they pray someone will bid higher."[6] The racial inflection of the caption, recalling the inspection of enslaved people's teeth at slave auctions, is undeniable. So is the sexualization of the girls and the derision of their preoccupation with their "value" in the marketplace. Yet, demonstrating the quotidian nature of the slave auction at SHS, the photo sits in the midst of a long article reporting on a survey of students about whether the Christmas dance should remain formal.

Before 1976, the auction did not appear in the yearbook, the *Sabre*. In 1976 and 1978, the *Sabre* devoted two pages to the Twirp Twirl, including photographs of some of the stunts that slaves were made to perform: "flagpole climbing, stuffing Freshmen into garbage cans, crawling along rooftops while singing the alma matter, and cleaning the band room."[7] For perhaps the first time, boys were also sold. One photograph features a triple-decker pyramid of slaves: two Black boys, two white boys, and eight white girls. Another photo features two boys—one white and one Black, shirts off—on display, in a visually arresting reenactment of slave auctions. During the sale, "the bidding was exciting, drawing a large crowd. In front of staring eyes, male slaves stripped to the waist for inspection."[8] But one fact subverted what might otherwise have been a visual reenactment of a slave auction: some boys were white.

From the vantage point of 2024, with the recent decades of emphasis on Black history, women's history, and the role of violence in our collective history, it is nearly impossible to grasp how students—girls and boys, white and nonwhite—interpreted this event at that time. How did it not offend? Did someone I did *not* interview find it disturbing? What anxieties did it create for those who participated, and those who did not? Why is it that many female athletes spoke forcefully and indignantly about the inequality of funding for uniforms and court space and time, but not about the fact that girls were routinely offered to the boys who bid the highest?

I could find no former students who reported that they had seen the slave sale as racially offensive at the time. Of the two student leaders I interviewed who had been responsible for pep and rally events, one had only a vague recollection of the slave sale and could not remember playing any part in organizing it. The other remembered an auction of lunches made by girls, not of the girls themselves.

Virtually everyone I interviewed who remembered the slave sale did not see it as a problem that required intervention by educators or students. What collective blind spot did students and adults share, which obscured, diminished, or denied the relationship between the sordid history of buying and selling human beings and this annual student activity? Those I interviewed who remembered the event said that, at the time, they did not see it as *intentionally* racist or sexist. This prompts me to ask: under what conditions does intent matter?

Significantly, when I asked alums about the slave sale in the interviews, many did not remember it at all. That absence makes it difficult to assess its situational meaning and significance. They recalled the dance, but not the slave sale. Was it erased from people's memories because they found it commonplace in popular culture? Or did students regard slavery as a human wrong that had been eliminated by the Civil War, which relegated it to the past and rendered it irrelevant? Alternatively, could people's inability to remember an event they witnessed be evidence of repressed memory?

Between 1969 and 1978, the period for which I have found documentation of slave sales, there is no sign that students protested the event. Nor is there any indication that teachers or parents took offense, tried to shut it down, or even thought to turn it into a teachable moment. Sunnyvale High's adults did not appear to blink at the activities. Did they not notice? Or did they dismiss it as the foolishness of clueless teenagers? These are not questions I can answer.

Even those champions of gender equality on campus, like Carolyn Buszdieker, who was a strong advocate for girls, have no recollection of attempting to shut it down. During his first term on the faculty in the fall of 1970, Doug Walker, who came to SHS to teach US Black History, noticed the slave sale. At the time, he saw no malevolent racial motivations and had no strong feelings about it: "It wasn't meant to demean anybody." He did not speak out against it because he did not regard it as harmful. He focused instead on teaching his US Black History course, which addressed what he regarded as pressing personal, experiential, and structural issues in the lives of students.

Some alumni who have no memory of the event could not imagine it being allowed or tolerated. Jackie Gooch '74 declared, "I don't recall that. Because honestly speaking, if they had done that while I was there, I would've had a problem with it. That's unacceptable to me. Because we're all human beings." Looking back, this African American woman saw nothing benign about the idea of a reenactment of slavery. Her attachment to Sunnyvale High is deep, and this event conflicted with her moral principles and her sense that SHS culture embraced those values.

Importantly, Sunnyvale High sponsored this event at the same time the administration and faculty increased their commitment to ethnic studies in response to student demands. Students demonstrated their enthusiasm for studying race and ethnicity by crowding into Doug Walker's US Black History classroom. They wanted to learn about race and collective efforts to end racial oppression from this charismatic teacher. But neither students nor their teachers saw nor felt a connection between the student slave sale and ongoing civil rights demonstrations across the country or the concurrent debates about race at SHS.

In sharp contrast, Smog-Free Locomotion Day, which was marked by intense emotions, serious conflict, and contradictory memories, was widely remembered as a day of racial conflict. Slave day did not evoke anything like such deep collective emotions. To the contrary, to most, it was a vague memory, completely untinged with strong negative feelings from the time.

Our challenge today is to put ourselves in the minds of high schoolers and high school educators half a century ago. How could something that is so racially and otherwise offensive today be seen as innocuous in 1970? How did people whose roles and contributions to racial and gender awareness we respect and admire not mark this ugly phenomenon as egregious? What shared understandings or misunderstandings of history and United States culture sustained this widespread myopia?

This conundrum prompts another question: what actions are we taking today in high schools, which we take for granted and cannot see, that will provoke revulsion and distress fifty years from now?

NOTES

1. Economic Opportunity Act of 1964. https://www2.ed.gov/about/offices/list/ope/trio/triohistory.html.
2. Nicholas Monroe, "No Roadmap? No Problem: First-Generation Students' Cultural Assets and the Path to Undergraduate Success" (PhD Diss., Brandeis University, 2021).
3. Some students, like Sandy Matteucci '70, countered this narrative. She insisted that she learned a fuller history, including the "truth about slavery, and maybe that's why we had hearts because we knew how horrible what had happened to the Indians."
4. Rudolfo A. Anaya, *Bless Me, Ultima* (Berkeley, CA: Tonatiuh-Quinto Sol International, 1972).
5. Sharon's adoptive father was Italian. Only after graduating did she discover that she had been adopted and that her birth mother had been Japanese and her biological father white. The Faeta family adopted her from an orphanage in Japan while her adoptive father was stationed there in the Navy. After this discovery, she changed her name to Keiko.
6. *The Skywriter*, December 14, 1971.
7. *Sabre*, 1977, "Costumes and Capers," 22–23.
8. *Sabre*, 1976, "Twirp Twirl," no page numbers.

Chapter 8

Informal Support Bolsters Resilience

Many SHS students lived in troubled families. Parents divorced, succumbed to alcoholism, or were violent. Single parents struggled to make ends meet; others lived with two parents but wished they did not. Adolescents dealt with these situations as best they could—sometimes not well enough, in other cases constructively, but almost never entirely by themselves. Their resourcefulness often depended on support and advice from others. Young people not only got each other into trouble but also they helped each other. Many found assistance from adults in their lives, sometimes family members, sometimes not. They got pushed in ways that both helped and hurt.

Some teachers were aware of some students' difficulties at home, but other students chose not to disclose their troubles. Sometimes teachers and counselors, as well as the parents of school friends, lent a helping hand. At that time, most schools did not provide wrap-around care, but teachers did not maintain the kind of distance from their students that is now the norm.

The stories in this chapter illuminate what some young people did to create livable circumstances for themselves. Gender determined what was possible: girls' and boys' opportunities differed. In addition to disparities in jobs and wages, social expectations were still entrenched in a 1950s vision of gender and sexuality. While feminist ideas and actions animated college campuses, "women's lib" still seemed strange in high schools. Unlike the civil rights movements, which linked Black, Chicano, and Asian youth at SHS to San Jose State University, the women's movement's critique of conventional femininity and radical rethinking of women's place in society had not yet fully registered in high schools.

DILEMMAS OF INDEPENDENCE

In the 1960s and 1970s, working-class childhood ended earlier than it does now: more teenagers held jobs, and parents did not see it as their responsibility to direct their children's education or supervise their social lives.[1] Many saw the age of eighteen as the moment when children became adults and needed to fend for themselves.

When middle-class young people sought independence from their parents, they could go away to college. For working-class youth of both sexes, employment, marriage, or the military was a more viable pathway to adult independence. Those bent on college had to support themselves, so they lived at home, worked part- or full-time, and took courses at the local community college. If they managed those multiple burdens well, they might transfer to a four-year institution and continue living at home.

Gender shaped when and how SHS students attained adult independence. Some ambitious young people began pursuing their goals as adolescents. Stretch Lakely '73, raised by a single mother with an older brother and younger sister at home, worked multiple jobs to help her family and buy things she needed. During the summer, she was a lifeguard, taught swimming, and worked at the cannery on swing shift. During the school year, she worked at McDonald's at lunchtime, between her classes and sports practices. Her athletic prowess led her to Chico State University. In this respect, Stretch followed a path taken by male athletes, but seldom open to talented and determined women.

In 1970s Sunnyvale, working-class families strongly encouraged legal marriage as the only acceptable way to have sex and raise children. It was not unusual for seniors at Sunnyvale High to get engaged before graduation. Sandy Matteucci '70 recalled girls flashing diamond rings, planning wedding showers, and being "married within six months out of high school." Working-class girls expected to join the paid labor force and be wives and mothers.

Young women who became pregnant "out of wedlock" were censured, ostracized, and often banned from schools.[2] "Reputation was still so important," Matteucci emphasized. While the birth control pill had made it possible to separate sex from reproduction, it was not universally available or universally used. Typically, boys whose girlfriends were pregnant either married them or abandoned them with impunity. Pregnant girls were sent away to suffer in shame until the baby was born and given up for adoption; only then could they return. But for those who kept their baby, finishing high school seemed impossible. JoAnn Vargas '73 had two older sisters who got pregnant and had to drop out of school; they completed GEDs later.

Sharon Prefontaine '65 began college at San Jose State but stayed with her high school boyfriend and soon found herself pregnant. "I just felt horrible. . . .

I didn't want this. I pounded on my stomach . . . trying to make that not happen." "Fortunately, I didn't know about coat hangers" or other ways to terminate an unwanted pregnancy that might endanger her own life. Her parents "made us get married. Always, always, always a sign that there will be great success," she commented sarcastically. Her father, a career Navy man, cried at her wedding, but his were not tears of joy. At the end of summer, she gave birth to twins and returned to school. Her husband was interested in sports. She was a brainiac, a speech and debate student, a reader and intellectual, and refused to give up. Sharon found childcare on campus and worked several jobs to shoulder the cost. When their daughters reached school age, "He abandoned us. And took the bank account. . . . He just left." Exhausted but determined, she finished her degree and earned a teaching credential in four years. She began teaching at Sunnyvale High as a single mother of twin girls.

Marriage offered an alternative to some pregnant high school students, although their parents' pressure did not make this step seem like a choice. An early influencer, Cece Padgett '72 often set trends—wearing nylon stockings and makeup to junior high school, adopting the latest fashions, becoming a Jet Girl. (See figure 8.1.) When she discovered she was pregnant at the end of her sophomore year at SHS, if she was not the first in her class, she was certainly in the vanguard. But figuring out how to handle her situation was an impossible dilemma. "I knew I did *not* wanna get married. I didn't; I cried." Her mother "was pushing it more." After marrying in a San Jose courthouse, she and her new husband, who had graduated the year before and was then nineteen, drove to Disneyland for their honeymoon. As he splashed in the pool, Cece, large with child, ran up to their room and called her mother, crying and pleading to let her come home. Her mother assured her, "You'll be okay. It's new to you."

The young couple moved into a room at his sister's house in Sunnyvale, and he worked alongside his father on the United Airlines loading docks in South San Francisco. Cece attended summer school so she could graduate with her class. A month later, after the baby was born, Cece recounted, "I went back to my mom's house." There she stayed, receiving help with parenting from her older sisters and mother. She found a job and managed to graduate. Her husband "just didn't know how to wrap his mind around . . . having a child." He wanted to surf every day and smoke pot. Like many, their early marriage was brief. It did not pave the way to autonomy from their parents.

RAISED BY FRIENDS

In the summer of 1972, a group of three white boys, fed up with their miserable home lives, took action to escape. (See figure 8.2.) After deciding that moving out was essential to their mental health and well-being, they

Figure 8.1 Cece Padgett (right) Talking with Cheryl Whincup and Two Other Girls, 1972. *Source: Sabre,* 1972.

attempted to act as adults despite being legally minors. The consequences were unpredictable and potentially dangerous. They had few resources except the jobs they were working and their strong ties to each other. While still attending high school, their perceptions of themselves as mature wage earners did not consistently match their actions.

Bob Hagg, Dan Steward, and Allan Taylor moved out of their parents' homes and into an apartment together. At the time, Bob was sixteen years old, while Dan and Allan were seventeen. They all worked in restaurants. Hagg called Taylor the "mastermind," the brave one who approached a manager and sweet-talked him into renting them an apartment. He had no idea they were underage. Two of them rode motorcycles, and with eighteen-year-olds fighting in Vietnam and working in factories, their self-sufficiency seemed plausible and appeared authentic.

Figure 8.2 Van McClung, Bob Hagg, and Gary Robinson, 1973 and 1974. *Source*: *Sabre*, 1973 and 1974.

They moved into a two-bedroom apartment near SHS. The group was soon joined by rising senior Van McClung, who was African American, after the family he was living with decided to move to San Jose. Later that summer, rising junior Gary Robinson, who was white, also moved in.

These boys were survivors: working, shouldering the responsibilities of adulthood, taking care of themselves and each other, playing sports, and aiming to finish high school. None of them was an outstanding student, nor did any of them imagine college in his future. They simply wanted to graduate and escape their destructive family situations.

Bob Hagg

Entering high school, Bob Hagg was a scrawny guy with a cocky attitude: "I was walking around like I could whip a bear with a switch." With a crop of dirty blonde hair, he stood at 5'6" and weighed only 112 pounds. Gary described him as "a small dude with a kind of a big head. He didn't grow into his head yet." He had played sports in junior high and had a penchant for fighting, which made him especially effective at wrestling.

Bob grew up in Lakewood Village, which he described as "the ghetto of Sunnyvale," and described himself as "poor white trash." Friends asked him why he didn't paint his house and why his family used lawn furniture in the living room. He refused to bring people over, embarrassed by his home and his parents' drinking and fighting. Bob's father, a Texan who had retired from the Air Force, argued incessantly with his belligerent mother. At the time, Bob's father worked for the post office; his mother found jobs in electronics factories, but had trouble holding onto them. Despite being confrontational outside his home, Bob attempted to be the family peacemaker. "I saw something developing very early and I would step in and stop it before it became a fight." But the police made regular visits to his house for "family disturbances."

Because his older sister was deaf, Bob learned to sign well enough to communicate with her but was not fluent in American Sign Language. He was quick to defend his sister when she became a target of ridicule. "It was well known that if you taunted my sister, you're gonna end up fighting her brother." He also felt responsible for his younger sister and brother. He claimed he rarely lost a fight because "I learned if you get in the first couple of licks . . . they don't want any more." As his reputation spread, he had to fight less. After his younger brother pulled a knife on his seventh-grade teacher, he was removed from the home and placed in foster care. "He never rejoined the family."

Bob's parents divorced around the time he entered high school. He had lots of friends but didn't care about academics. He struggled in math. Although he loved sports, Bob immediately clashed with the freshman football coach, quit, and got a job at a chain restaurant. He focused his athletic energy on wrestling, which helped him channel his anger. "I became a real good grappler and . . . it was just a natural ability. And then from being a dishwasher and lifting the plates up . . . I had real strong arms." At fifteen, he used his wages to buy a motorcycle.

Wrestling coach Steve McKeown appreciated Bob's zealousness on the mat and tried to run interference with his other teachers. Assistant football coach Steve Albrecht, who had Bob in his history class, asked McKeown: "What are you doing wasting your time on this Hagg kid? . . . He's gonna end up doing time or get killed in a violent crime." That comment provoked a visceral reaction in bystander Doug Walker. He believed that no teacher should ever talk about a student that way. He had previously witnessed the coach's cavalier denigration of an athlete under his supervision. For Walker, this was the last straw. He exploded at Albrecht, lunged toward him, and had to be held back by the other coaches in the room.

In the summer of 1972, before Bob's junior year, his father moved back to Texas and married his high school sweetheart. Bob protested but moved there along with his two sisters. He hated Texas and clashed with his stepmother. So, after two weeks, he boarded a Greyhound bus back to Sunnyvale to live with his mother, despite their tensions. That didn't last long.

After a month or so, Bob found the situation with his mother's drinking and her boyfriends "so unbearable that I said, 'Nah, I can't do this no more.'" One day, his mother showed up drunk at the restaurant where he was working and made a scene. Later that day, she told his wrestling coach that he had stayed out all night and shouldn't be allowed to compete. Bob burst with frustration. He told her, "I'm not living with you anymore. Don't bug me [or] come near me. If you do, I'm gonna make your life terrible; I'm gonna beat up your boyfriends." With that, she left him alone and he had to find someplace else to live.

Dan Steward

Dan Steward, a surly go-to guy, stood so straight that he almost leaned backward, his posture exuding pride and remoteness. Many people attributed his gruff demeanor to arrogance. A talented athlete, he led the basketball team as a point guard. Off the court, boys kept a respectful distance. Girls often confided in him because he was a reliable secret keeper.

Just weeks before freshman year started, Steward and his little brother had to move from their father's home in the East Bay to an apartment in Sunnyvale with their mother and her new husband. She had just remarried in an effort to support her two youngest sons, but the personality mix was toxic. Steward did not warm to his stepfather, his mother's erratic behavior, or her nighttime hours as a cocktail waitress.

Dan's father, who had immigrated from Greece as a boy, had moved out of his parents' house at age fourteen to make a living on his own. Dan reasoned, "He didn't know how to be a dad" because he had never been adequately fathered. Dan's two older brothers regularly got in trouble, while "I was always the good kid of the family." He excelled at baseball, basketball, and football. His father, a truck driver who was on the road for long stretches, hired Raymond Francis Libby, a former semipro boxer, to cook and clean. As a fellow athlete, Raymond appreciated Dan's talents, helped him train, and made a home for the boys.

In the summer of 1969, Raymond suddenly died. Two weeks before school started, his father announced that Dan and his younger brother would be moving to live with their mom. "That changed my life." He felt unsettled, resistant, and deeply unhappy, but he had no choice. In Sunnyvale, he had no friends and was a star to no one. He entered a multiethnic environment that contrasted profoundly with the mostly white community where he had lived. He did okay in school, but skipped football and tried out for "C" basketball.

Dan had responsibilities for his younger brother after school, but his greatest challenge was his mother's drinking, which got worse over time. He often came home and found his mother "passed out on the couch." Worried that "she didn't look right," he panicked and feared she was dead when he could not rouse her. "I'd shake her. 'Mom!' And she wouldn't move." While he checked to see if she was still breathing, she might suddenly wake up and exclaim, "What's the matter?" For a while, immersing himself in sports and spending every extra moment in the gym was a way to avoid the situation.

By the end of his junior year, Steward was working at McDonald's to earn spending money. He played varsity basketball, had many friends, and even a serious girlfriend whose family embraced him. But "it got so bad at home, I couldn't stand to be with my mom anymore." So, while hanging out with Bob and Allan, he found a path. He called his father, who wanted him to come back to the East Bay, but Dan refused. "This is my senior year." His father saw the wisdom of staying at SHS and moving out. He pledged $50 per month to help Dan pay rent and expenses until he graduated.

Van McClung

Van McClung's backstory differed profoundly from those of his roommates. Born in Greenwood, Mississippi, in August 1955, Van was the seventh child of a sharecropping family with thirteen children. They lived and worked on a white-owned plantation across the river from where Emmett Till had just been lynched. Like most rural Black southerners, the McClungs were very poor. Van's father, Dan Willie McClung, had played baseball on professional Negro League teams in Nashville and Atlanta, and he taught Van the sport in a way that served him well. In the summer of 1969, the Kraus family, who had been providing assistance to the McClung family, invited fourteen-year-old Van to spend the summer with them in Sunnyvale. He found living in their majority-white community unnerving.

Bill and Marti Kraus owned a business that manufactured and installed electrical circuit breakers. They lived in Lakewood, one of the two neighborhoods on the north side of the Bayshore freeway, and had four sons. The day Van arrived, they invited two white teenagers over to meet him. While he sat on the front lawn, the boy and girl approached him. After some chitchat, the girl asked, "What would happen if you kissed a white girl in Mississippi?" Van replied, "Stuff like that don't happen. . . . You don't do that." She laughed, then leaned over and kissed him "right smack in the mouth. And man, I'm having a heart attack." The boy and girl laughed uproariously, and Van felt scared half to death. The kidnapping, beating, and murder of Emmett Till, a fourteen-year-old Black visitor from Chicago, had sent a chilling message to African Americans in the Mississippi Delta and throughout the United States. Did white teenagers not know that history? Did this white girl simply act on her curiosity about a Black boy, safely wrapped in her racial privilege, assuring him that rules were different in California? Or was her action a form of racial harassment camouflaged as friendliness?

Van joined the local summer baseball league, where he met Bob Hagg, distinguished himself on the field, and sent his family newspaper clippings reporting on his athletic accomplishments. They came to understand, as did he, that he had more opportunities in California. At the end of the summer, when the Krauses invited him to stay through the school year, his parents agreed.

Van had no trouble with the social transition to Sunnyvale High. He already had buddies from baseball, and as an athlete, he "blended in." With the exception of the one altercation with the racist boy whom he replaced on the football team, he did not get into fights and made friends easily. The academic transition was much harder. The curriculum of schools for Black students in Mississippi lagged behind the curriculum in California, so he was unprepared for his classes. Van said, "Thank God for Ms. Pipal, my counselor." She got him placed in the right classes so he could catch up. Robert Handa offered to help him edit his papers.

When he went home to Mississippi the next summer, his family welcomed his return. While his mother didn't want him to leave again, Van's father recognized the opportunities California could offer and made a rare unilateral decision to let him go back for another year. Van returned to Sunnyvale and had a paid internship with the local police department.

The next summer, the Kraus family decided to move to San Jose. His host mother seemed to be having an emotional crisis and disagreed with her husband about Van's place in their family. She no longer wanted Van to live with them. From Van's perspective, the arrangement had worked well. He helped care for the children and cooked some meals; the kids liked him and he had been teaching them to play baseball. Van did not want to leave the social and athletic connections he had made at Sunnyvale High. His football prowess was attracting attention from colleges, and his coaches were helping him think through his future options. Another year with the Jets would be vital. So Van decided to move out and live with Bob Hagg and Dan Steward. He declined his host father's offer to help financially, assuring him that he could manage with his earnings and savings from his job at McDonald's.

Gary Robinson

Following a dispute with his mother, Gary Robinson joined the group of boys in the apartment later that summer. A taciturn white boy who was tall and muscular, Gary lived with his mother, a beautician who was deaf, and two older brothers in a modest house not far from SHS. Their father was nowhere to be seen, having left after the divorce years earlier. Gary's oldest brother had already graduated from Sunnyvale High; his other brother was the valedictorian in 1971. Gary had little in common with his brothers, however, and they were not close. At first, he had no aspirations for his future. Looking back, he saw himself as putting one foot in front of the other only when prodded. The movie "Jeremiah Johnson" (1972) gave him a glimmer of what he might want to do: move to the mountains, become a trapper, and live alone with a loyal dog.

His least favorite subject was math. Cynthia Stiles, who taught remedial math, insisted he finish his homework, which he did only episodically. She regularly sent him to the principal's office to insure it got done. He had to complete it before she would let him go home. "At the time, I couldn't stand her.. . . She didn't let me quit."

Gary loved motorcycles as much as he did football. His mom made little money, so Gary had a paper route, mowed lawns, and got a minimum wage job at Kentucky Fried Chicken to help out. He saved enough money to buy a Honda 150 motorcycle, which he used to get where he needed to go. Eventually, he bought a larger one, which is how he met Bob Hagg. Gary sold his old motorcycle to Bob for $150 and they made plans to ride together the next day.

> He shows up and the handlebars are really bent. And I go, "What the hell did you do? How are you even driving this thing now?". . . I was kind of mad at him. "Hey, that's a great bike. We gotta take care of this thing. And you wrecked it the first day."

When Gary and his mother disagreed about the kind of used car they would jointly buy and share, "that argument pretty much led me to say 'The hell with it. I'm leaving then.'" The other guys had already rented an apartment and were looking for a roommate.

Life in "Heartbreak Hotel"

Initially, very few educators at SHS knew that these boys were living independently. Their lives were ordered by work and school. All five continued to be employed and aimed to earn a high school diploma. Each felt deeply committed to his athletic team. Hagg bragged, "We had the best wrestler, football player, basketball player, living in the same apartment." The neat and tidy boys shared one bedroom, and the messy ones shared the other. Working in restaurants meant they had plenty of fried chicken and hamburgers to eat. They sponsored regular poker games at their place, inviting boys from school to play. Steward and Hagg got pretty adept at poker and were able to raise a significant portion of their rent from those games.

Steward described himself as "the mother hen," concerned about cleanliness and order in the apartment. When he came home and found a pile of ill-gotten goods in the living room, he shouted, "What the hell's the matter with you?! You guys, you're going to end up in jail." Taylor, who had a harebrained scheme to steal and resell televisions, also instigated crazy, loud weekend parties. Those invariably got them in trouble with the landlord, who threatened to evict them. Irritated but forgiving, Steward thought that "they didn't know any better. I mean . . . they had nobody giving them any guidance or support when they were growing up, so they just, they survived. I chose to deal the other way." He reasoned that he could provide his friends compassion and moral leadership. "I never had guidance; I never had support. . . . I just feel like it's important. If I can do that, that's great, because I never got it."

As Hagg put it, "We raised each other."

SUNNYVALE HIGH SCHOOL'S INTERVENTIONS

Their situation changed when Hagg and Taylor attempted to steal some beer from a convenience store. Hagg described what happened: "He opened the back door. I took the beer, put it on the fence. The cop found me, pulled his gun. I jumped, ran off."

Hagg's counselor, Bob Douglas, remembers the next morning when a police officer walked into his office and announced,

> "I almost shot your star pupil last night." I said, "You did?" And he said, "Yeah, Hagg." I said, "What did he do now?" The officer detailed the scene. "He was climbing the fence. And I was standing right on the fence with my gun at him saying, get off the fence."

When he looked away for a second, Hagg jumped. "I could have shot him, Bob." He then reassured the counselor, "We caught up with him. He's been arrested; he's in jail." The next day, the probation department phoned Bob Douglas: "I've got Bob Hagg here. You're his emergency contact." Shocked, Douglas replied, "I am?" He arranged to stop by the juvenile center on his way to work.

Douglas reflected on his importance to Bob Hagg and why he felt connected with the boy: "I think Bob touched something inside of me that reminded me of me." He had been a poor kid in a tough neighborhood.

> I had friends [who] ended up in prison or dead. And Bob was coming from that kind of an environment too. I always liked him. I felt that Bob never did anything violent toward anyone. He always had this kind of caring-ness to him. . . . He did some dumb things, but he also did some brave and resilient things.

Hagg's sweeter side was evident to all his friends. His fighting was triggered by specific situations, not by a violent temperament. Van recalled, "Bob was a really good guy. I think he did things outta anger with his parents or whatever. I mean, he had the biggest heart I know at Sunnyvale. . . . If you were friends with him, you had it."

So Douglas arrived early in the morning, met with the probation officer, and saw Hagg. "Bob's begging me to get him out of that place and get him back to school." But Douglas recognized the value of his getting caught and not getting hurt. "I said, 'Nah, I'm not gonna bail you out here. You're gonna sit in here for a while and think.'" When he picked up Hagg the next day, "We had some fairly father-to-son, heart-to-heart talks in that moment. . . . He didn't do things like that very often. I mean, he was wrestling, he was trying to do sports." That was when he discovered Robinson and Hagg were living independently and supporting themselves as high school juniors.

Once the police and the school realized Hagg was an unsupervised minor who had multiple brushes with the law and whose mother was in jail, they resolved that he should be placed in foster care. But he balked. Hagg discovered that he had an alternative: self-emancipation. When the manager at the restaurant where he worked found out about his living situation, he hired legal counsel for Hagg. At SHS, Linda Lewis, his other counselor, met with California Child Protective Services and the Catholic Church and wrote letters in support of Hagg's petition to be responsible for himself. So Hagg gained the right to live independently and be treated legally as an adult.

The question was how to keep him in school to finish his diploma. Douglas recalled, "He missed a lot of classes. . . . And trust me, as we got close to graduation that senior year in '74, I was sweating bullets about whether or not we were gonna get him outta school." Hagg was working the graveyard shift at the restaurant because he needed the money and benefits. He kept coming to school but often fell asleep, including in Doug Walker's US Black History class. Not all his teachers were clued into what was happening with these boys, but Walker figured it out and had a talk with Hagg. "So he would actually let me sleep in his class and wake me up and gimme my assignments and stuff. So he worked with me on that deal."

The load was heavy. Hagg had to quit wrestling that year because he needed to work. When the effort seemed impossible, Hagg decided that he just had to quit school. Douglas did not tolerate this option and played tough. Hagg recalls him saying, "You're not quitting school. I'll have Mike waiting, [to] beat you up." Mike was the officer who arrested Hagg when he stole the beer from the convenience store. Delivered this way, the message was powerful, and Hagg accepted it. "I had a real good relationship with" Douglas, he said.

The four boys eventually "got rid of Taylor," not just because of his parties and illegal activities but also because he took advantage of people. The shared apartment became easier to manage and more peaceful. Robinson reconciled with his mother and moved back home. McClung and Steward never got in trouble with police or teachers. The two older boys continued to go to school and work part-time, and no teachers knew about their situation. It was only forty years later that Steward told his basketball coach about it. At school, he was close to coach Paulson, but even he had no idea about Dan's living situation.

Steward did not know what he would do after graduating. "I don't remember anybody ever talking about college. I had no idea. I just wanted a job and a way to pay the bills." He knew that someday he wanted to get married and have children, aspiring to form a "stable household, 'cause I didn't have it. And I wanted to be a good role model for my kids." But the next steps were unclear. Playing basketball at a community college seemed like a good option. So, Dan moved back in with his father and played on the team at Diablo Valley Community College for a year. He discovered that he missed Sunnyvale and his friends and knew he needed a job. The father of his good friend Pat Alcares worked at Hewlett Packard and offered to help him get a job there. Dan started on the night shift as a janitor, and Pat's uncle up the street offered him lodging in his converted garage.

Van McClung's story evolved differently. By his senior year, he decided he wanted to go to college and that a football scholarship would get him there. With the guidance of coach Carroll, San Jose State recruited him and offered him a spot on their team. But during that critical summer before his senior year, when Marti Kraus became hostile to Van, she did not forward any of his mail. He never received the scholarship offers and registration forms. Van had eagerly anticipated his next step, and when it fell apart he could not explain it. "So I ended up going to Mississippi," where he felt isolated. Later he heard a rumor that when one school inquired, she told them Van had died.

The end of his time in Sunnyvale got no easier as he graduated. In typical senior fashion, Van circulated his yearbook for everyone to sign. He was startled when he discovered that someone he had considered his friend wrote a passage about the future and called him by the n-word. Not having had that racial slur directed at him at SHS, he was shocked to read it from someone he thought cared about him. He felt distraught that he had misjudged and began to wonder where else such sentiments might be hiding.

Van still had his sights set on college and decided that joining the Navy was a prudent step toward that goal. "I ended up going into the military and I played ball there for four years. . . . Then that paid for my education." He returned to California and got his bachelor's degree in finance.

Hagg, who had another year to finish, knew he had to keep out of trouble. He had a transformative moment in a class taught by Sharon Prefontaine. She teased him, "You're gonna have a job with your name on your shirt, wherever you work." One day, on a dare, he set off a firecracker and threw it just outside the classroom door before it exploded. She angrily let him have it. "What you did was *so stupid*, I can't even send you to the office." Bob suddenly realized that if she had sent him to the principal, "I would've got expelled, not suspended, expelled; kicked outta Sunnyvale. And then God knows what could happen." At that moment, Prefontaine's message clicked. "I realized that the end result of my actions can mess me up for life. So . . . I got it." He straightened up.

These boys found encouragement and help from the parents of their friends as well. Searching for adult guidance while he was still living at home, Bob Hagg spent a lot of time at the house of his best friend Dave Marquez. "His parents, especially his mom, were very kind to me. . . . I ate at their house all the time." Dan Steward had a close relationship with the parents of his long-time girlfriend; he walked her home from school every day and joined the family for dinner. Van McClung sought the wisdom of the father of his white friend Larry McCracken. Van trusted him; he had been a colonel in the military, and Van felt he could talk to him. "He treated me like I was his son, so I was always working at his house." When Hagg got involved with a serious girlfriend later in high school, they got engaged. "Then I called it off because I realized I was in love with the parents and not the girl." Her father had been his most important mentor, second only to his teachers and counselors.

Dan Steward reflected on the ups and downs of their independent living experiment. They all "were survivors. . . . We just did it in different ways." Bob Hagg thought that only Taylor, who had initiated the plan to get an apartment, did not make good. "We all took the high road and he took the low road." Taylor fell off of everyone's radar years ago, when it was rumored that he was doing time in prison.

It is hard to imagine a similar situation unfolding in 2024. The price of housing is so high that four people working minimum wage jobs would have a hard time making the rent. Would the California Youth Authority be more likely to intervene and find foster placements for the younger boys? Would parents allow their underage sons to live on their own?

GENDER DIVIDES

The boys who lived independently were able to separate from their parents and guardians legally and socially. Of the girls who did not live with a biological parent, virtually all lived with another family. Darci Daniels moved in with her best friend's family after her mother moved to another state.

Another girl's story reveals the challenges she faced trying to live as an autonomous adult. Dianna Good grew up in a family of athletes. Her dad had a career in the Navy and then worked at an electronics factory. Her mother died of breast cancer when Dianna was only thirteen. As the youngest child who was close to her mother, she felt the loss acutely.

Her father, lost without his long-term partner, sought another companion and remarried two months later. Stunned, Dianna nonetheless clicked with her stepmother emotionally and in their mutual love of art. But the marriage dissolved after two months. Two blows in less than six months left her reeling. Her older sisters had already graduated and were out on their own, leaving her and her brother home with their father. He was a man who liked order: "things had to be done precisely a certain way. There was a right and a wrong." He thought that Dianna had been babied by her mother and should grow up. Her older brother was supportive, played sports with her regularly, and encouraged her not to mope.

Dianna entered Sunnyvale High when her brother was a senior. As soon as he graduated, he joined the Air Force and left home. Their father met the partner he had been looking for, a woman with grown children. Dianna suddenly found herself in the uncomfortable position of being the only child at home with a new stepmother and a father who wanted to be free from the responsibilities of parenting. Dianna reflected, "I think people know when they're not wanted."

She knew she had to turn eighteen before she could legally act as an adult. She began saving money from her wages as a car hop at an A&W Drive-In so she could move out of the house. She counted down the years as she planned to get her driver's license, buy a car, and move out.

Her desire for autonomy grew more acute in her junior year when her father disparagingly accused her of hanging out with girls who were lesbians. Her first question was, "What is a lesbian?" When he explained, she asked, what's wrong with that? "People should be able to love who they want." He forbade her from seeing them. Shaken, she rebelled against her father's efforts to control her. At school later that week, her counselor, whom she had never saw, called her into his office. He asked her about her friends: "Do you know that this person [is] a lesbian?" Deeply offended, Dianna concluded he must have received a call from her father. Furious, she questioned what difference it should make to him or the school. "So of course, I stayed friends with them."

The next year, she realized that she too was a lesbian, and her quest for freedom intensified. In February 1976, the day she turned eighteen, she left home and moved into the one-bedroom apartment of the assistant manager from A&W, who made this offer when she discovered Dianna planned to sleep in her car. She proposed that Dianna sleep on the couch and contribute $60 per month to the rent.

That arrangement worked, but she was acutely aware that she needed more income to support herself while finishing high school. "I had this brilliant idea. I was going to work the midnight shift. I thought I could work from twelve to seven and then go to school and then come home and sleep, and then do my homework and whatnot." She got a job on an electronics assembly line and quickly found how boring and difficult it was. The job "lasted a week." She continued as a carhop at A&W, finished spring season in sports, and graduated with her class. She postponed going to college because she did not want to waste money and time floundering about; later, she earned a degree.

These stories speak not just to the determination of some young people, but also to the support provided them by their friends and by adults who were not their parents at school, in their neighborhoods, and at their workplaces. Those peers and grownups assisted them, advised them, guided them, offered them jobs, appreciated them, fed them, taught them things, goaded them, inspired them, let them make mistakes, gave them second chances, loved them, argued with them, nurtured them, and bolstered their efforts to become stand-up human beings.

Some young people who faced difficulties had more negative experiences. They fought with hurtful words and blows, sold drugs, and enticed others to join them in criminal activity. Some parents, counselors, and teachers undermined students directly and indirectly. A coach disparaged Bob Hagg and urged other teachers to give up on him. A counselor colluded with her father to insult Dianna Good and warned her not to associate with her friends because of their sexual identity. Conventional gender codes shaped adults' differential treatment of girls. Many pregnant teenagers were sent away from school to give birth and relinquish their babies in order not to shame their families. Cece Padgett's mother insisted that she get married at the age of fifteen, but when Cece wanted to return home, initially her mother refused. Some teachers stereotyped students because they were girls, Black, Brown, or Asian, or came from poor and immigrant families.

Nonetheless, Sunnyvale High School created the space for constructive relationships and cultivated a sense of possibility.[3] When life got tough for JoAnn Vargas, the PE teachers "had my back." She lived at home until she graduated and then proudly moved out and supported herself. When Bob Hagg was arrested, the school intervened on his behalf. Bob Douglas stepped into the role of advisor, father figure, and avid supporter, not just disciplinarian. He and another counselor informed the administration about his situation and wrote letters of support for Hagg's self-emancipation. They did not give up on Hagg; they held him accountable when he easily could have fallen through the cracks or gotten himself in even deeper trouble.

Not only did SHS create an environment that made empathic adult-student relationships possible, but it also respected the power of peer relationships. Even with its pockets of meanness, cluelessness, and disparagement, it was a place where young people wanted to be. Some felt that it saved their lives. Most schools, then and now, expected young people facing trouble to drop out. Yet at Sunnyvale High, they felt motivated to graduate. The school community made that goal both appealing and possible.

NOTES

1. Studies find that children who grow up in working-class and poor families experience an accelerated transition from adolescence to adulthood. Stefanie DeLuca, Susan Clampet-Lundquist, and Kathryn Edin, *Coming of Age in the Other America* (New York: Russell Sage, 2016).

2. See Margaret K. Nelson, *Keeping Family Secrets: Shame and Silence in Memoirs from the 1950s* (New York: New York University Press, 2022).

3. Contemporary studies affirm the power of these practices. See Barbara Cervone, and Kathleen Cushman, *Belonging and Becoming: The Power of Social and Emotional Learning in High Schools* (Cambridge, MA: Harvard Education Press, 2015).

Chapter 9

Legacies and Lessons

Few experiences in the United States are as universal as public high school. Although approximately 9 percent of students attend private schools and 5 percent are home-schooled, the vast majority of us pass through this common institution.[1] Legally mandated until adolescents are sixteen years old, the local high school is a "public square" where young people spend a great deal of time before adulthood. It has the potential not only to educate students in math, literature, history, and the arts, but to shape the kind of citizens they become.

SHS nurtured adolescents' thinking about themselves and others. In the school's diverse community, a shared sense of belonging prevailed over racial-ethnic divisions. Like most institutions, then and now, the school dealt with these tensions imperfectly and unevenly. The educators who ran the school fostered students' aspirations and promoted the tenets of a multicultural society. They valued the diversity of the school and sought to help students accept it, learn from it, and honor it.

They consciously created a space that invited students from all backgrounds to belong. Harold Benson '73 vividly recalled how he felt as a freshman, newly arrived from the Midwest. "It felt like I was the only one that didn't belong." But he made a place for himself through relationships with peers and teachers, speech and debate, and a telecommunications club he cofounded. "That cemented the feeling that Sunnyvale High was mine as much as anyone else's. This experience, this place, these people belong to me, at least in some way. And I've considered Sunnyvale my home ever since."

Educators sought to communicate their belief in students' worth and to demonstrate the personal and collective strength that comes from a robust learning community. They built on students' common class circumstances and cultivated a sense of shared purpose.

Sunnyvale High did not generate a college-bound culture or produce large numbers of famous or professionally prominent people. But its long-term impact on many students was profound. It cannot be meaningfully assessed by traditional outcomes like high test scores, graduation rates, and the proportion that attend four-year colleges.[2]

The stories told by SHS educators and alumni fifty years later attest to Sunnyvale High's impact on them. The school, broadly conceived as an innovative and welcoming community of students and teachers, bolstered young people at critical moments in their lives. Adults both preached and practiced mutual respect. They pointed many young people in the right direction when they had started to spiral downward and kept others going when events threatened their well-being. Sunnyvale High encouraged meaningful relationships between teachers and students and among peers. Teenagers believed in their fellow students' capacities, which made it easier for their peers to believe in themselves.

These oral histories point to mistakes and failures. But most narrators concluded that Sunnyvale High was a good school. Jackie Gooch '74 boasted, "I'm a proud Sunnyvale High schooler." As a paraprofessional teacher working with students who have learning and behavioral challenges, she understands the special quality of SHS. In retrospect, she said, "We had a great high school." She knew that she had tested the patience of her counselor Bob Douglas, who recalled:

> I probably . . . got more referrals from her teachers than anybody else in the entire school, because she'd cut class if there was something else going on. . . . And I chased her all over that school and all over Lakewood Village, to keep her in school. And she hated me for it. I just harassed her.

Now, with wisdom gained in adulthood and experience working in another high school system, Jackie's perspective has changed. She exclaimed, "Do you know that we had some of the best educators you could have ever asked for?" None of the teachers was "really, really mean. No, they cared about us." She now feels extremely grateful to Bob Douglas. Coming full circle, "I'm trying to give it all back now. That's what counts." She brings Douglas's perspective to her relationships with students and works from his starting assumption: "There are no bad kids."

For some teachers, principals, coaches, and counselors, SHS also had a lasting impact. It gave them creative license and energetic collaborators who were equally committed to working with a multiracial group of working-class and poor kids. It operated under the remarkable, far-sighted leadership of Adrian Stanga in the early years, Paul Sakamoto and Pete Mesa in the 1960s, and later the straightforward, door-opening encouragement of Walt Hale.

Studies of well-functioning schools almost universally point to the importance of principals.[3] Schools are extremely vulnerable to changes in leadership, which are, of course, inevitable. Sunnyvale High's early leadership established a foundation for inclusion and engagement with students that shaped it for twenty-five years. Remarkably, during a time of crisis, teachers and counselors stepped up when an ill-equipped principal failed.

The effective administrators trusted teachers to exercise leadership, use their own judgment, and explore their creative ambitions. They did not always agree with what teachers did and sometimes came down hard on their mistaken decisions, but they advocated for kids and teachers. Counselor Terry Dyckman, who later worked in human resources at Apple, remarked, "Two of the most brilliant people that I've ever seen were Paul Sakamoto and Pete Mesa."

FORECLOSING THE FUTURE

Two big changes in 1970s California altered the future of Sunnyvale High in particular and public schools in general: demographic shifts and the fiscal crisis resulting from a tax revolt.

The baby boom, from 1946 to 1964, ushered a huge cohort of young people into the educational system, which states and localities had to accommodate. Those born in its final year finished high school in 1982. Then public schools faced a dramatic drop in enrollment. Because state funding for local schools was tied to the number of students and their daily attendance, fewer students meant fewer funds. At the same time, inflation soared and property values rose, leaving homeowners increasingly pinched by taxes.

The 1970s also saw a demographic shift in the racial and ethnic makeup of children in schools. A recent report, *Unjust Legacy*, observed that in the 1970s the "state's foreign-born population doubled," and California had "the largest proportional increase in nonwhite children of any decade."[4] The diversification of the school population prompted some wealthy homeowners, who were predominantly white, to limit their support for public education.[5]

A conservative group mounted a campaign against both residential and commercial property taxes. They advocated cutting the tax rate and capping the tax increases that localities could impose. Moreover, they sought to embed these policies in the state constitution. Their ballot initiative, Proposition 13, won resoundingly in 1978.

Statewide budget cuts immediately followed. All state government services contracted, but school districts were hit particularly hard. While the "largest beneficiaries include commercial property owners," schools, especially in districts with lower property values, had to make do with much less.

The state generated more revenue by raising the income tax and sales tax, but schools were forced to cut programs, which "substantially narrowed the high school curriculum and other services like summer school."[6]

Speech and debate coach Sharon Prefontaine wryly assessed the policy shift in the district. The state standardized the curriculum and emphasized that high school was a path to college rather than fostering multiple avenues for student development.

> The motto of Fremont Union High School District used to be: "Every student is important. Every student has ability." And then they erased the programs for which certain students had very good ability, and put in programs where fewer students had ability.

To her that change meant that students had an equal opportunity to fail.

CLOSING SUNNYVALE HIGH SCHOOL

When the Fremont Union High School District decided that it had to close one of its six schools, it initiated a public deliberation about whether to shut down Homestead or Sunnyvale. Doug Boyd recalled: "They had . . . public open meetings in the gymnasiums in both" schools. "People were able to get up and say, 'Well, don't close my school because . . .'" They would point to the predictable consequences as students had to attend schools outside their neighborhood.

From the perspective of educators at SHS, based on residential distribution of students, the district should have closed Homestead High. But its middle-class parents showed up for public meetings, served on the school board, and had the time and resources to advocate for their school. The fact that Steve Jobs had graduated from Homestead implied that it was wildly successful at teaching young people and fostering innovation. How could they close the high school that educated the leader of a revolution in technology?

The district decided to close Sunnyvale High. According to Doug Boyd, "It was the path of least resistance." Teachers from SHS cried foul. Carolyn Buszdieker said, "They should have *never* closed Sunnyvale." Educators believed that they had created a vital and effective school, but they thought its character had been unfairly maligned and the district's decisions were politically motivated. "When we were told that Sunnyvale was a troubled school," Sharon Prefontaine protested indignantly, "we didn't get that. The kids didn't get that, and the faculty didn't see it that way."

Other educators agreed that the faculty was aware of students' family situations and languages. Astute teachers could anticipate when a student might withhold critical information about their academic performance from their parents who did not speak English. That connection made teachers more effective and parents able to hold students accountable.

Another rationale for closing Sunnyvale High, according to the district, was that it was a "segregated school." Prefontaine put it bluntly, "They called it segregated because all the Brown people were there." Ironically, fifteen years before, when the state of California was attempting to achieve what the courts called "racial balance," the district had argued that it was integrated because Sunnyvale High was in its district. The concentration of Black, Brown, and Asian kids at one school was inconsequential because SHS's integrated student body counted in the district's favor. In 1981, that same demographic profile was used against it.[7]

In effect, SHS's diverse student body had allowed the other high schools to remain predominantly white and middle class. With its closure, students were dispersed. The district divided up the neighborhoods that fed SHS by drawing straight lines on a map.[8] Teachers were also transferred to other schools in the district. But the district had no funds for transportation, so students from the far north of Sunnyvale had to take city buses to school. The punishing ride could sometimes take an hour and land students on the school's doorstep long before classes started. The burden of this transformation fell on the shoulders of the working-class students from Sunnyvale High and their families.

In the spring of 1981, Prefontaine organized a closing ceremony. She felt that people should not leave without marking the moment. Several teachers gave talks, and Robert Handa '73 was invited back to speak. The school's closure dissolved a vibrant community that had lasted twenty-five years. Sharon Faeta '70 said, "It's like we disappeared off the planet. Into the wild blue yonder." Other students lamented that closing Sunnyvale High meant not having "a place to come back home to for homecoming."

That changed in 2014 when John Amick '75, whose father had owned a gas station near the high school and generously supported it, persuaded the private school that occupied the campus to host a "homecoming" football game. They launched an annual event calling SHS alumni back to campus. Astonishingly, a decade later, hundreds of former teachers, administrators, and students continue this new tradition, celebrating a public school that closed decades before. Sunnyvale High School Marching Band alumni perform at the games, playing the SHS fight song and stirring participants with the soundtrack of their past.

SUNNYVALE HIGH CHANGED PEOPLE'S LIVES

Sunnyvale High School had an enduring impact on those who passed through its doors, young people and adults alike.

They learned important values in the classroom. Darci Daniels '72, whose defiant stance often challenged other students, absorbed a key message: "You can always ask questions. I think that's important." Gary Robinson '74 credited Cynthia Stiles with teaching him "how to learn." Her insistence that he stick with his homework taught him the power of persistence.

When teachers developed a new curriculum, students had to rethink some of their assumptions and learn new skills. Ron DeMedeiros '72 celebrated the computer classes designed and taught by Mike Summerbell and Jim Miller. They "gave me a jumpstart, an advantage over others in college," because programming was not yet taught in most high schools.[9] Tim Sanford '71 grounded what he learned in the values of his parents, who supported integration and the civil rights movement. In his English classes, he read *Invisible Man* and *Autobiography of Malcolm X*. These books deepened his understanding of the historical context and meaning of a racialized history, profoundly shaping how he thought about the world. That exposure "was *really* important to me." He also discovered theater, where he was able to take risks and perform, launching his lifelong passion and career.

The campus ethos of mutual respect and connecting across differences had lasting effects. Dan Steward '73 said: "I think that helped me get along with all kinds of people. I mean, there wasn't *anybody* that I couldn't get along with, manage, or be managed by, because of the experiences that I had at Sunnyvale." Mary Danziger '72 emphasized people learning to work together. Paul Fong '71 pointed to his "leadership skills. That's where I picked up my social justice values, my advocacy skills, my promotion of diversity and multiculturalism." Suzi Brink '72 summed up the shared sentiment: "Sunnyvale taught us tolerance."

Relationships with peers were the bedrock of students' high school experiences. Darci Daniels '72 claimed, "I walked away with friendships that last forever." Those deep connections built confidence in others' integrity, honesty, and loyalty. Gary Robinson '74 appreciated the power of high school friendships. "I can't believe that coming where I came from, that I'm at where I'm at right now. So, I'm very, very grateful." He credited his friends for setting him on a better path. They—not his parents, teachers, or coaches—taught him right from wrong.

The relational ethos of the school encompassed faculty members from all corners of campus. Students had many heroes, not just in art, music, and after-school sports, but also in home economics and business. In the English department, Marion Pierstorff discovered that Sharon Prefontaine '65 loved to read, but had few books at home. She recalled, "I just found him mesmerizing" for his ability to recite poetry or quote from a play. One day he invited her to walk with him to his car in the parking lot. He opened the trunk and revealed piles and piles of books. Pierstorff said, "Take some," and she did.

Sunnyvale High had a tradition of "senior wills" where those graduating could bequeath something to the peers and educators they left behind. In senior wills and their oral histories, students named a long list of educators who played vital roles in their lives: Sara Accornero, journalism; Carolyn Buszdieker, physical education; Barbara Clark, home economics; Bob Douglas, science and PAVE; Terry Dyckman, counseling and PAVE; Loretta Gutierrez, Spanish and Mexican American literature; Mike Honda, science; Peggy Hurt, English; Rich Knapp, science; Mike Mulvahill, history; Vauna Pipal, counselor; John Riggle, marching band; Cynthia Stiles, math; William Stretch, choral music; Doug Walker, history.

Ed Lizardo '73 was deeply attached to his mentor, John Riggle, but other teachers reached out and advised him about his future. Vernon Galliart and Sara Accornero were good at "recognizing certain attributes, telling me about them, and saying 'you'd be good at this.' And to me that was impactful." His aunt and uncle, who were raising him, felt they were aiming high by getting him to finish high school; they did not have the cultural capital to advise him about college. Ed's teachers were "a *guide* with purpose. I relished it."

Cece Padgett '72 felt respected at a vulnerable moment in her adolescence. When she became pregnant at the end of her sophomore year, her counselors helped her develop a plan to complete the credits she needed to graduate. She married, had the baby, got divorced, returned home to live with her parents—and graduated with her class. She relayed a later conversation with her counselor, Terry Dyckman. She told him, "You just don't know . . . you changed my life. You made me feel better about myself. You made me feel like . . . people weren't just totally looking at me for being this unwed mother, teenage mother."

Former teachers and administrators also held Sunnyvale High in high regard. Never an easy school to work at, it nevertheless provided many educators with one of the most meaningful experiences of their careers. Bob Douglas recalled SHS as "a wonderfully interesting multiethnic school with a faculty that [was] perhaps the strongest . . . and the most dedicated educational team I ever had the pleasure of working" with. After 43 years in education, he looked back on teaching science and becoming a counselor at SHS as "a phenomenal launch for me in this profession, and a great opportunity."

SHS attracted a cohort of younger educators who were dedicated to making things better. For the earlier generation, that sentiment also held true. Principal Adrian Stanga said that those were "my best years" in his thirty-year career. Walt Hale, who taught science, became boys' dean, then returned as principal in 1970, said, "If you were to get the faculty together, they would say their best years in education were at Sunnyvale High School."

Faculty often responded to the leadership of their peers. Counselor Terry Dyckman said:

> There were probably a dozen real difference-makers at Sunnyvale that created an environment and a culture that was really unique. . . . There was something almost magical about being a part of that staff. . . . We knew that we were on a mission of some sort. . . . You've got each other's back and you're willing to experiment and do some things.

He likened their work to a joint venture. "If it's an art project, we had great clay. The kids were all in." "Anybody you talk to that was at Sunnyvale at that time counts it as probably their most unique and special educational experience. I do. And I went on to work with people that were incredibly smart, incredibly bright," and had much more formal education.

The team of teachers shared concern for the students and supported each other. Sharon Prefontaine said, "We were the most united. It was the best teaching experience I will ever have in my life." The administration backed her experiments in teaching, even when they failed. Sunnyvale High taught teachers "how to teach." Staff at other schools where she worked often blamed the students when they did not learn. "It's a very wrong-headed notion about what teaching is." She recalled many kids whose lives turned around because of their experience at SHS. As a community, Sunnyvale High helped "kids get through life."

The mutuality of the relationships with students made teaching more satisfying. Bob Douglas mused, "Those kids made our lives richer. . . . We probably got back as much from them as we gave to them." Ironically, recent changes that have erected higher boundaries between faculty and students to protect both parties have made it harder for educators to help students. Terry Dyckman recalled driving a student to Planned Parenthood to get birth control after she confided that she was sexually active, on the verge of endangering her relationship with her family, and had no other sources of support. Recognizing that he could be fired, he nonetheless responded to her desperate need. "You just did things because the environment required it."

Prefontaine lamented, "We talk about the differences; we don't talk about the sameness. I think back in the day, we were much more aware of our sameness, not only student to student and teacher to teacher, but teacher to student. You know, we're alike."

PRINCIPLES AND PRACTICES OF TRANSFORMATIVE EDUCATORS

In many ways, despite similar institutional foundations, high schools today differ profoundly from those fifty years ago. Yet, SHS exemplified principles and practices that remain valuable today. It privileged student leadership, teacher-led innovation, and class and ethnic pride. Educators were most effective when principals treated them as collaborators rather than underlings who dispensed information to passive listeners. They created a dynamic teaching and learning environment that was satisfying for them as well as engaging for students.

Sunnyvale High embraced an ethos of belonging. Formative leaders like Adrian Stanga and Paul Sakamoto established values that endured after they left. The findings of multiple studies of high schools across the country over the last forty years align closely with the best practices of SHS educators.[10]

Here are ten ways public schools can reach multiracial, multicultural student bodies that are burdened by poverty.

1. Create a broad curriculum for all youth served by the school, both college-bound and those preparing to enter the workforce. Offer an abundance of opportunities in art, music, vocational education, sports, and theater.
2. Hire outstanding staff who excel at relating to teenagers. Encourage them to act as role models who share their own experiences as first-generation college graduates and persons of color. Treat their backstories and identities as assets.
3. Establish multiple arenas for belonging to the school community. Give every student access to connections that enable them to grow and develop. Recognize that when students feel like they belong to something, they are more likely to attend school and invest their energies in their own education.
4. Build a curriculum inside and outside the classroom that addresses the full diversity of the student body. Teach history and literature that reflects the range of students' racial ancestry, ethnic heritage, and social backgrounds and creates a basis for mutual understanding.
5. Allow educators to experiment with new ideas for classes and activities, even though not all of these will work. Adopt a flexible approach, giving students and teachers opportunities to exercise initiative, take on challenges, and solve problems.
6. Create forums for students to learn about and discuss racial inequality outside the classroom. Balance organizations and activities that foster solidarity among those who belong to marginalized groups with those that facilitate dialogue across differences of race and ethnicity, economic class, gender, and sexuality. Empower students with voice and agency.
7. Nurture students' pride in their school and each other. Develop multiple pathways for cultivating individuals' sense of worth and a collective commitment to shared values and goals.

8. Recognize potential in all students, not just high achievers. Create opportunities for those with different interests—or no special interests at all—to engage, explore, and develop talents they did not know they had. Combine vocational and academic experiences and embrace a wide range of learning styles.
9. When kids make mistakes, assume that they acted impulsively out of ignorance or fear. Do not give up on them. Be flexible in enforcing rules, giving young people a chance to learn from their mistakes.
10. Establish opportunities for students to engage with educators outside of the classroom. Help them get to know each other in a sustained way. Offer expansive extracurricular activities on and off campus.

We have reason for optimism, even when these conditions do not yet exist in most schools.[11] The reforms adopted at Sunnyvale High resulted from the synergy of broad thinking, concern for youth, and the wisdom of generations of educators. That some of their ideas seem cutting edge today is a testament to their vision. Many of these practices are being adopted in high schools across the country and can be implemented by committed principals and teachers. Some innovations come with price tags, but others simply require educators and students alike to rise to human challenges: expressing empathy, acting with determination, and respecting the minds and lives of young people.

NOTES

1. National Center for Education Statistics, 2024. https://nces.ed.gov/. On home schooling, see https://nces.ed.gov/programs/coe/indicator/tgk/homeschooled-children?tid=300.

2. Victoria Restler, *What Do You Do That Can't Be Measured? On Radical Care in Teaching and Research* (Leiden, Netherlands: Brill, 2023).

3. Jason A. Grissom, Anna J. Egalite, and Constance A. Lindsay, *How Principals Affect Students and Schools: A Systematic Synthesis of Two Decades of Research* (New York: Wallace Foundation, 2021).

4. Hahnel et al., *Unjust Legacy*, 5.

5. *Unjust Legacy* states that voters "were concerned that their property taxes were increasingly being diverted from their own (largely white) communities to fund schools in Black, Latino, and lower-income communities, that immigrants were taking unfair advantage of public services and programs, and that their own children would not benefit from the housing and economic security they felt they had built for themselves." Hahnel et al., *Unjust Legacy*, 11.

6. Hahnel et al., *Unjust Legacy*, 12, 9, 7.

7. See Clayton A. Hurd, *Confronting Suburban School Resegregation in California* (Philadelphia: University of Pennsylvania Press, 2014). For current data on the Latina/o population and how it has grown in the last forty years, see Mohamad Moslimani and Luis Noe-Bustamante, *Facts on Latinos in the U.S.* (New York: Pew Research Center, 2023).

8. Eve L. Ewing, *Ghosts in the Schoolyard: Racism and School Closings on Chicago's South Side* (Chicago: University of Chicago Press, 2018).

9. "The Wave of the Future: High School Computer Classes in the 1970s," www.colorized.com.

10. See John Hattie, and Klaus Zierer, *Ten Mindframes for Visible Learning: Teaching for Success* (New York: Routledge, 2017); Kim Marshall, "The Big Picture: How Many People Influence a Student's Life?" *Phi Delta Kappan* (October 2017), 42–45. Sueneal Kolluri, Liane L. Hypolite, Alexis Patterson, and Kimberly Young discuss the importance of giving students a way to talk about race in *The Racial Reckoning and the Role of Schooling: Exploring the Potential of Integrated Classrooms and Liberatory Pedagogies* (Los Angeles: The Civil Rights Project/Proyecto Derechos Civiles, UCLA, 2023). In their study of contemporary high schools in Pennsylvania and Virginia, Brooke Dinsmore and Karlyn Gorski find that few teachers, except former military leaders who taught in JROTC, talked about race with students; "'You Have to Give them Real Responsibility': Success Stories of Fostering Student Engagement in the JROTC and Performing Arts Classroom," paper presented at the Sociology of Education Association conference (Pacific Grove, CA, 2024).

11. Nel Noddings, *A Richer, Brighter Vision for American High Schools* (New York: Cambridge University Press, 2015).

Paul Sakamoto pen and ink drawing, 2013. Source: *Sakamoto Designs: Paul's Pen and Ink Drawings*, by Paul Sakamoto and Marilyn Mason, San Jose: self-published, 2014, p.11.

Appendix

Sunnyvale High School Interview Subjects

Table A.1 Educators, Staff, and Community Partners

Name	Position	Years	Gender	Race/Ethnicity	Education	Mother's job	Father's job
Boyd, Doug	teacher, coach, administrator	1956–1981	male	white	BA	hospital dietician	absent
Buszdieker, Carolyn	teacher, coach, administrator	1958–1981	female	white	BA	small business owner	engineer
Douglas, Bob	teacher, counselor	1967–1974	male	white	MA	housewife	oil field worker
Dyckman, Terry	counselor, dean	1968–1977	male	white	MA	acrobatic performer	cable splicer, phone co.
Furtado, Al	parent		male	white	high school	cannery worker	cannery worker
Furtado, Pat	parent		female	white	high school	housewife	steel worker
Gutierrez Morris, Loretta	teacher	1968–1980	female	Mexican American	BA	farmworker	farmworker
Hale, Walter	teacher, dean, principal	1962–1968; 1970–1975	male	white	EdD	unknown	unknown
Holte, Vern	staff	1971–1976	male	white	MA	farmer	farmer
Honda, Mike	teacher	1969–1971	male	Japanese American	BA	sharecropper	military; sharecropper
Miller, Jim	student, teacher, coach	1964; 1969–1971	male	white	MA, JD	electronics, Lockheed	US Postal Service
Olson, Charles J.	community partner	1962; 1968–1972	male	white	high school	fruit farmer	fruit farmer
Paulson, Eric	student, teacher, coach	1965; 1970–1981	male	white	BA	nurse's aide	truck driver
Prefontaine, Sharon Shull	student, teacher	1956–1969	female	Eurasian	MA	housewife	Naval Air officer
Sakamoto, Paul	teacher, dean, principal	1964; 1969–1981	male	Japanese American	PhD	sharecropper	farm worker
Shimoguchi, Joanne	student, teacher, coach	1958–1965	female	Japanese American	MA	housewife; secretary	gardener
Stanga, Adrian	vice-principal, principal	1970–1974	male	white	EdD	housewife	unknown
Walker, Doug	teacher, coach		male	Black	BA	teacher	Air Force officer

Table A.2 Students

Name or *Pseudonym	Class	Gender	Race/Ethnicity	Mother's job	Father's job	Education	Occupation
Alcares, Pat	1971	male	Hawaiian	Hewlett Packard farmworker; Raytheon	Hewlett Packard	high school	Air Force
Araujo, Peter	1971	male	Mexican American		absent	BA	firefighter
*Benson, Harold	1973	male	white	market analyst; psychologist	electrical engineer	MD	doctor
Blasquez Paulson, Carol	1962	female	white	housewife	miller at lumber yard	some college	clerk at school
Brink Logan, Suzi	1972	female	white	typist at Lockheed	unemployed	BA	teacher
Collins, Gloria	1973	female	white	housewife	tool and die machinist	MA	professor at San Jose State
Coombs Holdorf, Cathy	1972	female	white	housewife	engineer, Lockheed	some college	dress shop owner
Daniels Amaral, Darci	1972	female	white	various jobs	unknown	high school	director of human resources
Danziger, Mary	1972	female	white	physical therapist	scissor salesman	community college	food server; elder care provider
DeMedeiros, Ron	1972	male	white	housewife	engineer	BA	engineer
Epps, Max	1973	male	Black	nurse	Air Force officer	BA	professional bowler; college coach
Faeta Kelly, Sharon Keiko	1970	female	Japanese American	housewife, drug store clerk	Navy airplane mechanic	BA	teacher; professional cheerleader
Fong, Paul	1971	male	Chinese	flower grower	flower grower	BA	politician; business entrepreneur
Furtado, Sheree	1972	female	white	cable assembly, Hewlett Packard	janitor, Hewlett Packard	BA	nurse
Garcia, Yolanda	1972	female	Mexican American	housewife	calibration technician	some college	paralegal

(Continued)

Table A.2 (Continued)

Name or *Pseudonym	Class	Gender	Race/Ethnicity	Mother's job	Father's job	Education	Occupation
Gooch Hocker, Jacquelyn	1974	female	Black	lab assistant, NASA	airplane mechanic, NASA	community college	instructional paraprofessional
Good, Dianna	1976	female	white	housewife	Navy; Sylvania	some college	mortgage system administrator
Hagg, Bob	1973	male	white	varied short-term jobs	Air Force; post office; highway dept.	high school	firefighter
Handa, Robert	1973	male	Japanese American	cafeteria worker	Lockheed	BA	TV journalist; variety show host
Hernandez, David	1973	male	Mexican American	waitress	construction	some college	layout designer; investor
High, Malcolm	1967	male	white	housewife	PG&E	high school	meter reader, PGE
Huong Tong, Lorraine	1973	female	Chinese	housewife	engineer	BA	researcher, Library of Congress
*Lakely, Stretch	1973	female	white	purchasing manager	construction, odd jobs	BA	teacher, coach
Leone, Joe	1972	male	Calabrian American	collection agency office	building contractor	BA	materials management
Lizardo, Ed	1973	male	Filipino American	lived with aunt and uncle	occupations unknown	BA	tech, sales
Manley, Jane	1972	female	white	secretary; graduate student	jewelry salesman	MA	teacher; principal
Matteucci Henderson, Sandy	1970	female	white	housewife; Lockheed	Navy medic	BA	teacher
McClung, Van	1973	male	Black	sharecropper	sharecropper, Negro League baseball	BA	deputy sheriff; business entrepreneur

Appendix 149

Name	Year	Gender	Race	Mother's occupation	Father's occupation	Education	Occupation
Miller, Jim	1964	male	white	electronics, Lockheed	US Postal Service	MA, JD	teacher; lawyer
Padgett Anderson, Cece	1972	female	white	housewife	architectural engineer	high school	customer service manager, tech and financial services
Paulson, Eric	1962	male	white	nurse's aide	truck driver	MA	teacher; principal
Prefontaine, Sharon Shull	1965	female	Eurasian	housewife	Naval Air officer	MA	teacher
Robinson, Gary	1974	male	white	beautician	military	MBA	CEO, business entrepreneur
Romero Hernandez, Kathi	1973	female	Mexican American	Raytheon	government worker	high school	retail clerk
Sanford, Tim	1971	male	white	teacher	minister	BA	artistic director
Serna, Dan	1971	male	Mexican American	made and sold tamales	construction worker	high school	city worker
Shimoguchi, Joanne	1964	female	Japanese American	housewife; secretary	gardener	MA	teacher
Snook Mostes-Witherow, Karen	1973	female	white	housewife	airline mechanic	business school	executive assistant
*Steward, Dan	1973	male	white	cocktail waitress	truck driver	community college	purchasing management
Vargas, JoAnn	1973	female	Puerto Rican	housewife; cannery worker	construction worker	community college	security; floral design

Bibliography

Alcares, Pat. Interview by Karen V. Hansen. Sunnyvale, CA, October 6, 2017.

Alvarez Jr., Robert R. "The Lemon Grove Incident." *Journal of San Diego History* 32 (1986). https://sandiegohistory.org/journal/1986/april/lemongrove/.

Anaya, Rudolfo A. *Bless Me, Ultima.* Berkeley, CA: Tonatiuh-Quinto Sol International, 1972.

Araujo, Pete. Interview by Karen V. Hansen. Digital recording, July 24, 2023.

Baca Zinn, Maxine. "Family, Feminism, and Race in America." In *Families in the U.S.: Kinship and Domestic Politics*, edited by Karen V. Hansen and Anita I. Garey, 33–40. Philadelphia, PA: Temple University Press, 1998.

Banks, Cherry A. McGee. *Improving Multicultural Education: Lessons from the Intergroup Education Movement.* New York: Teachers College Press, 2005.

Bay Area Census. http://www.bayareacensus.ca.gov/cities/Sunnyvale50.htm.

Benson, Harold [pseud.]. Interview by Karen V. Hansen. Digital recording, December 7, 2023.

Bettie, Julie. *Women without Class: Girls, Race, and Identity*, 2nd ed. Berkeley: University of California Press, 2014.

Blanden, Jo, Matthias Doepke, and Jan Stuhler. *Educational Inequality.* Working Paper 29979. Cambridge, MA: National Bureau of Economic Research, April 2022.

Blasquez Paulson, Carol. Interview by Karen V. Hansen. Sunnyvale, CA, June 9, 2015.

Bloom, Joshua, and Waldo E. Martin Jr. *Black against Empire: The History and Politics of the Black Panther Party.* Berkeley: University of California Press, 2013.

Bonacich, Edna. "A Theory of Middleman Minorities." *American Sociological Review* 38 (1973): 583–94.

Brown v. Board of Education of Topeka, 347 U.S. 483 (1954).

Bowman, Kristi. "A Different Shade of Brown." *Judicature* 88 (2004): 85–90.

Boyd, Doug. Interview by Karen V. Hansen. Cupertino, CA, June 10, 2015.

Brink Logan, Suzi. Interview by Karen V. Hansen. Sunnyvale, CA, December 17, 2013; San Jose, CA, June 12, 2015; digital recording, April 19, 2017.

Buszdieker, Carolyn. Interview by Karen V. Hansen. Palo Alto, CA, March 28, 2014; San Jose, CA, March 29, 2014; Saratoga, CA, June 11, 2015; San Jose, CA, June 12, 2015; Saratoga, CA, October 14, 2016.

Camiré, Martin, Pierre Trudel, and Tanya Forneris. "Coaching and Transferring Life Skills: Philosophies and Strategies Used by Model High School Coaches." *The Sport Psychologist* 26 (2012): 243–60.

Carter, Prudence L. *Keepin' It Real: School Success Beyond Black and White.* New York: Oxford University Press, 2005.

Castillo, Elias. *A Cross of Thorns: The Enslavement of California's Indians by the Spanish Missions.* Fresno, CA: Craven Street Books, 2017.

Cervone, Barbara, and Kathleen Cushman. *Belonging and Becoming: The Power of Social and Emotional Learning in High Schools.* Cambridge, MA: Harvard Education Press, 2015.

Collins, Gloria. Interview by Karen V. Hansen. San Jose, CA, March 31, 2014.

Cooky, Cheryl, and Michael A. Messner, eds. *No Slam Dunk: Gender, Sport and the Unevenness of Social Change.* New Brunswick, NJ: Rutgers University Press, 2018.

Coombs Holdorf, Cathy. Interview by Karen V. Hansen. Watertown, MA, October 16, 2014.

Cox, Betty. "De Facto Segregation." In *Encyclopedia of Educational Reform and Dissent*, edited by Thomas C. Hunt, James C. Carper II, Thomas J. Lasley, and C. Daniel Raisch, 260–61. Thousand Oaks, CA: Sage, 2010.

Crawford, Matthew B. *Shop Class as Soulcraft: An Inquiry into the Value of Work.* New York: Penguin, 2009.

Daniels Amaral, Darci. Interview by Karen V. Hansen. San Jose, CA, June 12, 2015.

Danziger, Mary. Interview by Karen V. Hansen. Digital recording, March 12, 2023.

DeLuca, Stefanie, Susan Clampet-Lundquist, and Kathryn Edin. *Coming of Age in the Other America.* New York: Russell Sage, 2016.

DeMedeiros, Ron. Interview by Karen V. Hansen. Digital recording, May 18, 2023.

Dewey, John. "Looking Back: My Pedagogic Creed." *Language Arts* 59 (1982): 539–42.

Dinsmore, Brooke, and Karlyn Gorski. "'You Have to Give them Real Responsibility': Success Stories of Fostering Student Engagement in the JROTC and Performing Arts Classroom." Paper presented at the Sociology of Education Association conference. Pacific Grove, CA, February 2024.

Donato, Reuben, and Jarrod S. Hanson. "Legally White, Socially 'Mexican': The Politics of De Jure and De Facto School Segregation in the American Southwest." *Harvard Educational Review* 82 (2012): 202–25.

Douglas, Bob. Interview by Karen V. Hansen. Digital recording, March 26, 2023.

Duncan, Greg J., and Richard J. Murnane, eds. *Whither Opportunity? Rising Inequality, Schools, and Children's Life Chances.* New York: Russell Sage Foundation, 2011.

Dyckman, Terry. Interview by Karen V. Hansen. Cupertino, CA, July 25, 2018.

Eccles, Jacquelynne, and Bonnie Barber. "Student Council, Volunteering, Basketball, or Marching Band." *Journal of Adolescent Research* 14 (1999): 10–43.

Eckert, Penelope. *Jocks and Burnouts: Social Categories and Identity in the High School*. New York: Teachers College Press, 1989.

Economic Opportunity Act of 1964. https://www2.ed.gov/about/offices/list/ope/trio/triohistory.html.

Epps, Max. Interview by Karen V. Hansen. Mountain View, CA, June 10, 2015.

Epstein, Barbara. *Political Protest and Cultural Revolution: Nonviolent Direct Action in the 1970s and 1980s*. Berkeley: University of California Press, 1993.

Ewing, Eve L. *Ghosts in the Schoolyard: Racism and School Closings on Chicago's South Side*. Chicago: University of Chicago Press, 2018.

Faeta Kelly, Sharon (Keiko). Interview by Karen V. Hansen. Digital recordings, May 20, June 12, 2023.

Ferguson, Ann Arnett. *Bad Boys: Public Schools in the Making of Black Masculinity*, 2nd ed. Ann Arbor: University of Michigan Press, 2020.

Fong, Paul. Interview by Karen V. Hansen. Sunnyvale, CA, June 9, 2015.

Franke, Todd Michael, Anh-Luu T. Huynh-Hohnbaum, and Yunah Chung. "Adolescent Violence: With Whom They Fight and Where." *Journal of Ethnic and Cultural Diversity in Social Work* 11 (2002): 133–58.

Furtado, Al, and Pat. Interview by Karen V. Hansen. Sunnyvale, CA, December 17, 2013.

Furtado, Sheree. Interview by Karen V. Hansen. Sunnyvale, CA, December 17, 2013; San Jose, CA, June 12, 2015.

Galster, George. "Racial Discrimination in Housing Markets during the 1980s: A Review of the Audit Evidence." *Journal of Planning Education and Research* 9 (1990): 165–75.

García, Mario T., and Ellen McCracken, eds. *Rewriting the Chicano Movement: New Histories of Mexican American Activism in the Civil Rights Era*. Tucson: University of Arizona Press, 2021.

Garcia, Yolanda. Interview by Karen V. Hansen. Digital recording, March 20, 2023.

Gitlin, Todd. *The Sixties: Years of Hope, Days of Rage*, rev. ed. New York: Bantam, 1993.

Gooch Hocker, Jackie. Interview by Karen V. Hansen. Digital recording, April 6, 2023.

Good, Dianna. Interview by Karen V. Hansen. Digital recordings, October 10, October 22, 2023.

Gorski, Karlyn J. "In School for After School: The Relationship between Extracurricular Participation and School Engagement." *Sociological Forum* 36 (March 2021): 248–70.

Grant, Gerald. *The World We Created at Hamilton High*, rev. ed. Cambridge, MA: Harvard University Press, 1990.

Grissom, Jason A., Anna J. Egalite, and Constance A. Lindsay. *How Principals Affect Students and Schools: A Systematic Synthesis of Two Decades of Research*. New York: Wallace Foundation, 2021.

Gurin, Patricia, Biren (Ratnesh) A. Nagda, and Ximena Zúñiga, eds. *Dialogue across Difference: Practice, Theory, and Research on Intergroup Dialogue*. New York: Russell Sage Foundation, 2013.

Gutierrez Morris, Loretta. Interview by Karen V. Hansen. San Jose, CA, September 25, 2014.

Hagg, Bob. Interview by Karen V. Hansen. Digital recordings, March 6, June 7, 2023.

Hahnel, Carrie, Arun Ramanathan, Jacopo Bassetto, and Andrea Cerrato. *Unjust Legacy: How Proposition 13 Has Contributed to Intergenerational, Economic, and Racial Inequities in Schools and Communities*. Berkeley, CA: Opportunity Institute, 2022.

Hale, Walter. Interview by Karen V. Hansen. San Jose, CA, March 29, 2014.

Handa, Robert. Interview by Karen V. Hansen. San Jose, CA, December 17, 2013.

Hattie, John, and Klaus Zierer. *Ten Mindframes for Visible Learning: Teaching for Success*. New York: Routledge, 2017.

Hernandez, David. Interview by Karen V. Hansen. Sunnyvale, CA, July 25, 2018; digital recording, July 24, 2023; Sunnyvale, CA, September 22, 2023.

High, Malcolm. Interview by Karen V. Hansen. Saratoga, CA, June 11, 2015.

Hochschild, Adam. *American Midnight: The Great War, a Violent Peace, and Democracy's Forgotten Crisis*. New York: Mariner, 2022.

Holte, Vern. Interview by Karen V. Hansen. Palo Alto, CA, March 28, 2014.

Honda, Mike. Interview by Karen V. Hansen. San Jose, CA, October 9, 2017.

Huang Tong, Lorraine. Interview by Karen V. Hansen. Digital recording, September 10, 2018.

Hurd, Clayton A. *Confronting Suburban School Resegregation in California*. Philadelphia: University of Pennsylvania Press, 2014.

Ignoffo, Mary Jo. *Sunnyvale: From the City of Destiny to the Heart of Silicon Valley*. Cupertino: California History Center & Foundation, 1994.

Jackson v. Pasadena City School District. 59 Cal.2d 876. 1963.

Jackson-Jacobs, Curtis. "Constructing Physical Fights: An Interactionist Analysis of Violence among Affluent, Suburban Youth." *Qualitative Sociology* 36 (2013): 23–52.

Jacobson, Yvonne. *Passing Farms, Enduring Values: California's Santa Clara County*. Cupertino: California History Center Foundation, 2001.

Jones, Nikki. *Between Good and Ghetto: African American Girls and Inner-City Violence*. New Brunswick, NJ: Rutgers University Press, 2010.

Katznelson, Ira. *When Affirmative Action Was White: An Untold History of Racial Inequality in Twentieth-Century America*. New York: W.W. Norton, 2005.

Kerr, Clark. *The Uses of the University*, 5th ed. Cambridge, MA: Harvard University Press, 1963.

Kolluri, Suneal, Liane I. Hypolite, Alexis Patterson, and Kimberly Young. *The Racial Reckoning and the Role of Schooling: Exploring the Potential of Integrated Classrooms and Liberatory Pedagogies*. Los Angeles: The Civil Rights Project/Proyecto Derechos Civiles, UCLA, 2023.

Kuhlin, Fanny, Natalie Barker-Ruchti, and Carly Stewart. "Long-Term Impact of the Coach-Athlete Relationship on Development, Health, and Wellbeing: Stories from a Figure Skater." *Sports Coaching Review* 9 (2019): 1–23.

Lakely, Stretch [pseud.]. Interview by Karen V. Hansen. Digital recording. October 26, 2023.

Lareau, Annette. *Unequal Childhoods: Class, Race, and Family Life*, 2nd ed. Berkeley: University of California Press, 2011.

Le Espiritu, Yen. *Asian American Panethnicity: Bridging Institutions and Identities.* Philadelphia, PA: Temple University Press, 1992.

Lee, Erika. *America for Americans: A History of Xenophobia in the United States.* New York: Basic Books, 2019.

———. *At America's Gates: Chinese Immigration during the Exclusion Era, 1882–1924.* Chapel Hill: University of North Carolina Press, 2003.

———. *The Making of Asian America: A History.* New York: Simon & Schuster, 2015.

Leitz, Lisa. "Girl Fights: Exploring Females' Resistance to Educational Structures." *International Journal of Sociology and Social Policy* 23, no. 11 (2003): 15–46.

Leone, Joe. Interview by Karen V. Hansen. Digital recording, March 11, 2023.

Levenson, Marya R. *Pathways to Teacher Leadership: Emerging Models, Changing Roles.* Cambridge, MA: Harvard Education Press, 2014.

Licht, Erica, and Khalil Gibran Muhammad. "A Call for Anti-Bias Education." *Learning for Justice* 5 (Fall 2023): 28–31.

Lightfoot, Sara Lawrence. *The Good High School: Portraits of Character and Culture.* New York: Basic Books, 1983.

Lindsay, Brendon. *Murder State: California's Native American Genocide, 1846–1873.* Lincoln: University of Nebraska Press, 2012.

Lizardo, Ed. Interview by Karen V. Hansen. Patterson, CA, June 14, 2015.

Madley, Benjamin. *An American Genocide.* New Haven, CT: Yale University Press, 2016.

Manley, Jane. Interview by Karen V. Hansen. San Francisco, CA, August 15, 2014; San Jose, CA, June 12, 2015.

Marshall, Kim. "The Big Picture: How Many People Influence a Student's Life?" *Phi Delta Kappan* 99 (October 2017): 42–5.

Matteucci Henderson, Sandy. Interview by Karen V. Hansen. Digital recording, August 28, 2023.

Matthews, Glenna. *Silicon Valley, Women, and the California Dream: Gender, Class, and Opportunity in the Twentieth Century.* Stanford, CA: Stanford University Press, 2003.

McClung, Van. Interview by Karen V. Hansen. Digital recording, June 9, 2023.

McGhee, Heather. *The Sum of Us: What Racism Costs Everyone and How We Can Prosper Together.* New York: One World, 2021.

Medved, Michael, and David Wallechinsky. *What Really Happened to the Class of '65?* New York: Ballantine, 1981.

Mendez et al., v. Westminster School District of Orange County, 64 F.Supp. 544 (S.D. Cal. 1946), aff'd, 161 F.2d 774 (9th Cir. 1947).

Messner, Michael A. *Power at Play: Sports and the Problem of Masculinity.* Boston, MA: Beacon Press, 1992.

Miller, Jim. Interview by Karen V. Hansen. Cupertino, CA, 25 August 2014.

Minow, Martha, Richard A. Shweder, and Hazel Rose Markus, eds. *Just Schools: Pursuing Equality in Societies of Difference.* New York: Russell Sage Foundation, 2008.

Molina, John A. *Barnstorming America: Stories from the Pioneers of Women's Basketball*. Sikeston, MO: Acclaim Press, 2016.

Monroe, Nicholas. "No Roadmap? No Problem: First-Generation Students' Cultural Assets and the Path to Undergraduate Success." PhD Diss., Brandeis University, 2021.

Moore, Eli, Nicole Montojo, and Nicole Mauri. *Roots, Race, & Place: A History of Racially Exclusionary Housing in the San Francisco Bay Area*. Berkeley: Haas Institute for a Fair and Inclusive Society, University of California, Berkeley, 2019.

Moraga, Cherríe, and Gloria Anzaldúa, eds. *This Bridge Called My Back: Writings by Radical Women of Color*. Watertown, MA: Persephone Press, 1981.

Moslimani, Mohamad, and Luis Noe-Bustamante. *Facts on Latinos in the U.S.* New York: Pew Research Center, 2023.

National Center for Education Statistics. 2024. https://nces.ed.gov/.

Nelson, Margaret K. *Keeping Family Secrets: Shame and Silence in Memoirs from the 1950s*. New York: New York University Press, 2022.

Noddings, Nel. *A Richer, Brighter Vision for American High Schools*. New York: Cambridge University Press, 2015.

Noriega, Chon A., Eric Avila, Karen Mary Davalos, Chela Sandoval, Rafael Pérez-Torres, and Charlene Villaseñor Black, eds. *The Chicano Studies Reader: An Anthology of Aztlán, 1970–2019*, 4th ed. Los Angeles: UCLA Chicano Studies Research Center Press, 2020.

Oakes, Jeannie. *Keeping Track: How Schools Structure Inequality*, 2nd ed. New Haven, CT: Yale University Press, 2005.

O'Brien, David J., and Stephen S. Fugita. "Middleman Minority Concept: Its Explanatory Value in the Case of the Japanese in California Agriculture." *Pacific Sociological Review* 25 (1982): 185–204.

Office of Intergroup Relations. *Guide for Multicultural Education: Content and Context*. Sacramento: California State Department of Education, 1977.

Olson, Charles J. Interview by Karen V. Hansen. San Jose, CA, August 18, 2014.

Orfield, Gary, Jongyeon Ee, Erica Frankenberg, and Genevieve Siegel-Hawley. *Brown at 62: School Segregation by Race, Poverty, and State*. Los Angeles: Civil Rights Project/Proyecto Derechos Civiles, UCLA, 2016.

Ortner, Sherry B. "'Burned Like a Tattoo': High School Categories and 'American Culture'." *Ethnography* 3 (2002): 115–48.

———. *New Jersey Dreaming: Capital, Culture, and the Class of '58*. Durham, NC: Duke University Press, 2003.

Othering and Belonging Institute. Berkeley: University of California. https://belonging.berkeley.edu/.

Padgett Anderson, Cece. Interview by Karen V. Hansen. Digital recordings, March 17, March 31, 2023.

Pascoe, C. J. *Nice Is Not Enough: Inequality and the Limits of Kindness at American High*. Berkeley: University of California Press, 2023.

Patchen, Martin. *Black-White Contact in Schools: Its Social and Academic Effects*. West Lafayette, IN: Purdue University Press, 1982.

Paulson, Eric. Interview with Karen V. Hansen. Sunnyvale, CA, June 9, 2015.

Prefontaine, Sharon Shull. Interview by Karen V. Hansen. Digital recording, August 3, 2023.
Putnam, Robert D. *Our Kids: The American Dream in Crisis.* New York: Simon & Schuster, 2015.
Reese, William F. *The Origins of the American High School.* New Haven, CT: Yale University Press, 1995.
Restler, Victoria. *What Do You Do That Can't Be Measured? On Radical Care in Teaching and Research.* Leiden, Netherlands: Brill, 2023.
Robinson, Gary. Interview by Karen V. Hansen. Digital recording, April 7, 2023.
Romero Hernandez, Kathi. Interview by Karen V. Hansen. San Jose, CA, June 12, 2015.
Rothstein, Richard. *Color of Law: A Forgotten History of How Our Government Segregated America.* New York: W.W. Norton, 2018.
Ruiz, Vicki L. *Cannery Women, Cannery Lives: Mexican Women, Unionization, and the California Food Processing Industry, 1930–1950.* Albuquerque: University of New Mexico Press, 1987.
———. "South by Southwest: Mexican Americans and Segregated Schooling, 1900–1950." *OAH Magazine of History* 15 (2001): 23–27.
Rutter, Michael, Barbara Maughan, Peter Mortimer, Janet Ousten, with Alan Smith. *Fifteen Thousand Hours: Secondary Schools and Their Effects on Children.* Cambridge, MA: Harvard University Press, 1979.
Sakamoto, Paul. Interview by Karen V. Hansen. San Jose, CA, June 12, 2015.
Sandelson, Jasmin. *My Girls: The Power of Friendship in a Poor Neighborhood.* Berkeley: University of California Press, 2023.
Sanford, Tim. Interview by Karen V. Hansen. New York, NY, February 27, 2015.
Schneider, Jack. "Privilege, Equity, and the Advanced Placement Program: Tug of War." *Journal of Curriculum Studies* 41 (2009): 813–31.
Schofield, Janet Ward. *Review of Research on School Desegregation's Impact on Elementary and Secondary School Students.* Hartford: Connecticut State Department of Education, 1989.
Serna, Dan. Interview by Karen V. Hansen. Digital recording, July 24, 2023; Sunnyvale, CA, September 22, 2023.
Shimoguchi, Joanne. Interview by Karen V. Hansen. Saratoga, CA, June 11, 2015.
Sizer, Theodore R. *Horace's Compromise: The Dilemma of the American High School.* New York: Houghton Mifflin, 2004.
Slavin, Robert E., and Nancy A. Madden. "School Practices That Improve Race Relations." *American Education Research Journal* 16 (1979): 169–80.
Snook Mostes-Witherow, Karen. Interview by Karen V. Hansen. Digital recording, September 11, 2023.
Stacey, Judith. "Sexism by a Subtler Name? Postindustrial Conditions and Postfeminist Consciousness in Silicon Valley." *Socialist Review* 96 (1987): 7–28.
Stanga, Adrian. Interview by Karen V. Hansen. San Jose, CA, December 18, 2013; March 29, 2014; August 18, 2014.
State Board of Education. "Racial and Ethnic Distribution of Pupils in California Public Schools, Fall 1971. A Report to the State Board of Education," 1972. https://eric.ed.gov/?id=ED070789.

Steidinger, Joan. *Sisterhood in Sports: How Female Athletes Collaborate and Compete*. Lanham, MD: Rowman & Littlefield, 2014.

Steward, Dan [pseud.]. Interview by Karen V. Hansen. Digital recording, October 3, 2018.

Sunnyvale, City of. *Historical Context Statement*. Community Development Department, Planning Division. Sunnyvale, CA: City of Sunnyvale, 1988.

The Opportunity Atlas. 2018. https://www.opportunityatlas.org/.

"The Wave of the Future: High School Computer Classes in the 1970s." www.colorized.com.

Toobin, Jeffrey. *American Heiress: The Wild Saga of the Kidnapping, Crimes and Trial of Patty Hearst*. New York: Doubleday, 2016.

Townsend, Nicholas W. *The Package Deal: Marriage, Work and Fatherhood in Men's Lives*. Philadelphia, PA: Temple University Press, 2002.

Trottier, Christiane, and Sophie Robitaille. "Fostering Life Skills Development in High School and Community Sport: A Comparative Analysis of the Coach's Role." *The Sport Psychologist* 18 (2014): 10–21.

Vargas, JoAnn. 2024. Interview by Karen V. Hansen. Digital recordings, December 13, 2023; January 17, 2024.

Vietnam War Memorial, Capitol Museum, Sacramento, CA. https://capitolmuseum.ca.gov/learn/about-the-capitol/capitol-park/vietnam-war-memorial/.

Vinitzky-Seroussi, Vered. *After Pomp and Circumstance: High School Reunion as an Autobiographical Occasion*. Chicago: University of Chicago Press, 1998.

Waldron, Linda M. "'Girls Are Worse': Drama Queens, Ghetto Girls, Tom Boys, and the Meaning of Girl Fights." *Youth & Society* 43 (2011): 1298–1334.

Walker, Doug. Interview by Karen V. Hansen. San Jose, CA, December 16, 2013; October 17, 2016.

Ware, Susan. *Game, Set, Match: Billie Jean King and the Revolution in Women's Sports*. Chapel Hill: University of North Carolina Press, 2011.

———. *Title IX: A Brief History with Documents*. Boston, MA: Bedford/St. Martin's, 2007.

Wells, Amy Stuart, Jennifer Jellison Holme, Anita Tijerina Revilla, and Awo Korantemaa Atanda. *Both Sides Now: The Story of School Desegregation's Graduates*. Berkeley: University of California Press, 2009.

White, Richard. *Railroaded: The Transcontinentals and the Making of Modern America*. New York: W.W. Norton, 2012.

Wilkins, Amy C. *Wannabes, Goths, and Christians: The Boundaries of Sex, Style, and Status*. Chicago: University of Chicago Press, 2008.

Wolfe, Patrick. "Settler Colonialism and the Elimination of the Native." *Journal of Genocide Research* 8 (December 2006): 387–409.

Zarrett, Nicole, Philip Veliz, and Don Sabo. *Teen Sport in America: Why Participation Matters*. New York: Women's Sports Foundation, 2018.

Zavella, Patricia. *Women's Work and Chicano Families: Cannery Workers of the Santa Clara Valley*. Ithaca, NY: Cornell University Press, 1987.

Zinn Education Project. https://www.zinnedproject.org/.

Zussman, Robert. "Narrative Freedom." In *Narrative Sociology*, edited by Leslie J. Irvine, Jennifer Pierce, and Robert Zussman, 141–61. Nashville, TN: Vanderbilt University Press, 2019.

Index

Page locators in italics indicate figures and tables

Accornero, Sara, 9, 139
activity-based learning, 99–102
administration, 29–30, 48, 64, 88, 140; leadership in wake of conflict, 92–93, 95
affirmative action, 96
Alarcón, Ramon, 64–65, 85
Albrecht, Steve, 120
Alcares, Pat, 127, *147*
All American Red Heads basketball team, 42–43
American Civil Liberties Union, 64
Amick, John, 137
Araujo, Pete, 21, 41–42, 73–77, 102, *147*
art department, xii, 32
Asian American students, 8, 67, 78
Asian American Union (AAU), 78
Associated Student Body (ASB) council, 70–71, 78
athletics: as arena for integration, 43–45; badminton, 20, 46–47; basketball, boys', 35, 41, 47–49, 51–53; basketball, girls', 42–43, 47–48, *50*, 50–51; benfits of physical activity, 39–43; dance, 41, 52–53; football, 20, 25–26, 40–44, 58, 78, 123, 127; gender inequities, 28, 36, 39, 45–49; lack of parent attendance at, 39–40; power of coaches' mentoring, 51–54; soccer, 49; and success in school, 41–42; Sunnyvale as underdog, 40–41; swimming, girls', *46*, 52; teachers, 27–28; before Title IX, 39–54; Title IX, 45, 49–51, 54n9; track, 43–44; volleyball, 48–49, 53, 59; wrestling, 44, 49, 52, 126. *See also* coaches and coaching; marching band
Aztlán (Chicano homeland), 73

baby boom, 8, 15, 135
Bangle, Ed, 92
Bargman, Robert (Bob), 83–84, 88–89, 91, 92, 104
Barton, Rita, 101
belonging, 5, 23–25, 141; by participating, 34–*37, 36*
Benson, Harold (pseudonym), 133, *147*
Black Panther Party, 70, 71, 85, 89–90
Black Power, 71, 72
Black students, 11n6, 21, 33, 43, 67–68, 78, 83–84, 111, 123
Black Student Union (BSU), 7, 70–*73, 72*, 79–80, 88; alliance with CSU, 77; Black History Week, 84; divergence from CSU, 89–90, 92

Blasquez Paulson, Carol, 25, *147*
block schedules, 95–96
Boyd, Doug, 24, 50, 64, 84, 136, *146*
Brink Logan, Suzi, 56, 62, 71, 138, *147*
Brown, Barbara, 86
Brown, Benny, 43
Brown, Robert, 109
Brown Berets, 85, 90
Brown v Board of Education of Topeka, 3, 67
Bureau of Intergroup Relations, 68
Buszdieker, Carolyn (Buzz), 19–20, 27–28, 36, 41, 43, *46*, 52, 59, 91, 108, 112, 136, 139, *146*; in dangerous situation, 86–87

California: canneries, 14–15; contest over land, 13–14; Master Plan for Higher Education (1960), 7; Proposition 13, 135–36; tracking system, 26–27. *See also* Sunnyvale, California
California Alien Land Law, 14
California Canners, 14, 15
California Supreme Court, 67–68
canneries, xv, xvi, 14–15, 18
Capp, Al, 108
Carlos, Juan, 58–59
Chavez, Donna, 41, 52
"Chicano," as term, 73
Chicano Movement, 73, 103
Chicano students, 33, 80, 85, 88–92. *See also* Latino students
Chicano Student Union (CSU), 73–77, *75*, 85; alliance with BSU, 77; divergence from BSU, 89–90, 92; as Raza Latino, 77
Chinese Exclusion Act, 14
Chinese immigrants, 14
civil rights movement, 9, 55
class differences, 25–26
clubs, 70–71
coaches, 44, 51–54. *See also* athletics
cognitive, affective, and kinesthetic/psychomotor domains, 31
Collins, Gloria, xiii, 20, 47, 52, 89, *147*

Coombs Holdorf, Cathy, 20, *147*
counselors, xii–xiii, 33, 69, 75, 77, 92, 95, 135; and PAVE program, 68–70; and tracking, 33, 75, 77, 80
Cruze, James, 71
curriculum, 6; designed for everyone, 31–34, 141; for failing students, 33–34; hands-on activities, 30, 31, 34; multicultural, 95, 102–8

Daniels Amaral, Darci, 59, 61, 63, 91, 128, 138, *147*
Danziger, Mary, 41, 52, 138, *147*
De Anza College, 44–45, 70, 76, 102
DeMedeiros, Ron, 89, 91, 138, *147*
Department of Health, Education, and Welfare, 49
desegregation, 5, 67
Dewey, John, 4
Douglas, Bob, 29–34, 69, 83, 125–26, 130, 134, 139–40, *146*; and plans for changes to school, 92–93; and Wilderness Lab, 100–102
dress codes, 63–65
Dyckman, Terry, 26, 31, 43, 49, 68–69, 71–72, 88, 92, 101, 135, 139–40, *146*; fight intervention, 58–60

Earth Day, 84
educators: as coaches, 39, 40; creative teaching, 103, 134, 140, 141; discrimination toward students, 57–58, 80, 88, 120, 130; diverse backgrounds and skills of, 9–10, 28–30, 34, 68, 71, 96; leadership team in wake of conflict, 92–93, 95; principles and practices of transformative educators, 140–42; rapport with teenagers, 25–31; team teaching, 96, 101, 140. *See also* counselors; principals
environmental activism, 84, 87, 89
Epps, Max, 19, 20, 62, 72, 90, 99, 107, *147*
ethnicity and race: definitions, 10–11n4; and tracking, 33, 75–77, 108

ethnic studies. *See* multicultural curriculum
Executive Order 9066, 29
expulsions, of Latino boys, 24
extra-curricular activities, 34–*37, 36*, 37n7, 142; marching band, *98*, 98–99. *See also* athletics

Faeta Kelly, Sharon (Keiko), 20, 35–36, 52, 109, 113n5, 137, *147*
Fair Oak Park, Sunnyvale, 59, 64
families, 115; immigrant, 6, 20, 130; working class, 1, 24–25, 116, 119, 131n1. *See also* parents
Ferguson, Ann Arnett, 11n6
Ferrera, Bob, 92
fights, 55–66; broken up by counselors and teachers, 58–60; contested spaces, 60–61, 91; as personal rather than political, 86, 89–91; relationship ethos used to resolve, 86–87
fights between boys: conflicts over girls, 57, 90; easier to break up, 60
fights between girls, 60–61
first-generation college students, 102
Fong, Paul, 40, 41, 47, 57, 58, 86, 89–90, 138, *147*; as quarterback, 78
Fourteenth Amendment rights, 64, 67
Fremont High School, 15, 26
Fremont Student Alliance, 64
Fremont Union High School District, 1, 15, 47; "war against long hair," 64
friendships: across racial-ethnic boundaries, 61–63; raising each other, 63, 117–25, 138
Furtado, Al, *146*
Furtado, Pat, *146*
Furtado, Sheree, 65, 107, *147*

Gaebel, Beverly, 52–53
Galliart, Vernon, 139
Garcia, Mario, 73
Garcia, Yolanda, 20, 31, 52, 59, 74, *147*
gender: and independence, 115–17; inequities in athletics, 36, 39, 45–49; and living situations, 128–31; pregnancy and marriage for girls, 116–17, 130
Gerboe, Peggy, 32
Girls Athletic Association (GAA), 28, 47–48
Gobets, Dennis, xiii–xiv
Gooch, Johnny, 84
Gooch Hocker, Jackie (Jacquelyn), 21, 34, 36, 41, 62, 63, 77, 90, 112, 134, *148*
Good, Dianna, 47–48, *50*, 51, 128, 130, *148*
Great Depression, 15, 24
Guel, Jesse, 74
Gutierrez Morris, Loretta, 30, 61, 80, 88, 93, 139, *146*; as CSU advisor, 76–77; Mexican American Literature taught by, 103–4, 108

Hagg, Bob, 52, 62, 118, *119*, 119–21, 124–25, 128, 130, *148*
Hale, Walter, 25, 95–98, 134, 139, *146*
Handa, Robert (Bob), 23, 34, 37, 44, 62, 78, 90, 107, 123, 137, *148*
Hansen, Len, 91
Hanson, Gerry, 33, 95
Harold and Maude (1971), 99
Hart, Herb, 32
"Heartbreak Hotel," 124–25
Heller, Herm, 52
Hendy Iron Works, 14, 15
Hernandez, David, 19, 57, 75, 90, *148*
Hernandez, Vickie, 75
High, Malcolm, 25–26, 31, 35, 40, 52, *148*
high schools: dress codes, 63–65; low expectations for students in trouble, 130–31; principles and practices of transformative educators, 140–42; protests at, 85, 87
Holte, Vern, 36, 97, *146*
Homestead High, 58, 104
Honda, Mike, 76–78, 80, 86, 88, 90, 93, 104, 139, *146*; in US Congress, 77
Horachi, Ben, 32

Huang Tong, Lorraine, *148*

immigrants, 8, 14, 17, 20, 28, 35, 40, 68, 142n5
Indigenous peoples, 14
integration, 137; athletics at center of struggle for, 39; long-term impact of, 44–45
intergroup contact, 9–10, 67–82, 138, 141, 143n10; 1920s progressive ideas, 68; debate about racial-ethnic student groups, 79–80; friendships across racial-ethnic boundaries, 61–63; and sports, 43–45
Inter-Group Council (IGC), 70, 78, 83; "Brotherhood Week," 79–80; Paul Sakamoto convening, 70

Jackson v Pasadena City School District, 67–68
Japanese Americans: internment of, 28–29, 51, 68, 76; in school leadership positions, 78
Jenkins, James, 71
Jeremiah Johnson (1972), 123
Jetro (school mascot), 35
Jets, the (Sunnyvale High School), 6, 56, 123; pride in, 25–26; and "West Side Story," 23–24
Jobs, Steve, 58, 136
Johnson, Lyndon, 102

Katsarelis, Mike, 71
Kelley, Don, 71–72, 84–85, 88–90
Kelley, Oliver, 89
Kennedy, Robert, 55
King, Billy Jean, 45
King, Martin Luther, Jr., 55, 72
Knapp, Rich, 50–51, 139
Kraus, Bill, 122, 127
Kraus, Marti, 122, 127
Kuna, Russell, 62

Lakely, Stretch (pseudonym), 19, 39–42, 47, 49–52, 62, 116, *148*

Latino students, 8, 24, 44, 57, 64. *See also* Chicano students
Lee, Bruce, 78
Legal Aid Society, 64
Leone, Joe, 33, 62, *148*
Lewis, Linda, 126
Libby, Raymond Francis, 121
Libby's Cannery, 14, 15
Lightfoot, Sara Lawrence, 4–5
"Li'l Abner" (Capp), 108
living situations, 115–31; dilemmas of independence, 116–17; friends raising each other, 63, 117–25, 138; gender divides in choices, 128–31; interventions by Sunnyvale High, 125–28; self-emancipation, 126, 130
Lizardo, Ed, 43, 44, 62–63, 91, 139, *148*; as drum major, 57, 99, *100*; as student body president, 1–2
Lyon, Mary Lou, 104

Madden, Mike, 40
Malcolm X, 55
Manley, Jane, xiii, 20, 26, 40, 64, 65, 88, 91, *148*
marching band, 35, 98–99, *99*, 137
Martin, Pam, 99
Martinez, Mac, 79
masculinity, 39, 57
Mason, Marilyn, 48, 52, 59
Master Plan for Higher Education (California, 1960), 7
Mathiesen, Marty, 23–24
Matsumoto, Dale, 62
Matteucci Henderson, Sandy, 102, 113n3, 116, *148*
McClung, Dan Willie, 122
McClung, Van, 40, 41, 62, *119*, 122–23, 126–28, *148*; most valuable player award, 43–44
McCracken, Ellen, 73
McCracken, Larry, 62, 128
McGhee, Heather, 9
McKean, Dave, 70
McKeown, Steve, 44, 120

Mendez et al. v Westminster School District of Orange County, 67
Mendiola, Rose, 45
Mesa, Richard "Pete," 30–31, 33, 68–69, 134, 135
Mexican American literature course, 103–4
Mexican Americans, 67. *See also* Chicano students
Mexican-American War of 1846-1848, 13, 73; Treaty of Guadalupe Hidalgo, 104
middleman minorities, 86
Miller, Jim, 29, 51, 56, 60, 89, 93, 138, *146, 149*
Moffett Naval Air Station, 15
Moncallo, Bernie, 63
Monroe, Nicholas, 8–9, 102
multicultural curriculum, 95, 102–8; Mexican American literature, 103–4; US Black history, 104–8
Mulvahill, Mike, 69–70, 139
music department, 26, 32, 96. *See also* marching band

National Aeronautics and Space Administration (NASA), 15
National Federation of State High School Associations, 45
Negro League, 122
Neighborhood Youth Corps (NYC), 100, 102
Nolan, Kathy, 32
Norman, John, 63

Ohlone people, 13–14
O'Keefe, Tom, 33–34
Olson, Charles J., 21n6, *146*
Olympics, 43, 51, 58–59
Omagbemi, James, 44, 51
open campus, 95–96
Orange County school district, 67
Othering & Belonging Institute (University of California, Berkeley), 5
Outward Bound, 100–102

Padgett Anderson, Cece, 37, 52, 117, *118*, 130, 139, *149*
Palo Alto Times, 64, 84, 89
parents, 93; high school not completed by, 20, 75; lack of attendance at athletic events, 39–40; as mentors, 128. *See also* families
participation, and belonging, 34–*37, 36*
Paulson, Eric, 25, 29, 35, 40, 88, 127, *146, 149*
PAVE: Psychology and Vocational Education, 68–70
Peace Corps, 56, 76
Peckham, Robert, 64–65
Pep Club, 35; Twirp Twirl, 108–12
pep rallies, 35–36, *36*
Perez, Johnny, 74
Peterson High School, 77
Pierstorff, Marion, 138
Pipal, Vauna, 123, 139
Prefontaine, Sharon Shull, 29, 52, 69–70, 103, 116–17, 127–28, 136–38, 140, *146, 149*
pride, 25–26, 141
principals, 23–24, 27, 134–35. *See also specific principals*
Proposition 13 (California), 135–36

racial tensions: crisis as catalyst for change, 91–93; desegregation, 1970s, 5; face-off in cafeteria, 85; fight between two students, 85–91; "it's the people" version, 90–91; media reports of "race riot," 87–89; politics version, 89–90; Smog-Free Locomotion Day, 84–89
Ratcliff, Michael, 85
Ratcliff, Willie, 71
Riggle, John, 84, 98–99, 139
Roberto Alvarez v Lemon Grove School District, 67
Robinson, Gary, 41, 42, 51–52, 63, *119*, 123–24, 126, 138, *149*
Rohwer concentration camp, Arkansas, 28, 68

Romero Hernandez, Kathi, 42, 52, 63, 91, *149*
Roosevelt, Franklin Delano, 28–29
Ross, Chris, 79
Rutter, Michael, 5

Sabre (yearbook), 34, 36, 73; athletics in, 48–49
Sabrettes drill team, 19, 35–36, 52
Sadie Hawkins Day, 108
Sakai Brothers, 62
Sakamoto, Paul, 7, 17, 24, 27, *28*, 28–34, 36, 78, 134, 135, 141, *146*; departure of, 80, 83; and PAVE program, 68–70; as principal, 28, 68–70, 83
Sanchez, Eddie, 44
Sanford, Tim, 31–32, 138, *149*
San Francisco 49ers, 99
San Jose Mercury News, 89
San Jose State University, 70, 115; teacher education program, 27, 29–30
Santa Clara County: cherry and apricot orchards, 15, 21n6; racial makeup of, 17
Santa Clara Parade of Champions, 98–99
Santa Clara Valley, 13–14
Santa Clara Valley Athletic League, 26
Santa Clara Vanguard Drum and Bugle Corps, 35
schools: funded by local property taxes, 2–3; inequality perpetuated by structure of, 2–3; middle-class white norms of, 3, 11n6
science classes, 29–30, 32
segregation, 137; legal challenges to, 67–68; and stratified housing patterns, 15–17
"senior wills," 139
Serna, Chico, 85–86, 90
Serna, Dan, 21, 33, 74–77, *149*
Shimoguchi, Joanne, 29, 41, 48, 51–53, *146*, *149*

The Skywriter (school newspaper), 9, 30, 47, 64, 70; on class boycott, 91–92; "SHS Again Tries for Racial Harmony," 55; slave sale covered by, *110*, 111
slave sale, 108–13, *110*
Smith, Tommie, 58–59
Smog-Free Locomotion Day, 84–89, 95, 113; as "race riot" in media reports, 87–89
Snook Mostes-Witherow, Karen, *149*
solidarity dividend, 9
Soviet Union, 32, 51
Stanga, Adrian, 4, 7, 24–29, 31–32, 34–36, 95, 134, 139, 141, *146*
Steward, Dan (pseudonym), 40–42, 56, 118, 121–28, 138, *149*
Stiles, Cynthia, 124, 138, 139
Stretch, William, 139
student engagement, 6; pride, 25–26, 141; protests, 85–87. *See also* athletics; Black Student Union (BSU); Chicano Student Union (CSU); extra-curricular activities
study center, 96
Summerbell, Mike, 138
Sunnyvale, California, 13–14; discriminatory housing practices, 15–17; map, *16*; north side of town, 18–21. *See also* California
Sunnyvale High School (SHS); administrative team, 30–31; built on north side of town, 18–21; class, ethnic and racial diversity of, 20–21; closure of, 136–37; collective identity, 1–2, 25, 34–*37*, *36*; curriculum, diversity of, 6, 31–34; demographics, 8, 135, 137; disparagement of, 1–4; federal programs and philanthropic investment in, 95; former students as teachers at, 29; as good school, 4–7; gym, 17–18; impact of, 137–40; languages spoken at, 3, 136–37; Latino students, 73–77;

plan of, *18*; from prison to place of belonging, 23–25; rough reputation, 57, 61, 87; as safe place, 61–62, 91; student demands, 85, 87, 91–93, 95; successful graduates, 23, 30, 134; turnover rates/migratory rate, 4; Vietnam War, students drafted and killed, 56. *See also* Jets, the (Sunnyvale High School)
Sunnyvale Standard, 88–89
Swanson, Dennis, 71
symbolic inversion, 108
Szacacs, Ed, 51

Taylor, Allan, 118, 124–26, 128
Till, Emmett, 122
Title IX, 45; impact of, 49–51; and racial equality, 54n9
tracking, 37n5; according to race and ethnicity, 33, 75–77, 108; California system, 26–27
transformative changes, 95–113; block scheduling, open campus, and study center, 95–96; community outreach, 96–98; multicultural curriculum, 102–8; Neighborhood Youth Corps, 100, 102; slave sale as blind spot in school culture, 108–13; Wilderness Lab, 100–102
Trujillo, Charlie, 57, 90
Tuana, Pete, 51–52
Twirp Twirl dance, 108–12

United Cannery and Agricultural and Packing and Allied Workers of America, 15
United Farm Workers, 59, 73, 75
United States actual and attempted bombings in 1972, 94n7
United Student Union, 87

University of California at Santa Barbara, 89
Unjust Legacy (Opportunity Institute, University of California, Berkeley), 17, 135, 142n5
Upward Bound, 102
US Black History course, 6, 104–8, 112–13

Vargas, Alva, 58
Vargas, JoAnn, 19, 21, 35, 52, 57–58, 60–61, 73, 74, 76, 77, 90, 116, 130, *149*
Vietnamese refugees, 20, 53
Vietnam War, 55–56, 89

Walker, Doug, xi–xii, 44, 52–53, 104–8, *105*, 112–13, 120, 126, 139, *146*
Ware, Susan, 49, 54n9
War on Poverty, 102
Washington Park, 56
"West Side Story" (Sondheim and Bernstein), 23–24
Whincup, Cheryl, *118*
white students: middle-class, 1–3, 19–20, 26, 137; working-class and poor, 40, 58, 71
Wisely, Kathy, 71
women's movement, 115
working class, 1, 24–25, 119; accelerated transition to adulthood, 116, 131n1
World War II, internment of Japanese Americans, 28–29, 51, 68, 76

Yamamoto, Wesley, 62
Youth Involvement Program (Sunnyvale), 64

Zinn, Maxine Baca, 10n4
Zukov, Cathy, 89

About the Authors

Karen V. Hansen is the Victor and Gwendolyn Beinfield Professor, Emerita of Sociology at Brandeis University, with appointments in Women's, Gender, and Sexuality Studies and History. Her most recent, award-winning book, *Encounter on the Great Plains*, explores the consequences and meanings of structural shifts in people's daily lives as they struggle with racial hierarchies in bounded communities. She currently co-leads the Cascading Lives project, an in-depth study of downward mobility in the contemporary United States (www.brandeis.edu/cascading-lives).

After graduating from Oberlin College in 2009, **Nicholas Monroe** worked as a middle school social studies and reading teacher in Chicago and Gary, Indiana. He earned a PhD in sociology from Brandeis University in 2021 with a dissertation on the social and cultural resources first-generation college students use to navigate higher education. Monroe currently works at Gartner, conducting research and writing reports for enterprise marketing executives and lives in Chapel Hill, North Carolina.